LABOUR BEYOND COSATU

LABOUR
BEYOND
COSATU

LABOUR BEYOND COSATU

MAPPING THE RUPTURE IN
SOUTH AFRICA'S LABOUR LANDSCAPE

EDITED BY
ANDRIES BEZUIDENHOUT & MALEHOKO TSHOAEDI

WITS UNIVERSITY PRESS

Published in South Africa by:
Wits University Press
1 Jan Smuts Avenue
Johannesburg 2001

www.witspress.co.za

First published 2017

978-1-77614-053-4 (Print)
978-1-77614-150-0 (Web PDF)
978-1-77614-151-7 (EPUB)

We acknowledge the support of the Dean of the Humanities Faculty of the University of Pretoria.
The publication of this volume was made possible by funding from the Rosa Luxemburg Stiftung
with funds from the Federal Ministry for Economic Cooperation and Development of the
Federal Republic of Germany.

ROSA
LUXEMBURG
STIFTUNG

Copyeditor: Monica Seeber
Proofreader: Lisa Compton
Indexer: Sanet le Roux
Cover design: Fire and Lion, South Africa

CONTENTS

FIGURES AND TABLES

ABBREVIATIONS AND ACRONYMS

AFL-CIO	American Federation of Labour and Congress of Industrial Organizations
Amcu	Association of Mineworkers and Construction Union
ANC	African National Congress
Apso	African Professional Staffing Organisation
AsgiSA	Accelerated and Shared Growth Initiative for South Africa
Azactu	Azanian Congress of Trade Unions
Azapo	Azanian People's Organisation
Bawsi	Black Association for the Agricultural Sector
Bawusa	Bawsi Agricultural Union of South Africa
Bcawu	Building, Construction and Allied Workers' Union
BEC	Branch Executive Committee
Capes	Confederation of Associations in the Private Employment Sector
Case	Community Agency for Social Enquiry
CEC	Central Executive Committee
Ceppwawu	Chemical, Energy, Paper, Printing, Wood and Allied Workers' Union
Consawu	Confederation of South African Workers' Unions
Cope	Congress of the People
Cosas	Congress of South African Students
Cosatu	Congress of South African Trade Unions
Cusa	Council of Unions of South Africa
CWIU	Chemical Workers' Industrial Union
CWU	Communication Workers' Union
DA	Democratic Alliance
Denosa	Democratic Nursing Organisation of South Africa
DoL	Department of Labour
EFF	Economic Freedom Fighters
ELRC	Education Labour Relations Council
EPWP	Expanded Public Works Programme

Fawu	Food and Allied Workers' Union
Fedsal	Federation of South African Labour
Fedusa	Federation of Unions of South Africa
FFC	Financial and Fiscal Commission
Force	Federation of Organisations Representing Civil Employees
Fosatu	Federation of South African Trade Unions
FPD	Forum for Public Dialogue
GDE	Gauteng Department of Education
Gear	Growth, Employment and Redistribution
GPSSBC	General Public Service Sectoral Bargaining Council
Hospersa	Health and Other Services Personnel Trade Union of South Africa
HSRC	Human Sciences Research Council
IDP	Integrated Development Plan
ISS	International Institute of Social Sciences
Limusa	Liberated Metalworkers Union of South Africa
LRA	Labour Relations Act of 1995
MDC	Movement for Democratic Change
MTT	Ministerial Task Team
Mwasa	Media Workers Association of South Africa
Nactu	National Council of Trade Unions
Naledi	National Labour and Economic Development Institute
NDP	National Development Plan
NEC	National Executive Committee
Nedlac	National Economic Development and Labour Council
Needu	National Education Evaluation and Development Unit
Nehawu	National Education, Health and Allied Workers' Union
NMMU	Nelson Mandela Metropolitan University
NNF	National Negotiating Forum
Nulaw	National Union of Leather and Allied Workers
NUM	National Union of Mineworkers
Numsa	National Union of Metalworkers of South Africa
NWC	National Working Committee
PAC	Pan Africanist Congress
Pawusa	Public and Allied Workers' Union of South Africa
PHSDSBC	Public Health and Social Development Sectoral Bargaining Council
Popcru	Police and Prisons Civil Rights Union
PSA	Public Servants Association of South Africa
PSBC	Public Service Bargaining Council

PSC	Public Service Commission
PSCBC	Public Service Coordinating Bargaining Council
PSLRA	Public Service Labour Relations Act of 1993
RDP	Reconstruction and Development Programme
RLS	Rosa Luxemburg Stiftung
Saapawu	South African Agriculture, Plantations and Allied Workers Union
Saccawu	South African Commercial, Catering and Allied Workers' Union
SACP	South African Communist Party
Sactwu	Southern African Clothing, Textiles and Allied Workers' Union
Sacwu	South African Chemical Workers' Union
Sadtu	South African Democratic Teachers' Union
Saftu	South African Federation of Trade Unions
SAIRR	South African Institute of Race Relations
SALGBC	South African Local Government Bargaining Council
Sama	South African Medical Association
Samwu	South African Municipal Workers' Union
Sanco	South African National Civics Organisation
Sanpad	South Africa-Netherlands Research Programme on Alternatives in Development
SAOU	Suid-Afrikaanse Onderwysersunie
SAPS	South African Police Service
Sasawu	South African State and Allied Workers' Union
Sasbo	Finance Union
Satawu	South African Transport and Allied Workers' Union
Satu	South African Typographical Union
SSSBC	Safety and Security Sectoral Bargaining Council
StatsSA	Statistics South Africa
Swapo	South West African People's Organisation
Swop	Society, Work and Development Institute
TAC	Treatment Action Campaign
TUACC	Trade Union Advisory and Coordinating Council
Tucna	Trade Union Congress of Namibia
Uasa	United Associations of South Africa
UCT	University of Cape Town
UDF	United Democratic Front
UDM	United Democratic Movement
UF	United Front
UIF	Unemployment Insurance Fund

UJ	University of Johannesburg
UKZN	University of KwaZulu-Natal
Unisa	University of South Africa
UP	University of Pretoria
UPE	University of Port Elizabeth
UWC	University of the Western Cape
Wasp	Workers and Socialist Party
WCED	Western Cape Education Department

Andries Bezuidenhout and Malehoko Tshoaedi

This volume is the fourth in a series of books published on the basis of five surveys of members of trade unions affiliated to the Congress of South African Trade Unions (Cosatu) that have been conducted over the past twenty years. As a series of longitudinal surveys of trade union members, this database is most probably one of the very few of such resources available to researchers anywhere in the world. The history of the survey itself is a remarkable story. In this Preface to the book we trace the outlines of this history briefly and comment on how the fifth survey is situated in the tradition.

The first survey was conducted shortly before South Africa's first democratic elections in 1994 and was called Taking Democracy Seriously. The aim was to understand the impact that South African traditions of trade union democracy would have on the country's emerging system of parliamentary and constitutional democracy. The findings were published in a book, *Taking Democracy Seriously: Worker Expectations and Parliamentary Democracy in South Africa* (Ginsburg et al. 1995). At the time, the authors engaged what was known as transition theory, a body of literature interested in the conditions under which societies moved from authoritarian rule to consolidated democratic rule without sinking back into authoritarianism. The authors critiqued Adam Przeworski's (1991) argument that successful democratic transitions mostly resulted from some form of elite pacting where parliamentary democracy was accompanied by conservative economic policies. They argued that, in the case of South Africa, Cosatu's strategic alliance with the African National Congress (ANC) and its history of participatory democracy could prevent this form of elite pacting:

> By initiating and committing itself to the RDP (Reconstruction and Development Programme), Cosatu has made clear its commitment to broad national goals … In this way, the possibility of deepening democracy by operating as a left pressure within the Alliance holds open the prospect that democracy in South Africa might transcend the conservative limits predicted by leading exponents of transition theory (Ginsburg et al. 1995: 109).

This statement was qualified with a cautionary note: 'It will be difficult but not impossible for the labour movement to remain in the Alliance but not be co-opted, and to neither alienate itself from its base nor lose its militancy.'

These sentiments reflected the optimism of the early 1990s. The Reconstruction and Development Programme (RDP) contained a Marshall Plan-type intervention to bring about a process of wealth redistribution through massive state investment in physical and social infrastructure. The document initially came out of the National Union of Metalworkers of South Africa (Numsa) and became the ANC's election manifesto. Jay Naidoo, Cosatu's general secretary, became part of the new government and was tasked with the implementation of the RDP. Shortly after the elections, a new framework for labour legislation was negotiated in the National Economic Development and Labour Council (Nedlac), a body in which Cosatu was the dominant labour voice. But we also know that two years after the first elections the ANC government had adopted the controversial Growth, Employment and Redistribution (Gear) programme. In so doing, the ANC government bypassed Nedlac and presented the policy to Parliament as 'non-negotiable'. Needless to say, this policy shift to the right led to considerable strain in the relationship between the ruling party and its Alliance partner Cosatu.

This was the context of the second survey that was conducted before the elections in 1998. Surprisingly, the 1998 survey showed high levels of support for the ANC despite the policy shift. In their analysis of the data, Sakhela Buhlungu and Christine Psoulis (1999) referred to this as 'enduring solidarities'.

Following the adoption of Gear in 1996 came a period of tensions in the Alliance. Neoliberal policies started to bite and new social movements emerged as a result. Many of these, such as the Anti-Privatisation Forum and the Soweto Electricity Crisis Committee, were openly critical of the ANC, and because of its loyalty to the ANC Cosatu refused to engage with many of these movements. During this time the provision of antiretroviral treatment to sufferers of HIV also became a major issue, around which new movements emerged. Sensitive to the politics of the Alliance, the Treatment Action Campaign downplayed party politics and was able to work with Cosatu against the policies of then president Thabo Mbeki. In 2004, a third survey was conducted, this time culminating in the publication of an edited volume entitled *Trade Unions and Democracy: Cosatu Workers' Political Attitudes in South Africa* (Buhlungu 2006). Again, the findings showed continued levels of support for both the ANC and the Alliance, even though there was evidence of a steady decline from levels in earlier surveys. A major theme in the book was the changing social composition of Cosatu members. Findings showed an upwardly mobile membership base, with significantly higher levels of education than in the early 1990s. It also raised concerns over the inability of Cosatu unions to organise vulnerable workers in precarious tiers of the labour market.

The fourth survey was conducted shortly before the elections in 2009. Cosatu had intervened decisively in what became known as the ANC's 'succession battle' and the 'Polokwane moment' and hoped that Jacob Zuma, the candidate they had supported, would shift government policies away from Gear (and the Accelerated and Shared Growth Initiative for South Africa (AsgiSA) policy that followed) towards a more progressive developmental path. Nevertheless, the fact that Cosatu had directly involved itself in the ANC's succession battle also made an impact on levels of unity in the federation and its affiliates. Congresses were characterised by pro-Mbeki and pro-Zuma camps, and conflict was often resolved by the expulsion of opponents by means of disciplinary hearings over corruption or other alleged misdemeanours. Another edited volume, entitled *Cosatu's Contested Legacy: South African Trade Unions in the Second Decade of Democracy* (Buhlungu and Tshoaedi 2012), raised a number of political and organisational challenges faced by the strategies of the labour federation and its affiliates. It had become clear that labour was not only influencing the transition to democracy, but that the transition had a number of contradicting effects on the labour movement itself, which was still equated with Cosatu at the time. Interestingly, levels of support for both the ANC and the Alliance remained at levels similar to those of 2004 – a short-lived moment of optimism.

As we know, this optimism was not to last. Although the rollout of antiretroviral treatment was a major victory, government economic policy did not fundamentally shift to the left. A new policy, the National Development Plan (NDP), was formulated and duly critiqued by the unions, notably Numsa. The massacre of thirty-four mineworkers at Marikana by the South African Police Service (SAPS) fundamentally shook the organisation, with mineworkers striking against not only their employers but also their union, the National Union of Mineworkers (NUM).

This even led to a number of trade unionists questioning their commitment to the Alliance with the ruling party. Levels of support for both the ANC and Cosatu remaining in the Alliance dropped to below 50 per cent of the sample. Cosatu leaders also started openly to criticise levels of corruption in the state, with references to 'hyenas' by Zwelinzima Vavi, Cosatu's general secretary, who was later expelled from the federation. A further tectonic shift has taken place in the expulsion of Numsa from Cosatu at the end of 2014, in part due to political differences over whether Cosatu should remain in an alliance with the ANC after its failure fundamentally to shift the ruling party's approach to economic policy. This led to the formation of the South African Federation of Trade Unions (Saftu) in 2017, in opposition to Cosatu and with 'union independence' as one of its key principles.

This book is the result of the fifth Taking Democracy Seriously survey, conducted shortly before the elections in 2014. We call it *Labour Beyond Cosatu*, because it has become clear that the federation is no longer the only dominant or significant force that influences the country's labour landscape. That things have changed rapidly while we write – both terrifying and exciting at the same time – has made the project particularly difficult. Because we were living and conducting research in a time of rapid social change, we decided to also conduct a number of in-depth interviews with key players in the labour movement. The findings presented in this book are therefore also based on an analysis of the interview transcripts of these conversations. Often, unionists were only willing to talk on the basis of anonymity, and we respected this wish. We were struck by the levels of trauma they were exposed to at a time when a movement they had contributed to was fragmenting in such a tragic and spectacular way. We would like to thank these participants and each and every worker who spent time with us and our fieldworkers for their effort to contribute to research and scholarship.

We don't call the book *Labour* After *Cosatu*, since the federation will clearly continue to play a significant role even if it fragments further. We use the word 'beyond', because it signifies that the field is opening up and that references to the South African labour movement and Cosatu can no longer be treated as synonymous. In researching the field we realised how little work has been done on other federations and independent trade unions. As the labour landscape changes, so will the field of labour studies. New connections between academics and trade unions will be formed and new traditions will result from this. We attempt to understand the reasons behind the rupture in South Africa's labour landscape. In so doing we also try to consider what the future landscape might look like. As editors of this book and members of a project team we are less interested in supporting factions than in opening up the field for further inquiry. We think that there is a need for a fiercely independent but critically engaged labour scholarship and that the entire community can benefit from continued social research of this nature. Future surveys can clearly no longer include Cosatu members only and we are sure that negotiating this space would be a major challenge to ourselves and future generations of labour scholars.

South African labour studies as a field of study has had an impact beyond the borders of the country, in part because of the historical relationship between the movement and scholars (Keim 2011; Keim et al. 2016), yet this has always been a dynamic and, at times, a conflictual relationship. Upon completing the project we attempted to present the research findings to Cosatu in a closed meeting, as has been the tradition, before going public. Owing to divisions in Cosatu we were unable to convene such a meeting. Instead, in order to provide members of both opposing groupings the opportunity to engage with us on the findings, we decided to make two presentations: one at the head office of the NUM and one at the head office of Numsa. We also indicated our willingness to make further presentations and did another at the head office of the Democratic Nursing Organisation of South Africa (Denosa) at their request.

We would like to thank participants of these seminars for their feedback and advice, as well as participants of a later presentation at the office of the Rosa Luxemburg Stiftung (RLS) in Rosebank, Johannesburg. Those who are familiar with the participants' personal histories with the labour movement will find it hard to link us as a collective to any one grouping in the labour movement. At stake is not only the consolidation of democracy in South Africa (the concern of this survey from its inception in 1994), but also democratic traditions in trade unions themselves. Authoritarian societies often succumb to paranoia and conspiracy theories. We hope that this project does not fall prey to this worrying trend in both the labour movement and the public arena.

The previous two surveys (2004 and 2008) were funded by the South Africa-Netherlands Research Programme on Alternatives in Development (Sanpad), a programme that drew to a close and that was therefore no longer available as a source of funding. Also, the academic labour market had taken previous project participants in new directions. This institutional flux meant that the network was not as coordinated or prepared for the survey as in the past. At the end of 2013 a group of researchers involved in previous projects drew up a funding proposal and approached the RLS as a possible alternative source of funding. We were delighted when Armin Osmanovic, director of the RLS, expressed interest and, after our meeting with him, agreed to fund the project. We convened a workshop to plan the project and were just in time to conduct our fieldwork before the elections.

We would like to thank the RLS for their generous financial support. Without this grant and their speedy response to our request for funding, this project would not have happened and what has become an institution in South African labour studies would have died a tragic and premature death. Of course, none of the opinions and interpretations of data necessarily reflect those of the RLS or its staff.

We were delighted when Wits University Press, after a review process, agreed to publish this volume. In addition to the anonymous reviewers, we would like to thank Roshan Cader as commissioning editor and Kirsten Perkins who oversaw the production process. We would also like to thank Monica Seeber, who did so much more than just a language edit. We would like to acknowledge the work of Wits University Press staff who worked behind the scenes and who assist in keeping academic publishing in South Africa alive and well.

The research project team consisted of Malehoko Tshoaedi from the University of Pretoria as project leader, as well as (in alphabetical order) Andries Bezuidenhout (University of Pretoria), Christine Bischoff (University of the Witwatersrand), Janet Cherry (Nelson Mandela Metropolitan University), Nkosinathi Jikeka (Nelson Mandela Metropolitan University), Boitumelo Malope (University of Pretoria), Johann Maree (University of Cape Town), Sandla Nomvete (University of Pretoria), Ntsehiseng Nthejane (University of Pretoria), Ari Sitas (University of Cape Town), Bianca Tame (University of Cape Town) and Nomkhosi Xulu (University of KwaZulu-Natal). We were particularly privileged to have Janet and Johann on board, since they were involved in the first survey conducted in 1994, as well as Christine Bischoff (née Psoulis), who has been involved in several of the surveys. We would also like to thank Musa Malabela from the University of Johannesburg for conducting many of the in-depth interviews, as well as Mondli Hlatshwayo from the University of Johannesburg and Sarah Mosoetsa from the University of the Witwatersrand for their encouragement and involvement in earlier stages of the project. Sakhela Buhlungu (formerly from the University of Cape Town, now the University of Fort Hare), as previous project leader, was also available as a sounding board and provided excellent advice as well as encouragement – especially to follow through on the in-depth interviews.

BIBLIOGRAPHY

Buhlungu, Sakhela (ed.). 2006. *Trade Unions and Democracy: Cosatu Workers' Political Attitudes in South Africa.* Cape Town: HSRC Press.
Buhlungu, Sakhela and Christine Psoulis. 1999. Enduring solidarities: Accounting for the continuity of support for the Alliance amongst Cosatu members. *Society in Transition* 30(2): 120–130.

Buhlungu, Sakhela and Malehoko Tshoaedi (eds). 2012. *Cosatu's Contested Legacy: South African Trade Unions in the Second Decade of Democracy*. Cape Town: HSRC Press.

Ginsburg, David, Edward Webster, Roger Southall, Geoffrey Wood, Sakhela Buhlungu, Johann Maree, Janet Cherry, Richard Haines and Gilton Klerck. 1995. *Taking Democracy Seriously: Worker Expectations and Parliamentary Democracy in South Africa*. Durban: Indicator Press.

Keim, Wiebke. 2011. Counter hegemonic currents and internationalization of sociology: Theoretical reflections and one empirical example. *International Sociology* 26(1): 123–145.

Keim, Wiebke, Ercüment Çelik, Christian Ersche and Veronika Wöhrer (eds). 2016. *Global Knowledge Production in the Social Sciences: Made in Circulation*. London and New York: Routledge.

Przeworski, Adam. 1991. *Democracy and the Market: Political and Economic Reforms in Eastern Europe and Latin America*. Cambridge: Cambridge University Press.

1

Democracy and the Rupture in South Africa's Labour Landscape

Andries Bezuidenhout and Malehoko Tshoaedi

INTRODUCTION: BETWEEN PARTICIPATORY AND REPRESENTATIVE DEMOCRACY

The decision in the early morning hours of Saturday, 8 November 2014, to expel Numsa from Cosatu was taken by the federation's Central Executive Committee (CEC). Cosatu's CEC is made up of the federation's national office bearers and the chairperson and provincial secretary of each of the federation's provincial structures. The CEC also includes two representatives from affiliate unions with fewer than 80 000 members and four representatives from affiliate unions with more than 80 000 members; these representatives are usually the presidents, deputy presidents, general secretaries and assistant general secretaries of such affiliates. Thirty-three CEC members voted for the expulsion of Numsa and twenty-four against. Numsa was quick to point out that a momentous decision had been taken by a small number of elite labour leaders, and challenged the federation to call a special national congress to reconsider the decision. Such a congress would constitute the federation's highest decision-making body and would be made up of shop stewards with voting rights in proportion to the number of paid-up members of each affiliate union.

One of the key agitators for the expulsion of Numsa from Cosatu was Frans Baleni, then the general secretary of the once powerful NUM. When conducting fieldwork for another project in the Free State, we were told by NUM shaft stewards of how Baleni had been challenged from the floor at the NUM's regional congress there. He was asked why such an important decision had been taken at the federation's central level, and was also questioned on whether he had received a mandate from his union to expel Numsa. Baleni's response was that he had been elected as general secretary. At the following NUM national congress, Baleni lost his position to David Sipunzi, the union's secretary for the Free State region. Irvin Jim, Numsa's general secretary, was quoted in the media: 'The mine workers said we need new leadership that will champion accountability and take mandate direct from the workers' (eNCA 2015). The NUM nevertheless ratified Cosatu's decision to expel Numsa at this congress, so even though Baleni was defeated in the election, the NUM congress ratified the controversial decision to expel Numsa. Union politics, like national politics, tend to be messy.

In the end, and after much delay and legal wrangling, the CEC decision to expel Numsa was ratified by a special national congress, but only after debates over whether the vote would be secret or by the showing of hands. At the heart of these battles is the nature of union democracy. Two issues are at stake. The first is the way in which unions make decisions internally, traditionally structured as participatory democracy that values the notion of worker control and the principle that leaders may only take important decisions with clear mandates from the workers they represent; it is on this point that Frans Baleni was challenged at the NUM's Free State regional congress. The second issue is the way in which trade unions relate to representational democracy under a constitutional dispensation in which political parties are allocated parliamentary seats according to proportional representation. They do not have to take direct mandates from their electorate, who can recall them by voting for another party in the next election. In this book we are interested in both these forms of democracy and how the traditions intersect.

Democracy, according to Iris Marion Young (2010: 52), entails political equality, such that all members of the polity are included equally in the decision-making process and have an equal opportunity to influence the outcome. Carole Pateman (2012) further notes that efficient participation in a democratic system also requires that individuals possess specific capacities, skills and characteristics that will enable them to have meaningful engagement with democratic authority structures. She argues:

> Participatory democratic theory is an argument about democratisation. That is, the argument is about changes that will make our own social and political

life more democratic, that will provide opportunities for individuals to participate in decision making in their everyday lives as well as in the wider political system. It is about democratising democracy (Pateman 2012: 10).

Worker control in Cosatu is based on the understanding that workers can directly influence decision-making processes through the mandate system – and, therefore, control of the trade unions. This means that power is distributed to the trade union rank-and-file membership and not necessarily concentrated in the hands of a few union officials. Within this conceptualisation, the system of mandates, consultation and reporting back to workers has always been central. In the words of one of the union officials we interviewed for this project:

> So worker control as conceived in Cosatu in my view it's not out of context, it should be understood in terms of how it was conceived in the democracy of the eighties. There was a strong slant towards participative democracy; there was cross-pollination of what happened in the labour movement and what happened in the civic movement, what happened in the student movement and what happened in the labour movement ... So in a nutshell the point I'm making is that the notion of worker control it articulates a notion of democracy and we are into a space that, we are a defined democracy in a particular way that it was direct, it was participatory, it was driven from below and it was not kind of an elite where the elite decide and therefore ... (interview, Ceppwawu official, 2014).

Participatory democracy within Cosatu unions is largely practised at the shop-floor level, where rank-and-file members directly elect their shop stewards and have the power to hold them accountable. This was confirmed by workers' responses to a question in the Taking Democracy Seriously survey's interview schedule: 'If a shop steward does not do what the workers want, should the workers have a right to remove her/him?' About 89 per cent of the workers responded in the affirmative – that workers should have a right to remove their shop steward – and this finding on strong practices of trade union democracy at the shop-floor level is also supported by other studies such as the shop-steward survey conducted in 2012 by the National Labour and Economic Development Institute (Naledi) (see Masondo et al. 2015).

In consideration of the workers' responses above, it is no surprise that Cosatu workers are still in favour of participatory democracy, where leaders only act on the full mandate of workers. About 49 per cent of the workers expect their leadership to 'only do what the membership tells them to do' and 74 per cent stated that their leadership 'must report back to the workers every time'. What this actually suggests is that workers firmly support participatory democracy and expect their leadership to consult them in decision-making processes.

However, what the Taking Democracy Seriously survey suggests is that this tradition of worker democracy has weakened in the last twenty years, specifically at the regional and national levels of Cosatu trade unions (see Maree 2012; Wood and Dibben 2006). When it comes to decision making at the regional and national levels, workers may have little influence or control over their leadership's decisions at the level of their own unions or over decisions made at the level of Cosatu as a federation. This is not only evident from the controversy in the NUM over the expulsion of Numsa from Cosatu – our findings regarding workers' knowledge of policies (such as Cosatu's involvement in Nedlac, where it plays a central role in influencing policies that may affect workers) that have been central to Cosatu's campaigns show a general lack of awareness. The second area where workers were found to be lacking knowledge is on specific policies such as the NDP and youth wage policy, to which Cosatu has taken critical opposition. The survey demonstrates that, within our sample of shop stewards, few had knowledge of these policies. How do we explain this?

In their analysis of the 2004 survey, Geoffrey Wood and Pauline Dibben (2006) note that since 1994, Cosatu has devoted fewer resources to political education and training of workers in the workplace as a result of prioritising its focus on influencing national policy. As a result, both shop stewards and rank-and-file membership became increasingly remote from the issues in which the federation was centrally involved (Wood and Dibben 2006: 52). Similarly, Sakhela Buhlungu and Malehoko Tshoaedi (2012) further note that democratisation, within the context of globalisation and economic restructuring, has deepened the social distance between leadership and rank-and-file workers:

> Union responses to the challenge of democratisation, globalisation and economic restructuring of the workplace have alienated the leadership from the rank and file member of the unions. The focus on specialised training and education for elected worker leaders and full-time union officials has resulted in the emergence of sharp differentiation between workers and leaders, and between leaders at the lower levels and those at the provincial levels and national levels (Buhlungu and Tshoaedi 2012: 19).

Trade union education in Cosatu has been crucial in the mobilisation of workers and ensuring that workers actively participate in trade union structures and the broader civil society movements. But, more significantly, trade union education was not restricted only to training workers; it was also important in keeping workers informed on key political debates and policy positions of Cosatu and the broader civil society movement. The RDP, for example, was a broad-based policy that was informed by a consultative process within the trade union movement, which included the views of the trade union rank-and-file members. The process in which the RDP was derived challenged the elite model of policy making, which often excludes the masses on the assumption that they lack knowledge and understanding.

It is important to emphasise the importance of trade union education in our analysis of the weakening worker democracy in Cosatu in the post-apartheid era. We argue that the focus on 'specialised training and education' for union leadership has influenced the erosion of internal trade union democracy in Cosatu unions. It has disempowered the rank-and-file membership in terms of their ability to actively take part in broader national debates of the labour movement.

The consequences of this, as suggested by the Taking Democracy Seriously survey, is that the decision-making processes at the national level, and specifically on national policies such as the NDP and youth wage subsidy, have mostly been informed and driven by the leadership. This has resulted in the elite model of policy making, where the rank-and-file members are not empowered or given the opportunity to participate meaningfully. Consequently, participatory democracy has been replaced by representative democracy. However, even representative democracy within this context is problematic. As Buhlungu and Tshoaedi (2012) noted in their analysis of the previous survey:

> Workers' lack of knowledge and information about the macroeconomic and political issues that Cosatu and its unions are involved in renders representative democracy meaningless and increases the alienation of the workers from their leaders, something which the leaders should be concerned about (Buhlungu and Tshoaedi 2012: 20).

Cosatu's weakening of internal democracy has serious implications for their role in the consolidation of democracy in post-apartheid South Africa. One of the key objectives of the Taking Democracy Seriously survey when it was initiated in 1994 was to assess workers' conceptualisation of internal democracy and how they see it influencing democracy in post-apartheid South Africa. The assumption underlying this objective was that Cosatu would play a key role in deepening democratic processes at the broader national level. However, our argument in the current volume is that Cosatu's inability to maintain strong internal democratic processes within their own structures undermines their role in the reconstruction and development of a post-apartheid South Africa.

We would like to briefly discuss two additional issues related to the nature and texture of internal democracy in Cosatu. The first is a challenge to Cosatu around what some have called a 'crisis of representation'. This relates to the rise of a segment of non-standard workers in the labour market and the inability of the federation and its affiliates to represent and organise this rising precariat (see Standing 2011, 2014) into trade unions. We discuss this matter in the section that follows and then we go on to the second challenge, the shift in trade unions from what we call 'solidarities of similarity' to 'solidarities of difference'. Solidarities under apartheid were necessarily based on a working class that was discriminated against by the apartheid state, and this produced solidarity around identities defined as 'black' and 'working class'. Potential fractures and fissures were underplayed in the interests of a common enemy – white capital and a white state. These solidarities are now challenged by a new dispensation in which difference has become more pronounced. Following on from this, and in order to follow through on our focus on trade unions and democracy, we look briefly at trade unions and party politics in Africa and what we may learn from post-colonial experiences in other countries. We do this because the Alliance has come under strain and the field is wide open after the rupture in Cosatu and the labour landscape more broadly. What can we expect in the longer run? We conclude this introductory chapter with a brief outline of the eleven chapters that follow this one.

THE POLITICS OF THE PRECARIAT

One of the major challenges facing Cosatu in post-apartheid South Africa has been the growth in non-standard forms of employment, what Guy Standing (2011) terms the precariat, workers who are on the margins without any job security or social benefits. On the one hand, the Taking Democracy Seriously survey reveals that over the years, the composition of Cosatu membership has changed from that of a dominantly unskilled and semi-skilled workforce to an increasingly skilled workforce with full security of tenure. This should be regarded as a positive development, but, on the other hand, it is disappointing that with the increase in precarious forms of employment, Cosatu's membership has not diversified its ranks to include outsourced workers, casual workers or informal sector workers who are often on the margins of society.

The precariat, as Standing (2011) refers to them, are workers who are often not protected by the legislative framework, and often do not have standard working contracts or access to social benefits. The struggle against the employers and the apartheid regime on the reform of the industrial relations system mostly aimed at ending the racialised segmentation of the labour market, which made protective provisions for white workers at the exclusion mainly of black workers. Workers' struggles centred on inclusion and extending protection of all workers through the legislative framework.

In their analysis of the consequences of outsourcing cleaners at the University of the Witwatersrand, Andries Bezuidenhout and Khayaat Fakier (2006: 462) note that there are similarities and continuities with regard to the structure of the labour market between the apartheid labour regime and the neoliberal regime in post-apartheid South Africa. They argue that although there have been some gains, in that the labour laws have been extended to include all workers, the neoliberal agenda has effectively reversed these gains. The result is that there is now a re-segmentation of the labour market, where large numbers of workers in non-standard contracts continue to be excluded by the same legislative framework drafted with the aim of being inclusive.

The continuities between the apartheid labour regime and the neoliberal post-apartheid regime has major consequences for the transformation agenda. The working class in South Africa is still predominantly black, and the unskilled labour force is largely black and female. Therefore, the 'precariat', in the post-apartheid neoliberal regime, refers mainly to black people and women, whom the new legislative framework aimed at incorporating into the industrial relations system. More significantly, these continuities raise questions about the relevance of the trade union movement if unions cannot expand their membership to include the marginalised sectors of society.

The point about the relevance of trade unions has been highlighted through the nationwide student protests and #FeesMustFall campaigns which have included demands for ending the outsourcing of support services at all universities in South Africa. With most universities (including the universities of Cape Town, the Witwatersrand and Pretoria) conceding to this demand, it has been noted by many that students have in a matter of weeks/days achieved what the labour movement has failed to achieve in the last twenty years.

With the advancing of globalisation and the neoliberal agenda in the last twenty years, trade unions have retreated into the workplace, consolidating and defending gains made in the past era (Mosoetsa and Tshoaedi 2013). Trade unions have not strengthened their efforts to develop new strategies of mobilising and expanding their membership to incorporate the precariat:

The problem is that Cosatu's organising strategy is still industrial based and it has not worked on the realities of emerging forms of work. [Cosatu] is defining employee in the traditional sense. Cosatu will always be faced with the decline of membership. No work has been done on the informal economy, migrant labour, casual and contract workers (Anonymous, interview, September 2009, cited in Hlatshwayo 2012: 233).

Although Cosatu has been engaged in campaigns against outsourcing and the outlawing of labour broking, these efforts, one could argue, have been reactive and aimed largely at protecting the interests of their traditional membership base. Cosatu's responses to globalisation and the emergence of precarious forms of labour have been reformatory or at the policy-intervention level, challenging government to amend the laws on labour broking. The organisation has not forcefully engaged in the transformation and redefinition of trade union mobilisation and organisation in post-apartheid and global contexts. Their continued reliance on the organisation of workers within the traditional workplace points to the slowness of the workers' movement to reinvent itself in the face of a capitalist system that is in a continuous process of renewal moving at the pace of a whirlwind.

THE POLITICS OF DIVERSITY AND MARGINALISATION IN COSATU UNIONS

Diversity in the South African trade union movement is often an issue treated with scepticism and therefore not prioritised. The history of the South African labour movement is built on the notion of solidarity based on common identity and struggles (Tshoaedi and Hlela 2006). In the context of apartheid, the politics of diversity were often discouraged for fear of weakening the collective strength of the working class. However, Young (2010: 43) warns that in contexts that are highly unequal the emphasis on common interests often privileges the interests of the powerful groups in the majority and in essence excludes the interests of minority groups – which reproduces social inequality. Further arguing against what she sees as 'privileging unity' over difference, she states:

The idea of a generalised and impartial public interest that transcends all difference and division makes it more difficult to expose how the perspective of the privileged dominates the public agenda than it is when people believe that politics is nothing but the naked competition of interest (Young 2010: 43).

However, in post-apartheid times, with advances in democracy and equality, diversity has been inevitable. The constitutional guarantees for equality have given rise or visibility to the often marginalised struggles and interests of heterosexual women, lesbian women, gay men, and disabled women and men – often groups that experience the worst forms of discrimination in the labour market and the workplace. The visibility of these interest groups in the labour market and trade unions challenges the traditional and narrow conception of trade union democracy which is often biased towards the hegemonic interests of heterosexual able-bodied men (Colgan and Ledwith 2002). Diversity in the labour market and trade union movement challenges the unions to re-evaluate their strategies on how they engage with the politics of difference and represent the diverse interests of the broader working class.

Instances of brutal physical and sexual violence against women in the mining sector and in the workplace demonstrate the fault lines in our democracy that fail to protect women even in spaces that are meant to be safe (Benya 2013b). More so, such experiences raise questions about the commitment of the labour movement to addressing the safety and protection of women workers from their own male comrades. How is the labour movement raising issues of gender-based violence against women in the workplace? Is rape and sexual harassment being defined as a health and safety issue in the workplace? Are trade unions making demands for women to refuse to work under unsafe working conditions and for women to be protected from dismissal? These are questions that require a significant shift in how the labour movement currently defines the working class and workers' issues. The working class is diverse, and therefore workers' interests are also diverse – and this has to be taken into consideration at the collective bargaining level.

The politics of diversity and marginalisation also refer to the lack of transformation in the leadership structures of Cosatu and its affiliates. Cosatu has been in existence for the last thirty years and in this period no woman has come close to securing the position of general secretary or president. No woman has ever been nominated to contest these positions. Cosatu's record in terms of advancing the politics of gender and gender equality within its organisational structures is disturbing considering its power and significance in the broader political landscape. Given this poor record in championing gender equality rights for women workers within its very own structure, can women rely on Cosatu to advance gender interests at the collective bargaining level?

The representation of women's voices has not been sufficiently addressed by Cosatu and its affiliates. The politics of domination, where consensus is reached through the silencing of minority views within the labour movement, has seen the voices of women (and other minority groups) on key political debates and decisions being sidestepped (Tshoaedi 2012). This is highlighted by the results of the Taking Democracy Seriously survey in 2008 which demonstrate that women's political interests and attitudes diverge significantly from those of their male counterparts. In responding to the question 'Cosatu has entered into an alliance with the ANC and the SACP [South African Communist Party]. What do you think of this arrangement?', about 50 per cent of women (as opposed to 69 per cent of men) agreed that 'it is the best way of safeguarding workers' interests in Parliament'. This was a significant decline from 2004, when 66 per cent of women (and 65 per cent of men) agreed with the statement. In 2014, however, the difference is marginal (42 per cent of women and 46 per cent of men), showing that support of both for the Alliance had dropped. During the 2008 and 2014 surveys about 42 per cent (in 2008) and 43 per cent (in 2014) of women indicated that they would vote for the ANC in the national elections.

The sharp political differences between women and men in Cosatu demystify the notion that the working class is a homogeneous group that speaks with one voice (Tshoaedi 2012). However, what is also significant is that as much as we know about the tensions in Cosatu on the politics of the Alliance, the gendered differences and opinions are not sufficiently highlighted in the analysis of these political developments within the labour movement. How, then, do we make sense of the fact that women's views on the Alliance, or support for the ANC, have not generated debates within the broader labour movement in South Africa? Tshoaedi (2012) argues that the political space in Cosatu is a contested arena in which women have largely been excluded. The rules of engagement in political debates and decision making exclusively privilege the dominant male majority in the unions. Young (2010: 53) calls this 'internal exclusion', where minority groups are superficially included in decision-making processes but the terms of discourse make assumptions that some do not share; the interaction privileges specific styles of expression; and the participation of some people is dismissed as out of order. 'If dialogue succeeds primarily when it appeals to what the participants all already share, then none need revise their opinions or viewpoints in any serious way in order to take account of other interests, opinions or perspectives' (Young 2010: 42).

TRADE UNIONS AND POLITICAL PARTIES

Relationships between trade unions and post-colonial ruling parties in Africa have always been complicated and contested. Indeed, this is the case in many other parts of the world as well. Trade unions may wish to use relationships with political parties to gain influence, but in the process they may be corrupted or incorporated into elite projects that do not necessarily advance the interests of their members. It is still unclear in which direction Numsa may go. Our interviews with union leaders have revealed that there is considerable internal contestation in Numsa around the relationship between the union and the United Front, as well as over the kind of politics and alliances the United Front should pursue. What is clear is that Numsa has decided on a path of oppositional politics, rather than remaining in an alliance with the ruling party.

Björn Beckman, Sakhela Buhlungu and Lloyd Sachikonye (2010) have brought together a range of case studies that shed light on the various configurations of alliances between trade unions and political parties in post-colonial Africa. These range from cases where trade unions become incorporated into the programmes of political parties and lose their independent voice in the process, to trade unions that refuse to enter into any kind of structured relationship with political parties and prefer to rely on the electoral process and their membership as a voting bloc to influence the political process. For the purpose of the discussion here we draw on their book to identify four possible ideal-typical configurations shown in Table 1.1 (see also Cohen 1974; Cooper 1996; Davies 1966; Freund 1988).

The first configuration is where the historical link between trade unions and liberation movements results in the labour movement becoming subservient to the liberation movement reinvented as political party. The Namibian case is a possible example of this, where the Trade Union Congress of Namibia (Tucna) is formally affiliated to the South West African People's Organisation (Swapo), the ruling party. Another example would be Zimbabwe immediately after independence, even though this has shifted somewhat over time. Uganda would also be an example. Some would argue that the alliance between Cosatu and the ANC runs the risk of turning into this kind of scenario.

The second configuration is an attempt by trade unions to form an alliance with a ruling party, maintaining their independence nonetheless. In South Africa, the early stage of the alliance between Cosatu, the ANC and the SACP is cited as an example, but one could also mention the relationship between the labour movement in the United Kingdom and the Labour Party there, as well as the American

Federation of Labour and Congress of Industrial Organizations (AFL-CIO) in the United States and the Democrats there. Such relationships tend to shift over time and may be close at certain times (in the UK before Labour became New Labour) and more removed at others (in the post-Blair UK). In such cases trade unions tend to use the relationship in order to influence policy, but the relationship may also be turned against trade unions and be used by political parties to legitimise anti-worker policies. In the case of Numsa, the trade unions wanted the ANC to commit to the RDP that initially was developed from within the union. Some Numsa leaders wanted the RDP to be more than an election manifesto in the form of a binding accord between the unions and the ANC. When the principles of the RDP were replaced by the Gear programme, many in Cosatu felt that a core agreement had been reneged upon. This illustrates the complexities that such alliances produce for trade unions.

In the third configuration, trade unions actively pursue party politics by supporting an oppositional party. There are two interesting cases from southern Africa that produced different outcomes. In both, trade union leaders made a transition to become leaders of opposition parties. In the case of Zambia, Frederick Chiluba successfully contested elections against the long-standing president of the country, Kenneth Kaunda, with the support of the Zambian Congress of Trade Unions. However, as president of the country he engaged on an aggressive privatisation drive to the dismay of some of the union leaders who had put him in power by supporting him. In this case, some of the dilemmas of the previous configuration faced the trade unions following election victory. In the case of Zimbabwe, Morgan Tsvangirai left the Zimbabwean Congress of Trade Unions to form an opposition party, specifically after the impact of structural adjustment was felt by union members. Up to the present his opposition party, the Movement for Democratic Change (MDC), remains largely unsuccessful and a stint of being incorporated into a unity government with the ruling Zimbabwe African National Union – Patriotic Front (Zanu-PF) left it weakened. Numsa's setting up of the United Front (UF) may signal a move in this direction – however, some of the tensions between Numsa and the UF may be explained by an optimistic reading of the UF's electoral chances in the long run, combined with the Zambian experience and Numsa's experience with the ANC post-RDP.

The fourth and final configuration is when trade unions decide not to be aligned politically. Ghana and Senegal provide examples. In Ghana, the labour movement uses its members as a voting bloc to influence electoral politics. It is not aligned to any political party, though, and may shift this support according to policies and the performance of parties as governments or opposition. In South Africa itself, the Federation of Unions of South Africa (Fedusa) and the National Council of

Table 1.1: Variations of relationships between trade unions and political parties in Africa

Trade unions subservient to ruling party	Trade unions in alliance with ruling party	Trade unions in alliance with an oppositional party	Trade unions politically non-aligned
Namibia, Uganda	South Africa (historically)	Zambia, Zimbabwe	Ghana, Senegal
Cosatu?	Cosatu	Numsa?	Nactu, Fedusa, Numsa?

Trade Unions (Nactu) may be cited as examples. Fedusa remains completely independent and does not advise its members on political affiliation or who to vote for. In line with its pan-Africanist and black consciousness history, Nactu maintains a loose association with the Pan Africanist Congress (PAC), but in the 2014 elections advised its members to vote for either the PAC or the Economic Freedom Fighters (EFF). Remaining politically independent but using membership as a voting bloc remains an option for Numsa. To be sure, the option of being politically independent, rather than aligned, was a very popular position among Numsa members surveyed by us.

CHAPTER OUTLINE

In Chapter 2, Ntsehiseng Nthejane, Sandla Nomvete, Boitumelo Malope and Bianca Tame reflect on the politics of doing research in workplaces in a politically contested environment. Never before has the team of Taking Democracy Seriously researchers faced such challenges of getting access to workplaces to conduct the research. In the past, Cosatu formally vetted the researchers and sent a letter to shop stewards to introduce the team. This time around the situation in Cosatu was so tense that it was impossible for us to get people who perceived each other to be from different camps into one room in order to discuss the research strategy, let alone the findings once we had conducted the research. Because many of us have historical connections to the labour movement, our research team was able to draw on personal connections in the provinces in order to get access to workplaces. The process also allowed us to forge new relationships. Often the process of doing fieldwork reveals as much as the findings themselves – for example, it happened on more than one occasion that our fieldworkers would arrive at a factory formerly organised by a certain Cosatu affiliate, only to find that another affiliate had taken over the representation of members. The authors of this chapter reflect on these experiences, as well as on the sample we were able to get after overcoming these and many other challenges.

In Chapter 3, Ari Sitas explores the social character of labour politics. What explains what others have called the 'fragmentation of Cosatu' (see Satgar and Southall 2015)? Sitas argues that the decomposition of old solidarities alongside the waning of the hegemony of the ANC means, that new variables have to be taken seriously as analytical concepts. He reflects on past surveys, and argues that educational and generational differences have already affected long-established but now reconfigured solidarities. He adds to these different experiences of working life, gender, migrancy, ethnicity and religion and explores each as independent variables making an impact singularly, but also in interaction, on political cultures and support.

In Chapter 4, Andries Bezuidenhout, Christine Bischoff and Ntsehiseng Nthejane turn to the changing class composition of Cosatu members. They draw on the Taking Democracy Seriously data set, but supplement it with data from other surveys, including the Naledi survey of Cosatu members and Labour Force Surveys conducted by Statistics South Africa (StatsSA) on behalf of the Department of Labour (DoL). They use a framework of understanding the new class composition of societies under neoliberal globalisation proposed by Standing to make sense of these shifts. The notion that the tensions in Cosatu are the result of a clash between the working class and a rising middle class is critiqued.

In Chapter 5, Christine Bischoff and Bianca Tame elaborate further on the changing social composition of Cosatu members. They respond to approaches that present trade union members as a labour aristocracy and point out that trade union members often share households with people who are unemployed and that it is problematic to single union members out as an individualistic elite. Nevertheless, the fact is that Cosatu unions have never really succeeded in organising the 'precariat' – those in vulnerable and marginal positions in the labour market, or so-called nonstandard employment – which means that trade union members are often in a better position than the precariat. They suggest that the term 'marginal labour elite' is a better description than the problematic notion of a 'labour aristocracy'.

In Chapter 6, Janet Cherry, Nkosinathi Jikeka and Boitumelo Malope provide a detailed analysis of what our data set tells us about changing attitudes among trade union members on matters of worker participation in national politics through negotiating forums such as Nedlac and their participation in politics through elections, as well as the state of alliances between workers' organisations and political parties. They trace shifting attitudes back to previous surveys, but also comment on the dynamic in the Eastern Cape, where Numsa has a particularly strong base.

In Chapter 7, Janet Cherry presents a detailed analysis of survey findings on Cosatu members' participation in service delivery protests and community politics. She looks at the potential for a growing alienation between Cosatu members and the 'precariat' or 'underclass' who often drive community protests and the danger of a divided working class as a result. She reviews results from the survey, but also looks at a number of interesting case studies, in particular a case in Nelson Mandela Metro where a former ANC councillor stood successfully in local government elections as an independent candidate in a working-class area, and won. In her conclusion she explores the implications of this for the United Front and other efforts to re-establish links between organised labour and community-based movements.

In Chapter 8, Malehoko Tshoaedi takes a closer look at the politics of sexual harassment in post-apartheid trade unions. Since the person of Zwelinzima Vavi was so central to the split between Cosatu and Numsa, the incident at Cosatu head office involving him and a staff member became a key issue of contention. Vavi described the incident as an 'own goal' and made light of it at times, whereas opponents, at times opportunistically, gained political leverage through how it was presented. The chapter deepens our understanding of the politics of sexual harassment in the labour movement on the basis of the survey findings.

In Chapter 9, Johann Maree draws on the survey results to explore dynamics around union democracy internally. He finds that basic structures are in place and that shop-steward elections are held regularly, even though elections happen less frequently and shop-steward terms in office have become longer. However, when it comes to structures of mandating and accountability between these workplace structures and national leaders, some tendencies of what Robert Michels (1959) calls the 'iron law of oligarchy' seem to be emerging – Maree calls this a democratic rupture.

In Chapter 10, Christine Bischoff and Johann Maree use the survey data to compare public sector unions to private sector unions in light of the fact that Cosatu has become dominated by public sector unions. They find that members of public sector unions tend to be in more secure jobs and receive on average significantly higher wages than their counterparts in private sector unions. They also find that there seem to be significant differences in terms of interests and opinion on key policy matters. More public sector workers, for example, support the NDP and the idea of a youth wage subsidy than do members of private sector unions. These emerging organisational cleavages may explain some of the tensions and the resulting fragmentation happening in Cosatu.

In Chapter 11, Johann Maree asks whether Cosatu's public sector unions have become too powerful. This chapter follows on from the previous chapter and develops an international framework for understanding the role of public sector unions in democratic societies. Maree argues that public sector unions have significantly increased the benefits of their members, but that this has potentially happened at the expense of broader development goals. He also draws on a case study of the South African Democratic Teachers Union (Sadtu) to point to the danger of civil service trade unions becoming entrenched and to the vested interest of officials and members which may undermine the effective delivery of a public good such as education.

In Chapter 12, Andries Bezuidenhout explores the broader and changing labour landscape, drawing on the concepts of business unionism, political unionism, social movement unionism and entrepreneurial unionism to make sense of how the different labour formations are located in this landscape. The chapter maps the other major federations – notably Fedusa and Nactu, but also groupings such as Solidariteit and independent unions such as the Public Servants Association (PSA). He argues that South African labour studies will have to take seriously these formations, as well as the new formation emerging from the split between Cosatu and Numsa. The implication is that future surveys of the kind that this book is based on will have to cover labour beyond Cosatu alone.

BIBLIOGRAPHY

Beckman, Björn, Sakhela Buhlungu and Lloyd Sachikonye (eds). 2010. *Trade Unions and Party Politics: Labour Movements in Africa*. Cape Town: HSRC Press.

Benya, Asanda. 2013a. Gendered labour: A challenge to labour as a democratising force. *Rethinking Development and Inequality* 2: 47–62.

Benya, Asanda. 2013b. Women in mining: A challenge to occupational culture in mines. Master's dissertation, University of the Witwatersrand.

Bezuidenhout, Andries and Khayaat Fakier. 2006. Maria's burden: Contract cleaning and the burden of social reproduction in post-apartheid South Africa. *Antipode* 38(3): 462–485.

Buhlungu, Sakhela and Malehoko Tshoaedi. 2012. A contested legacy: Organisational and political challenges facing Cosatu. In *Cosatu's Contested Legacy: South African Trade Unions in the Second Decade of Democracy*, edited by Sakhela Buhlungu and Malehoko Tshoaedi. Cape Town: HSRC Press.

Cohen, Robin. 1974. *Trade Unions in Nigeria, 1945–1971*. London: Heinemann.

Colgan, Fiona and Sue Ledwith. 2002. Gender and diversity: Reshaping union democracy. *Employee Relations* 24(2): 167–189.

Cooper, Frederick. 1996. *Decolonisation and African Society: The Labour Question in French and British Africa*. Cambridge: Cambridge University Press.

Davies, Ioan. 1966. *African Trade Unions*. Harmondsworth: Penguin.

eNCA. 2015. NUM has new general secretary. *eNCA.com*, 6 June. http://www.enca.com/ south-africa/num-has-new-general-secretary (accessed 21 August 2015).

Freund, Bill. 1988. *The African Worker*. Cambridge: Cambridge University Press.

Hlatshwayo, Mondli. 2012. Cosatu's attitudes and policies towards external migrants. In *Cosatu's Contested Legacy: South African Trade Unions in the Second Decade of Democracy*, edited by Sakhela Buhlungu and Malehoko Tshoaedi. Cape Town: HSRC Press.

Maree, Johann. 2012. Cosatu, oligarchy and the consolidation of democracy in an African context. In *Cosatu's Contested Legacy: South African Trade Unions in the Second Decade of Democracy*, edited by Sakhela Buhlungu and Malehoko Tshoaedi. Cape Town: HSRC Press.

Masondo, Themba, Mark Orkin and Edward Webster. 2015. Militants or managers? Cosatu and democracy in the workplace. In *Cosatu in Crisis: The Fragmentation of an African Trade Union Federation*, edited by Vishwas Satgar and Roger Southall. Johannesburg: KMMR Publishing.

Michels, Robert. 1959. *Political Parties*. New York: Dover Publications. (First published in 1911 in German.)

Mosoetsa, Sarah and Malehoko Tshoaedi. 2013. Cosatu retreating to the workplace in post-apartheid South Africa: What about community struggles? *Rethinking Development and Inequality* 2: 28–46.

Pateman, Carole. 2012. Participatory democracy revisited. APSA Presidential Address. *Perspectives in Politics* 10(1): 7–19.

Satgar, Vishwas and Roger Southall. 2015. Cosatu in crisis: Analysis and prospects. In *Cosatu in Crisis: The Fragmentation of an African Trade Union Federation*, edited by Vishwas Satgar and Roger Southall. Johannesburg: KMMR Publishing.

Standing, Guy. 2011. *The Precariat: The New Dangerous Class*. London: Bloomsbury.

Standing, Guy. 2014. *A Precariat Charter: From Denizens to Citizens*. London: Bloomsbury Academic.

Tshoaedi, Malehoko. 2012. Making sense of unionised workers' political attitudes: The (un) representation of women's voices in Cosatu. In *Cosatu's Contested Legacy: South African Trade Unions in the Second Decade of Democracy*, edited by Sakhela Buhlungu and Malehoko Tshoaedi. Cape Town: HSRC Press.

Tshoaedi, Malehoko and Hlengiwe Hlela. 2006. The marginalisation of women unionists during South Africa's democratic transition. In *Trade Unions and Democracy: Cosatu Workers' Political Attitudes in South Africa*, edited by Sakhela Buhlungu. Cape Town: HSRC Press.

Wood, Geoffrey and Pauline Dibben. 2006. Broadening internal democracy with a diverse workforce: Challenges and opportunities. In *Trade Unions and Democracy: Cosatu Workers' Political Attitudes in South Africa*, edited by Sakhela Buhlungu. Cape Town: HSRC Press.

Young, Iris Marion. 2010. *Inclusion and Democracy*. Oxford: Oxford University Press.

2

Research in a Highly Charged Environment: Taking Democracy Seriously, 2014

Ntsehiseng Nthejane, Sandla Nomvete, Boitumelo Malope and Bianca Tame

INTRODUCTION

At times, the process of conducting fieldwork can be as revealing as the analysis of the data itself. Our experience of conducting the 2014 Taking Democracy Seriously workers' survey, the fifth of its kind, is an example of such a moment. Over a period of twenty years, members of our teams have been visiting the same factories, mines and workshops in order to interview Cosatu members. In the process we have seen some factories close down and others restructured through various kinds of outsourcing arrangements, especially after trade liberalisation in the mid-1990s. This has had a profound impact on trade unions, especially since they often lose members to unemployment or vulnerable positions in the casualised labour market. In spite of this, insofar as trade unions themselves and the federations they are affiliated to are concerned, the organising landscape itself has remained stable for roughly twenty years.

However, in conducting the 2014 survey we encountered a range of new research challenges related to this seismic rupture in the country's trade union dispensation. It was the first time we were unable to get formal approval from the federation.

Instead, we had to rely on cooperation from affiliates. It was also the first time we encountered real rivalry at the workplace between trade unions from the same federation. In some cases we would go to factories previously organised by one Cosatu affiliate, only to encounter the leadership of a rival union from the same federation representing workers. We also conducted our fieldwork during the longest mining strike in South African history, led by the Association of Mineworkers and Construction Union (Amcu), a union that is not affiliated to Cosatu. In Rustenburg we even received death threats in the course of attempts to interview mineworkers for the survey, raising new ethical challenges not encountered before. In short, we conducted the research in a highly charged environment.

Some of the challenges we have faced are not entirely new. Since 2008, with the launch of the Congress of the People (Cope) as a party split off from the ANC, the Taking Democracy Seriously research teams have noted how the political climate has affected the research process (Bischoff and Tshoaedi 2012; Buhlungu 2006). In 2014 this was no different, but the impact was more profound and presented us with unusual research challenges that determined how we negotiated access to the workplaces. In this chapter we document the strategic choices we had to make under the circumstances. In spite of these challenges we were determined to see the survey through.

In this chapter we first comment on the main features of a highly charged research environment. We then discuss the research process. We discuss the preparatory phase in which we refined our research instruments and planned the selection of participants, and then we look at the process of conducting fieldwork and how this was affected by the charged environment we refer to. We focus in particular on access, and how this shaped our strategies and the outcomes of the survey. We then outline the sample achieved and compare it to those of previous surveys. Finally, we discuss the implications of all these elements for the credibility of the survey, highlighting what we see as strengths and weaknesses.

THE CONTEXT

Three political moments had a powerful effect on our survey, namely the formation of the EFF, the Marikana massacre and the process of the expulsion of Numsa from Cosatu. The first moment refers to the birth of the EFF, which followed the expulsion of the then ANC Youth League leader Julius Malema after he had been found guilty of sowing divisions within its mother body. A few months later, the charismatic leader had amassed substantial support and sought to contest the 2014 general elections, thus creating tension in the country's political landscape. Unlike Cope, the EFF is a left-orientated political party, deriving its inspiration from Marx, Lenin and Fanon, and positioned itself as representative of working-class interests in opposition to the ANC. In the run-up to the elections Amcu advised its members to vote for either the EFF or the PAC. AgangSA, in contrast, was founded by the highly respected academic and businesswoman Mamphele Ramphele, with an emphasis on clean governance. Nevertheless, AgangSA was set up as alternative to the Democratic Alliance (DA) rather than the ANC, and failed to attract significant electoral support.

The second moment we refer to is the Marikana massacre and the five-month strike that shook Rustenburg's platinum belt – and the country. The former occurred over a week-long period with the killing of two security guards while workers were striking, and was violently suppressed on 16 August 2012 when thirty-four mineworkers were gunned down by the police. The Marikana massacre was then succeeded by the longest strike ever seen in the platinum belt, led by Amcu, an offshoot of the NUM. The rise of Amcu is seen by some as a direct result of the NUM's organisational failures, particularly the servicing of its members (Alexander et al. 2012; Chinguno 2013).

This brings us to the third moment, which relates to tensions within Cosatu and its affiliates that eventually led to the split between Cosatu and Numsa. Cosatu has always participated formally with the surveys. However, the 2014 survey presented new difficulties owing to contestations that led to changing power relations within the federation and between competing affiliates. As mentioned, previous surveys had also witnessed political divisions – primarily the survey conducted in 2009 after the ANC's conference at Polokwane, which saw the formation of Cope by mostly disgruntled ANC leaders and national leaders who had been expelled from Cosatu (we refer here to Willy Madisha, Cosatu's former president). Yet, unlike the EFF, Cope did not pose a significant threat to ANC's claim to represent working-class interests.

The threat of Numsa splitting from Cosatu was seen by many as having the potential to split the federation in half. Following the threat, events took the inevitable turn when Numsa was expelled from Cosatu on 7 November 2014. From Cosatu's point of view the reasons for Numsa's expulsion included:

- that Numsa's declarations and resolutions taken after its special national congress were at odds with Cosatu's constitution;
- that Numsa withheld subscriptions that were due to the federation;
- that Numsa expanded its scope of operation to areas outside its domain;
- that Numsa was seen as organising a march and dividing the Alliance.

Cosatu affiliate officials interviewed by us indicated that the tensions were due to ideological and/or personality clashes. Phrases such as the 'paralysis within Cosatu' and 'the paralysis starting from the workplace' were used to describe the current rupture in the federation. A Numsa official said that 'Cosatu is in the state of decay' and a number of leaders explained that these factions stemmed from leaders pursuing self-interests – referred to by one official as 'stomach politics':

> ... stomach politics, leadership of trade unions generally now are looking at what is going to benefit them ... maximise kickbacks for them to benefit. Use the banner of the union to build more networks for them and not the organisation ... So that means the focus is not on what they were mandated to do, the focus is on what they want to achieve using the banner and platform of the trade union ... So the leaders of the trade unions some of them are collaborating with the private sector closely for the private sector to make money at the expense of workers (interview, Satawu official, 2015).

The failure to serve members was seen not only as a serious concern but also an area of tension within Cosatu. Others suggested that these divisions stemmed from polarised views regarding policy (specifically the National Development Plan (NDP)) and the tensions among those for or against the Alliance. This is discussed by Janet Cherry, Nkosinathi Jikeka and Boitumelo Malope in Chapter 6 of this volume.

PLANNING AND RESEARCH INSTRUMENTS

The Taking Democracy Seriously survey is traditionally based on semi-structured face-to-face interviews with a sample of members and shop stewards of unions affiliated to Cosatu that take place immediately in the run-up to national elections. Workers are typically selected from workplaces organised by Cosatu unions, and access to these members is gained through the unions of which they are members. The survey is traditionally conducted in Gauteng, the North West, KwaZulu-Natal, the Eastern Cape and the Western Cape. Initially this was due to the institutional affiliations of the 1994 research team, and subsequent teams have decided to keep this constant for reasons of continuity.

The research team for this project was assembled during the course of 2013. As mentioned in the Preface to this volume, a certain amount of institutional flux (such as members of previous project teams moving to different institutions and a former project leader taking up a position of academic leadership) negatively affected the preparatory phase. Nevertheless, generous funding from the Rosa Lux-emburg Foundation enabled us to embark on the fifth Taking Democracy Seriously survey. Members of the project team for the 2014 survey, as well as members of previous surveys, are listed in Table 2.1.

Before researchers took to the field, we met at a workshop in Braamfontein, Johannesburg, in early December 2013 to discuss the way forward for the 2014 Taking Democracy Seriously survey. By this time, and as had been the practice up to then, we had already approached Cosatu to seek the federation's approval and cooperation. We used formal channels as well as informal networks, but to no avail. One of the trade union general secretaries we spoke to informally responded with a blunt 'Good luck'. It should be noted that Zwelinzima Vavi had still not been formally expelled at the time and that the contestation among the leadership had been intense and fierce. Given this lack of support the team had to make a number of decisions. Also, following changes on the political party front since the 2009 elec-tions, including formations of new political parties and additions of new national policies (such as the NDP), we needed to update and amend the interview schedule used for face-to-face interviews with trade union members and shop stewards.

We also needed to refine the phrasing of certain questions based on the expe-rience of previous surveys. In addition to this and in keeping with recent femi-nist and other critiques of South African labour studies, a number of new ques-tions were included in the interview schedule to broaden our understanding of the lives of workers outside of the workplace, as well as matters of sexual harassment. For example, questions were asked relating to weekly or monthly earnings, how many households union members supported, how many dependents they had and whether they had access to alternative sources of income. These questions were considered important, given the recent scholarship on household dynamics and the decline of the significance of wage earners in the economy as a whole. Apart from these adjustments to the interview schedule, our aim was to maintain as much con-tinuity as possible with previous surveys.

In light of the turmoil in Cosatu and the possibility of a split at the time, the research team decided to expand the scope of the survey to include members from other federations as well – primarily Fedusa and Nactu. Our sense was that Nactu was also important, since Amcu was affiliated to this federation and many of Amcu's members would have been former members of the NUM. However, through lack of time to consult with these federations, as well as the fact that Amcu was involved in a protracted strike in Rustenburg, our attempts to interview adequate numbers from unions affiliated to these federations were not successful.

Table 2.1:   Taking Democracy Seriously, survey teams, 1994–2014

1994	1998	2004	2008	2014
Sakhela Buhlungu (Wits University)	Sakhela Buhlungu (Wits University)	Sakhela Buhlungu (Project leader) (Wits University)	Sakhela Buhlungu (Project leader) (Wits University, UJ, UP)	Malehoko Tshoaedi (Project leader) (UP)
Janet Cherry (UPE)	Janet Cherry (UPE)	Janet Cherry (HSRC)	Wilson Akpan (University of Fort Hare)	Janet Cherry (NMMU)
David Ginsberg (Project leader) (University of Natal)	David Ginsberg (Project leader) (University of Natal)	Hlengiwe Hlela (Wits University)	Philip Hirschsohn (UWC)	Andries Bezuidenhout (UP)
Richard Haine (UPE)	Christine Psoulis (Wits University)	Devan Pillay (Wits University)	Carol Christie (NMMU)	Christine (Psoulis) Bischoff (Wits University)
Gilton Klerck (Rhodes University)	Gilton Klerck (Rhodes University)	Pauline Dibben (University of Sheffield)	Christine (Psoulis) Bischoff (Wits University)	Nomkhosi Xulu (UKZN)
Johann Maree (UCT)	Johann Maree (UCT)	Freek Schiphorst (ISS, Netherlands)	Stephen Ellis (Leiden University, Free University of Amsterdam)	Johann Maree (UCT)
Roger Southall (Rhodes University)	Roger Southall (Rhodes University)	Roger Southall (HSRC)	Aisha Lorgat (UCT)	Ari Sitas (UCT)
Edward Webster (Wits University)	Edward Webster (Wits University)	Edward Webster (Wits University)	Edward Webster (Wits University)	Sandla Nomvete (UP)
Geoffrey Wood (Rhodes University)	Geoffrey Wood (Rhodes University)	Geoffrey Wood (Middlesex University)	Malehoko Tshoaedi (Wits University, UJ, Unisa)	Bianca Tame (UCT)
		Malehoko Tshoaedi (Leiden University)	Ikechukwu Umejesi (University of Fort Hare)	Ntsehiseng Nthejane (UP)
		Roger Tangri (University of Botswana)	Themba Masondo (Wits University)	Nkosinathi Jikeka (NMMU)
			Yusuf Small (UWC)	Boitumelo Malope (UP)
			Nomkhosi Xulu (UKZN)	

Teams of fieldworkers were assembled in four provinces at the beginning of 2014. Workshops were held in the four provinces and team leaders trained fieldworkers in the history of the survey so that they could begin by understanding the context. They were also thoroughly trained in how to administer the questionnaire to respondents. Fieldwork commenced in February 2014 and continued until the day before the elections on 7 May 2014. The host for the workers' survey was the University of Pretoria. Teams from five other collaborating institutions participated in the survey process: the University of Cape Town, the University of the Witwatersrand, the University of KwaZulu-Natal, the University of Fort Hare and the Nelson Mandela Metropolitan University. As with previous surveys, we were fortunate to have input and experience from former team members to guide the process and mentor first-time contributors, most of whom were postgraduate students, to the study.

ACCESS

We mentioned at the beginning of this chapter that the actual process of collecting data is often as revealing as the analysis of data itself. In this section on access we would like to expand on this point. Ultimately, the levels of distrust encountered also made us reflect on the role of research in a democratic society. Conducting research in such a charged environment and in the absence of formal cooperation from Cosatu meant that we often had to adopt a pragmatic approach in the field, taking advantage of existing networks among senior researchers (networking and snowballing); improvising as and when a situation arose (when networks did not work); and, most importantly, persisting despite challenges such as general gatekeeping due to union and company bureaucracies, as well as occasional threats or warnings from workers.

As with previous surveys, every attempt was made to contact workplaces with Cosatu affiliates that had been surveyed in previous years across the different provinces. Previous survey data was collected and archived at the Sociology of Work Unit (Swop), now the Society, Work and Development Institute, at the University of the Witwatersrand. Where companies denied us access, or no longer existed, suitable substitutes were found, often with assistance from trade unions. At each workplace, ten union members were surveyed. Managers and shop stewards were asked to assist us in gaining access to eight ordinary members, with a gender and age mix, and two shop stewards.

The typical access-related challenges we faced were, for example, gatekeeping constraints from companies and unions and the general suspicion and doubt regarding our political intentions. This was somewhat expected, and consistent with former experiences in the field, especially since the survey is conducted immediately prior to the elections. However, the doubt and mistrust expressed by managers, workers and union leaders was amplified in 2014. An added constraint was the fact that we had only three months in which to complete the fieldwork. As mentioned above, this survey takes place each time before the general elections and does not continue beyond them, as some of the important questions are directly linked to the upcoming election.

In general, gaining access to workplaces was a slow process. For example, in certain regions, and for certain affiliates, leadership officials were reluctant to grant access to their union members or to participate in interviews, and referred us to their national office. This way of gaining access presented its own set of challenges because in many cases the provincial, regional and local offices had incoherent communication structures. At times, formal protocol and vertical communication structures were imposed even when it seemed unnecessary. Where structures were horizontal and levels of distrust lower, we could go straight to the branch or local office and they would contact the regional office for support.

Where possible, we used team members' networks to gain access to workplaces and/or union officials. In the hope of fast-tracking the bureaucratic process through unions or workplaces, even 'name-dropping' of established academics participating in the survey was deployed (although with the sensitive climate prior to the elections this did not always work). For the most part and across different provinces, we found ourselves negotiating access through laborious gatekeeping processes. In Gauteng, we had to meet with one union during its provincial congress at the Johannesburg Zoo to do a presentation on the survey, and only then were we granted access.

We were also struck by the fact that there was evidence of a certain level of institutional memory of the survey and of previous practice. For example, a Communications Workers' Union (CWU) official noted that our approach differed from that of previous years and explained why, without communication from Cosatu, affiliates were reluctant to participate in the survey:

> … the way now you guys are doing it, it's different with the way you did it in the past. Because in the past we receive a correspondence a month before you start these interviews that was going to all of the affiliates. So we were waiting for you … now even our correspondents were not told about you. We are only hearing now about you (interview, CWU official, 2014).

When we asked a Cosatu official why access was so challenging, he explained:

> I think in part the access may be linked to the fact that Cosatu just has got so much on its plate at the moment, that the survey done by somebody is not the priority for them. Ordinarily I mean we do it as a merely a favour to an organisation … I think it's wrong because they have got to give academics the benefit of the doubt to just come on to getting a reflection of what the environment is. But people respond to things differently, that just our biggest failure as a people, that we are clouded by our personal issues and so it comes out in a variety of ways. And I think that could just have been part of it but I don't think there's any instructions from anywhere that people shouldn't be responding to surveys. Some people, some shop stewards, have been phoning me from Pep stores, they said some people were coming to do surveys there and asked them about political parties they supported and so on. And they ended up chasing those people doing the survey out of the factory because they felt they were pushing a DA agenda. You know people defend what they think is important in their own ways, in their own environments. It's just how things are (interview, Cosatu official, 2014).

What exacerbated the situation, especially where Cosatu affiliates were concerned, was a recent experience of research results being released with what was interpreted as a political agenda. The research in question was commissioned by Moeletsi Mbeki through his think tank, the Forum for Public Dialogue (FPD) and conducted by the Community Agency for Social Enquiry (Case) (2013). An interpretation of some of the study's findings was released by one of the researchers involved before the ANC's 53rd conference in 2012 in Mangaung, and was seen to favour a certain faction. Our research was conducted before the 2014 elections and, in part due to the controversy around the shop-stewards survey, our motives were routinely questioned. Equally, while Cosatu did not endorse our research, there was no directive given to affiliates not to participate in the survey either. This caused confusion and, more importantly, paved the way for our research to be construed as politically motivated, especially by those who were not familiar with the history of the Taking Democracy Seriously survey. In one instance, some unions thought we were spies, given that the 2014 elections were looming. However, while Cosatu may have had too much on its plate or generally supported research as merely a favour to organisations, officials acknowledged that research was important for reflecting changes within the organisation and among workers; giving workers a platform to express their opinions freely; and allowing 'leaders

[to] use such research outcomes as a way of making an introspection among themselves' (interview, Sadtu official, 2014).

What came across strongly among a number of officials is that there was some discomfort (or fear) regarding the outcome of research findings. A NUM official, for example, indicated that access to their members was not a problem because they had nothing to hide, whereas those who were concerned with the frank or honest views of 'ordinary members' at the plant level were more likely to block access. Linked to the theme of workers speaking their minds and how they portray leadership members, a Sadtu official had the following to say about the 'negative attitude', particularly among leadership members, towards research findings:

> Including the [National Labour and Economic Development Institute] Naledi research arm of the federation, leaders at that highest level have been exposed by what the ordinary members are saying generally around how their organisation and how their trade unions are run, to an extent that comrades have taken a very negative attitude now in the publishing of the outcome of the research because they do expose a serious dichotomy, a difference of understanding of what these unions are supposed to be doing, the leadership and ordinary members. So ordinary members expressing themselves that the leaders don't seem to be prioritising their issues. Leaders are using the union as the stepping stone or the ladder to jump in the ladder of state, be it government, be it Parliament, be it offices in the bureaucracy. Members have expressed the views. Surely some leaders do not appreciate … those comments of members of how they view their leaders (interview, Sadtu official, 2015).

From our experiences in the field and the frank views shared with us by trade union officials, it is evident that there are fissures within the federation, especially between leadership and ordinary members. The bureaucratic process to gain access to workers differed from workplace to workplace. Sometimes we were referred to human resource managers, 'employment officers', plant managers, company managers or shop stewards. Regular follow-ups had to be made with most companies because responses were not prompt, owing to internal workplace bureaucratic processes. In other instances certain workplaces would not participate in the survey unless they were given the go-ahead from the union directly. This meant that in addition to securing access to workplaces we also had to communicate with unions at a regional and/or national level to ensure the surveys could be conducted.

In some instances managers agreed to grant us access to their premises but union members refused to participate because they had not been informed by their regional office about the survey. In other instances the opposite occurred. Union officials granted us access but management refused to participate. In one case we had agreed with a union to conduct the survey at a plant in Gauteng, but twenty minutes into the interviews, a plant manager called us to his office and inquired what was going on. After we explained the survey to him, he informed us that he had no knowledge of it and as proper channels of communications had not been followed he ordered us to leave the plant. We were escorted off the premises by security guards. After a number of phone calls to a regional organiser, we later found out that the union in question had lost its majority position at the plant and was not aware of it.

Two issues emerge from the above incident. The first is that Cosatu affiliates continue to fight each other for membership at workplace level. Where Numsa has contested and won over membership from its former sister unions, it has been labelled as a union that 'poaches' members. This has seen a number of other affiliates expressing frustration with Numsa. Animosities and divisions among Cosatu affiliates are likely to continue if grounds to mobilise in industries are not clearly defined. The second issue is that of a union understanding its position in a company. In this case, shop stewards seemed unfamiliar with the content and procedures resulting from their own recognition agreement with the company where they were supposed to represent their members. However, it is also possible that those procedures were misrepresented on purpose in order to attempt to exclude a rival union from gaining an organising foothold in their company. What we see in this situation is the contestation of space and power among two sister unions. The most important question to ask is what this contestation at branch level means for the federation, but the end result for us of this scenario was that we were ejected from the company premises by management.

Incidents differed from one organisation to the other. The next case was of a public sector union. Here we received very good cooperation from the regional offices, but after being received at the given public institution by the union we faced a challenge because the union had not communicated adequately with the human resources (HR) department. We were invited to the HR manager's office. He told us that he was the employer and therefore the workers belonged to him before they belonged to the union and that nothing would happen until he had been approached properly for consent – and by the researchers, not the union. In that case we referred back to the manager and then sent the consent letter (which we had sent earlier, without receiving a response). We followed this with a phone call from one of our senior researchers and were welcomed openly the next day.

What transpired here was another instance of power contestation, this time between union and management. What struck us was the powerlessness and inability of the union to negotiate with management about an initiative it was fully aware of and one that it had used its resources and time to organise. This makes one question the union today, and how it has changed since the 1970s and '80s in relation to its autonomy – and how a union is able to claim its members during working hours for a union-related initiative.

When bureaucracy prevented interviews in workplaces, researchers had to improvise by conducting the survey with workers outside company premises, and at times while workers were picketing, but also at trade union offices or the workers' homes during a public holiday, when it was necessary. Almost all the interviews were, however, conducted at workplaces, in keeping with the original research design, and where they were not, workers were identified by shop stewards, the examples above being the exception.

So far, we have documented how our efforts to gain access through trade unions was difficult (or impossible) at times. In such cases the alternative was resorting to the human resources departments at workplaces sampled in previous surveys. We assumed that the HR departments would be familiar with the study and would easily enable us to do fieldwork. This was not always the case and at times we were only able to gain access to companies after extended negotiations with HR managers and with trade union branches. Our impression was that in Gauteng it was easier to negotiate with HR management and union leadership in the metal industry than in other industries. Many managers, however, were reluctant to participate, partly because of their concern that such a study could jeopardise the internal dynamic among workers in the workplace. Some managers requested a copy of the questionnaire prior to granting us access. In one instance, the manager asked that questions on wages be omitted. Some workplaces were in the middle of wage negotiations or retrenchments and thus were reluctant to allow us to conduct the survey among their disgruntled workers. In KwaZulu-Natal, a few managers refused to participate without providing any reason. Health and safety issues, as well as production deadlines, were the main reasons managers said they could not accommodate us. In a number of companies, managers granted us access to workers but only during their thirty-minute lunch break, although our research brief to managers clearly indicated that an average survey per worker took forty-five to sixty minutes. Despite our efforts to negotiate extra time, we often had no choice but to seek alternative workplaces or conduct the survey with workers at a time and place convenient for them. Our efforts were aided by helpful shop stewards and ordinary union members as well as regional secretaries who played an active facilitating role. For instance, in the Western Cape a determined shop steward suggested that we conduct surveys with his workers at the Khayelitsha stadium on Workers' Day. Another shop steward took two fieldworkers from house to house in the evening so that they could complete the survey. In the Eastern Cape a regional office called workers and set up interviews at the office.

Given the political climate under which the research was undertaken, the Rustenburg region posed a number of complications in terms of gaining access to workers, at the level of the union office as well as the workplace. Access challenges were exacerbated by the unprotected strike that took place from January to June 2014. The strike not only posed a physical threat to researchers, but also brought to the fore ethical issues that had not been experienced in previous surveys. When we arrived in the Rustenburg region, the atmosphere was hostile. Workers blatantly refused to participate, and the community was also unreceptive. The question that related to community involvement in union affairs was of great importance. This came with the realisation of how union activities deeply affected the community. Community members expressed as much anger as did the workers. The level of distrust towards researchers appeared to be at its peak during the strike. There were speculations that we were working for the mine companies, which had allegedly sent people into the communities to inquire about workers' standpoints regarding the strike. This had allegedly resulted in the loss of employment for many individuals. Fear of job losses and distrust of researchers' intentions resulted in many workers refusing to participate in the survey. A number of death threats were made to deter us from continuing with our interviews.

The seemingly unethical behaviour of previous researchers in the area, or individuals pretending to be researchers, also surfaced as a major obstruction in a politically volatile climate (this is also a concern for future research endeavours where mistrust is high due to possibly unethical practices). We learned that some research publications and journalists' reports had put the subjects of interest (in this case, workers) at risk. One observer who refused to participate in the study said, 'I don't have time to participate. But be careful, there are many people who come here and pose as researchers and as a result people have been victimised, people have lost their jobs.' By explaining our research intentions, showing our proof of identification, and assuring workers that anonymity was guaranteed, we gained access to workers.

Nevertheless, fieldwork in Rustenburg was unpredictable and required improvisation. The majority of respondents, who worked underground, were reached through personal connections and door-to-door efforts. We relied almost entirely on a key contact who worked at the mines, was familiar with the environment, and was able to predict the reception we were likely to encounter. Driving to different parts of Rustenburg with our key contact person became the order of the day on our three-day visit in the region to meet our target sample. We met some union officials at their workplace in one of the mine hospitals: after a brief meeting with the hospital manager in which we formally identified ourselves, union members were organised, and all willingly participated. This was the only group with whom we met easily – unionised civil servants in the region were much more accessible than mineworkers, who were directly affected by the strike.

SAMPLING

Our data-collection method involved face-to-face semi-structured interviews with leaders of Cosatu and Cosatu affiliates, as previous surveys had done. Our aim was to increase the sample size from previous years and to conduct 1 500 interviews. We wanted to increase the sample size partly because we knew that future surveys would have to cover more than one federation. Because of the access challenges, we managed to conduct only 708 interviews. Although not meeting our target, the sample size compares well to previous surveys (see Table 2.4). As mentioned, for the 2014 survey Fedusa and Nactu affiliates were included in the sample. Included in most of the following tables is also the number of interviews conducted with federations other than Cosatu. One notices that Cosatu constitutes 87.7 per cent of the sample; this was because other federations were included at short notice and was also due to a lack of historical connections to officials and office bearers of these other federations, which made it difficult to arrange access to relevant workplaces. Below are summary tables that outline federations that participated, provinces where the research was conducted and the names of Cosatu affiliates that participated. In some cases, we compare our sample to those of previous years, to show that we succeeded to a large extent to achieve broadly similar numbers and proportions despite the access challenges.

Table 2.2:   Taking Democracy Seriously, interviews by federation, 2014

	Number of interviews	Percentage of sample
Cosatu	621	87.7
Fedusa	54	7.6
Nactu	6	0.8
Independent	27	3.8
Total	**708**	**100**

Table 2.3: Taking Democracy Seriously, interviews by province, 2014

	Number of interviews	Percentage of sample
Gauteng	195	27.5
North West	35	4.9
KwaZulu-Natal	142	20.1
Eastern Cape	163	23
Western Cape	173	24.4
Total	**708**	**100**

Table 2.4: Taking Democracy Seriously, interviews by province, 1994–2014

	1994	**1998**	**2004**	**2008**	**2014**
Gauteng	199	223	239	248	195
North West	13	–	43	21	35
KwaZulu-Natal	116	123	103	113	142
Eastern Cape	206	166	129	133	163
Western Cape	109	127	141	115	173

As one would expect, Gauteng has, over the years, dominated in terms of the numbers in the sample. One of the reasons is that the province of Gauteng has, by far, the largest number of trade union members. Also, it is the most industrialised province, from which people can be sourced as participants. However, in comparison to the previous surveys, the numbers in Gauteng have dipped, and this one would attribute to the absence of an access letter from Cosatu as referred to earlier in this chapter. The low sample in North West also reflects the ambivalence over and hostility towards the fieldwork in this province because of the strike.

In Table 2.5 we compare 2014 interviews, with Cosatu members only, to the two previous surveys, 2004 and 2008. We see that the number of interviews with Numsa members roughly doubles in 2014 relative to 2008 (possibly because Numsa had broadened its scope in terms of representation). For NUM the number remains more or less the same, in spite of the reduction in NUM membership after the emergence of Amcu. Our findings of political support have to be read with this in mind.

Table 2.5:   Taking Democracy Seriously, interviews by Cosatu affiliates, 2004–2014

	2004	**2008**	**2014**
Ceppwawu	34	67	47
CWU	30	28	19
Fawu	48	29	25
Nehawu	44	62	67
NUM	55	51	56
Numsa	90	69	136
Popcru	88	45	58
Saapawu	1	–	–
Saccawu	40	50	36
Sactwu	80	59	24
Sadtu	46	74	51
Samwu	49	29	39
Sasbo	10	13	30
Satawu	20	49	24
Denosa	–	5	14
Pawusa			7
Other	15	–	N/A
Non-members	7	–	N/A

Table 2.6:   Taking Democracy Seriously, interviews of shop stewards and union members, 2014

	Number of interviews	**Percentage of sample**
Shop stewards	162	22.9
Union members	546	77.1
Total	**708**	**100**

Table 2.7:   Taking Democracy Seriously, interviews of shop stewards and union members, 1998–2014

	1998	**2004**	**2008**	**2014**
Shop stewards	153	171	160	162
Union members	486	481	447	546

Our interviews have traditionally involved shop stewards as well as ordinary union members. In Tables 2.6 and 2.7, we present the proportions for 2014, as well as the actual figures, compared to previous surveys. Proportions remain roughly stable over the years, including the 2014 survey.

Table 2.8 illustrates that male and female representation in our sample is more or less consistent over the years. As pointed out, our fieldworkers make an effort in workplaces to ensure a gender balance when conducting interviews. In practice, this does not always work out owing to high levels of male leadership, even in unions with high numbers of female members. We expand on this in Chapter 8 of this volume.

Table 2.9 represents the different age categories of union members in our sample over the years. What is observable is that from 1994 to 2014, the age categories 26–35, 36–45, and 46–55 have represented the ages of the majority of union members. The lower representation in ages 18–25 could be argued as indicative of the times at which the majority of that age group are still battling with entrance into the labour market. On the other hand, the lower representation of the ages of 56–66+ could be attributed to the likeliest retirement age. From the table we can conclude that since the end of apartheid in 1994, a large number of young people (according to the South African definition) continue to take part in union activities.

Table 2.8: Taking Democracy Seriously, interviews by gender, 1994–2014

	1994	1998	2004	2008	2014[1]
Male	431	448	430	393	468
Female	212	191	225	232	233

Table 2.9: Taking Democracy Seriously, interviews by age cohort, 1994–2014

	1994	1998	2004	2008	2014[2]
18–25	19	36	37	33	31
26–35	244	233	198	206	217
36–45	219	226	259	229	234
46–55	135	123	130	109	169
56–65	26	21	29	32	47
66+	–	–	2	–	–

IMPLICATIONS

As the initial title of this longitudinal survey suggests, our research has always focused on the impact of democratic mandate-based forms of trade union representation (participatory democracy, representative democracy). The first survey was conducted prior to the 1994 elections that ushered in the new democratic dispensation. In this historical moment it was considered important to assess what workers expected from democracy and, more importantly, to consider ways in which to track these changes over time. With this is mind, the first Taking Democracy Seriously workers' survey was described by David Ginsburg et al. (1995: 15) as a modest endeavour to contribute to contemporary debates and demonstrate 'some of the possibilities of survey research in the context of a changing South Africa'. With minor changes to the questionnaire over the years, the Taking Democracy Seriously workers' survey has continued to examine workers' conceptions of democracy on the shop floor in order to understand how these conceptions extend to the broader political arena.

The use of a longitudinal study has allowed us to achieve this task, to build a wealth of data collected over a twenty-year period and to assess key trends. Targeting primarily workers belonging to Cosatu, and to a lesser extent other union federations, as well as supplementing this data with semi-structured in-depth interviews with trade union officials, our research offers important insights into how change has come about and where these changes are taking place. The temporal element of a longitudinal study has certainly proved that it 'can increase the explanatory power of empirical analysis' when individuals are tracked over time (Ruspini 1999: 219). This remains a major strength of this data set.

The Taking Democracy Seriously workers' survey has always been located within the context of the broader political and socio-economic climate that is sensitive prior to elections – a social context that has played a major role in shaping the research process, not only in terms of gaining access to workers, but also in terms of reflecting and interpreting the findings based on workers' dispositions in the workplace. With the former surveys, Cosatu has always played a supportive role by endorsing this research initiative to all its affiliates. This has been helpful to a certain extent. In 2014 this changed. While Cosatu did not object to the survey, they did not endorse the research to their affiliates, and this had a serious impact on the research process.

Even with careful planning and preparation, researchers cannot completely control the influence the socio-political climate will have on the research process. The implications of a changing political climate are that gatekeeping was experienced from both unions and employers. During this survey we noted the reluctance of certain unions to participate due to researchers 'coming and collecting what they need and never reporting back to us [unions]', to quote a union official. Others feared that researchers were spies for employers or political parties. Their concern, that research results could be used for political horse-trading, only heightened mistrust and ambivalence towards our research.

To address concerns and fears raised by unions, we have done our best to report back to them after the completion of the study. In spite of challenges we have managed to maintain some old and nurture some new networks, in keeping with the tradition since the first study in 1994. The fifth survey has opened up space for us to view more closely the perspectives and opinions of the historical rupture that has taken place in the labour movement at the time of the survey and thereafter. South African labour studies, like the labour movement, will face new challenges.

NOTES

1   Of the 708 participants interviewed, 7 participants did not respond.
2   Of the 708 participants interviewed, 10 participants did not respond.

BIBLIOGRAPHY

Alexander, Peter, Luke Sinwell, Thapelo Lekgowa, Botsang Mmope and Bongani Xezwi. 2012. *Marikana: A View from the Mountain and a Case to Answer.* Auckland Park: Jacana.

Bischoff, Christine and Malehoko Tshoaedi. 2012. The experience of conducting a longitudinal study: The Cosatu Workers' Survey, 2008. In *Cosatu's Contested Legacy: South African Trade Unions in the Second Decade of Democracy*, edited by Sakhela Buhlungu and Malehoko Tshoaedi. Cape Town: HSRC Press.

Buhlungu, Sakhela (ed.). 2006. *Trade Unions and Democracy: Cosatu Workers' Political Attitudes in South Africa.* Cape Town: HSRC Press.

Chinguno, Crispen. 2013. Marikana massacre and strike violence post-apartheid. *Global Labour Journal* 4(2): 160–166.

Community Agency for Social Enquiry (Case). 2013. *Cosatu Shop Steward Survey Findings Report.* Commissioned by the Forum for Public Dialogue (FPD). Braamfontein: Case. http://www.fpd.org.za/ (accessed 12 January 2016).

Congress of South African Trade Unions (Cosatu). 2012. *Findings of Cosatu Workers' Survey.* Johannesburg: Cosatu.

Ginsburg, David, Edward Webster, Roger Southall, Geoffrey Wood, Sakhela Buhlungu, Johann Maree, Janet Cherry, Richard Haines and Gilton Klerck. 1995. *Taking Democracy Seriously: Worker Expectations and Parliamentary Democracy in South Africa.* Durban: Indicator Press.

Ruspini, Elisabetta. 1999. Longitudinal research and the analysis of social change. *Quality and Quantity* 33: 219–227.

3

The Social Character of Labour Politics

Ari Sitas

THE ANC'S WANING HEGEMONY IN COSATU

The vital comradeships of class and nation shared by trade union members and shop stewards during the 1990s and the early 2000s (Sitas 2010) have been on the wane. Past Taking Democracy Seriously surveys, conducted from 1994 to 2004, showed how workplace democracy on the one hand and a commitment to the Alliance and support for the ANC on the other defined the character and political consciousness of the membership of Cosatu. For example, 75 per cent of members interviewed in 1994 expressed the intention to vote for the ANC, and 83 per cent and 84 per cent respectively supported the existence of the Alliance between the ANC, the SACP and Cosatu, and supported its continuance (Ginsburg et al. 1995).

Such quantitative measures dovetailed well with more qualitative work that enunciated forms of consciousness that blended class analysis and nationalism: the national idea spoke of a black nation, the producer of all wealth and values, exploited by white capitalists in the workplace (Sitas 2010); and, despite critical comment of Cosatu's shift from 'social movement unionism' towards a 'strategic unionism' (Von Holdt 2002) or a politics of 'cooperative alterity' and the adoption of a language that placed the ANC as the leading and hegemonic force in South Africa's National Democratic Revolution, workers and shop stewards expressed

Table 3.1:   Proportion of Cosatu members surveyed intending to vote for the ANC

	1994	1998	2004	2008	2014
Percentage	75	74	72	58	50

Table 3.2:   Proportion of Cosatu members surveyed who think the Alliance is the best way of securing workers' interests in Parliament

	1994	1998	2004	2008	2014
Percentage	82	70	65	62	45

unreserved support for such a post-1994 politics. To put it bluntly: between 1994 to 2004, the ANC was hegemonic. Period.

But as our continuous monitoring of all this has demonstrated, by 2014 such a hegemony has been receding.

Similarly, support for the Alliance has been receding.

In the volatile current environment it is appropriate to note that alongside this trend an increasing number of respondents would prefer that Cosatu is not aligned to any political formation or party. They constituted a bloc of 15 per cent of respondents in 1994; by 2014 this had doubled to 30 per cent. Furthermore, the call that Cosatu should abandon the Alliance and form its own political party was supported by 3 per cent of the 1994 respondents and 8 per cent of the 2014. The latest figure is at odds with a recent survey conducted by Case (2013), which found that such support would be six times our estimate. According to Terry Bell (2013), '65 per cent of the federation's shop stewards surveyed said they would vote for such a party if it existed – and was backed by Cosatu. In the absence of such a choice, 90 per cent pledged their votes to the ANC' (see also Pillay 2015: 121–126).

Such a view is very active in Numsa respondents in our survey, but not so evident in the rest. What is evident is support for the EFF at 8 per cent and the DA at 4 per cent. These phenomena of support are more vivid in Gauteng (EFF) and the Western Cape (DA). What is obvious is that there is disenchantment with the ANC and the Alliance as the majority, 52.5 per cent and 55 per cent respectively, are distancing themselves for a variety of reasons that can only be addressed through qualitative work. To use Gramscian language, the cement that held the ANC's hegemonic project together is crumbling as concerns organised labour. Ironically, this turn away starts from 2008, the year that also marked the post-Polokwane 'defeat' of the '1996 class project'.

My brief here is not to provide a socio-political analysis of these phenomena but, as a sociologist, to focus on a range of sociological variables that are linked to possible differentiation of disposition or attitude among our respondents, and to throw some light on them in order to deepen our understanding of this epochal shift in consciousness. In this chapter, I draw on the 2014 survey, as well as previous surveys, to provide an analysis of broad trends mainly at the quantitative level. But this demands a digression to make a serious theoretical point about hegemony.

In the past, whether one talked of blue- or white-collar cleavages, young or old workers, men or women, migrant or urban workers, Sesotho or isiZulu respondents, it was to give studies some depth and nuance, as such variables did not play a defining role. They acted as decorative inflections because they did not trump the political consciousness of the period between 1994 and 2004.

Such an emphasis could point to the fact that there was a lot to be shared between women nurses and clothing workers who headed households as single women and that, for example, the migrant workers in the mining industry did not share the same dispositions as those in the construction industry. But, in the main, shop-floor democracy and support for the Alliance coexisted with a variety of differentiating sociological variables.

Hegemony was and is the capacity of a movement to turn all possible contradictions, divisions and plausible fissures into a question of difference and, through that, establish an emotive and cognitive sway over and a unity between people. Questions of class, race, caste, gender, ethnicity, and so on get diffused into a mere difference. The work of Ernesto Laclau (2015) on Latin American populism, originally published in 1978, and my own work on Zulu ethnicity and Natal's working class (Sitas 1985) used this notion of hegemony to understand the creative construction of collective identities. In this sense, then, the ANC was hegemonic.

The fact that working-class respondents showed such dispositions and attitudes irked many left commentators who thought that all this was false consciousness. The subtext was that all this was a misrecognition of their real interest. The abandonment of the RDP by the '1996 class project' and the consolidation of the market-friendly Gear policy between 1996 and 1998 ought to have created a distance between the ANC and Cosatu. Furthermore, social movement activists were at a loss as to how Cosatu continued to enjoy such support even through the government's denialism about the AIDS epidemic that was ravaging workplaces, and the labour federation's affiliates and leadership's refusal to participate in service delivery protests and anti-neoliberal movements. Nevertheless, both Gillian Hart and I tried to elucidate the reasons for the sturdiness of such a hegemonic project (Hart 2002, 2013; Sitas 2010).

Whereas sociological variables were about inflections within a narrative of hegemony, since 2008 they have become serious points of differentiation and fissure. Obviously, the main cleavage is political: workers' dispositions are pulled apart by what were Cosatu's two largest trade unions: the NUM, whose members' support for the ANC has indeed increased to 82 per cent of respondents; and Numsa, whose members' support for the ANC has decreased to 36 per cent. The rest of trade union memberships of unions still affiliated, or formerly affiliated, to Cosatu are somewhere in between, pulled by both statistical poles. But in between, too, there is a range of sociological variables that demand attention. It is to these we now turn in order to elucidate seven of them. The following has to be read with an important caveat in mind: the sample size does not permit complex inferential statistics, save some explicit cross-tabulations that act as proximate indicators for basic trends. Suffice it to say that, at least in the following pages, such trends are strong enough to give some veracity to the argument that is unfolding here.

SOCIAL CHARACTERISTICS

The 2008 Taking Democracy Seriously survey announced the first two important variables that made an impact on political shifts: education and age. As the edited volume of the 2008 survey (Buhlungu and Tshoaedi 2012) showed, they were the most active variables affecting divergences in respondents' attitudes. This has continued as a point of divergence in the current survey.

Education

The more educated Cosatu members were, the more distant they were from the Alliance and the ANC; the less educated they were, their attitudes showed a tendency to be closer to the ANC and the Alliance. This is serious, because the educational character and profile of the trade union federation is changing. Table 3.3 demonstrates this pattern succinctly.

As can easily be seen, there is a staggering increase of people with technical diplomas and university degrees: from 3 per cent in 1994 to a combined 35 per cent by 2014. There is a concomitant decrease of respondents from Standard 10 and below: from 65 per cent in 1994 down to 17 per cent in 2014. There is a steady increase of those with Standard 11–12 levels of education: from 31 per cent in 1994 to 45 per cent by 2014. This shift is accompanied by a 48 per cent support of the ANC among the more educated categories in 2008 and a further decline to 41 per cent by 2014. Ironically, the

Table 3.3: Educational qualifications of Cosatu members (as percentages)

	1994	1998	2004	2008	2014
Below Standard 7	21	16	8	4	4
Standards 8–10	44	39	28	16	13
Standards 11–12	31	37	38	44	45
Technical Diploma	3	5	13	18	19
University Degree	0	2	7	13	16
Other	1	1	6	5	3

Source: Taking Democracy Seriously surveys, 1994–2014

higher concentration of diplomates and degree respondents will be found in Sadtu, the National Education, Health and Allied Workers' Union (Nehawu), the Finance Union (Sasbo) and Denosa. There is little variation between such dispositions, no matter what the trade union is. The irony is that the first two unions are formally very much two of the strongest supporters of the Alliance.

The opposite is also significant. The lower the educational endowment, the more commitment to the Alliance – with the exception of Numsa-linked respondents. Of course, lower education correlated strongly with skill levels, and the bulk of the unskilled and semi-skilled shows above-average levels of support for the ANC (50 per cent to 54 per cent). This perception will be modified later, when some refinement will be brought in through a focus on workplace conditions and working life. There is 100 per cent support for the ANC and the Alliance from signed-up and paid-up members of the SACP, half of whom belong in equal portions to the NUM and Numsa; 43.5 per cent of them are diplomates and/or degreed individuals. It is the opposite with the ANC members – the majority would be of Standard 12 and below, with a significant 36 per cent having higher education attainment.

Generation

Educational attainment seems to be co-weighed by age. The younger cohorts in Cosatu are better educated than the older, and the 1994 younger cohorts would now be the over-50-years-old members constituting close to a third of the shop-steward and member respondents. The variations between education and age are insignificant, which means that it is difficult to disaggregate the two. What reinforces the difficulty is that older workers (forty years plus) who are also better educated (usually technical diploma) do not display the same dispositions as younger workers with high qualifications. The former would be closer to the political culture of the Alliance.

So there is a generational divide beginning to emerge since 2008 which is reinforced by educational attainment. The older generation would have lived through the 1980s as young people at a time when their generation would have been the shock troops of the insurrection; they would have matured during the transition years and would have had a serious involvement in the decision towards strategic unionism. The younger generation would have picked up the relay stick in the 1990s and 2000s, a time of higher mobility and access to qualifications. The former would have been part and parcel of the establishment of structures on the shop floor and the deliberations around the establishment of an industrial relations system; the younger cohort would have found the structures in place.

There would undoubtedly have been an experiential divide, given the recent history of the country, but it need not, in and by itself, have created a divergence. That it does is a point of concern.

So if education and age were already appearing in the 2008 survey as points of cleavage, the 2014 survey points to another five points that need critical attention: working life-linked experiences, gender, migrant or non-migrant status, ethnicity and religion.

Working life

There is an implicit assumption that shop-floor experience of working conditions shapes consciousness. Such literature was at the heart of historical work on the transition from craft to industrial unionism (Lane 1974) and the transition of industrial life to mass production and Fordism. It has been assumed therefore that the more mechanical, repetitive, deskilled and like an assembly-line working life is, the more workers are dissatisfied and available to militant trade unionism. Such an assumption in the early 1960s (Blauner 1964) led to studies of 'alienation' which demonstrated that the more production was like an assembly-line, the more workers felt dissatisfied, powerless and contrary.

We tried to group together in this survey all mass-producing manufacturing plants (metal, food, clothing and chemical) where the work process approximated the modality of mechanical and assembly-line work. Unfortunately, the rest (save services) did not constitute a cohort large enough for a meaningful analysis. Furthermore, 'services' were so variegated that a coherent working-life model could not be put together – so we left them as a contrasting 'other'.

The support for the ANC (42 per cent) and the Alliance (43 per cent) becomes less in the former mass-producing clump. The constructed other (non-manufacturing cohort) tends to 'support' at higher rates both the ANC (49 per cent) and the Alliance (48 per cent). Removing metal- and rubber-producing shop floors

Table 3.4:   Manufacturing workers and support for the ANC

Category of working life	Proportion supporting the ANC
Manufacturing workers	42 %
Composite other	49 %
Manufacturing (rubber and metal excluded)	45.5 %

(Numsa strongholds), the support goes slightly up to 45.5 per cent (ANC) and 45 per cent (Alliance), which is below the study's average overall report. If one removes the more educated diplomates and university graduates from the mass-production cohort, it ranges from 41 per cent (with Numsa) to 45 per cent (without Numsa). This is an interesting inversion of the above educationally linked findings: in the mass-producing sector one finds more support for the Alliance among white-collar rather than among semi-skilled shop-floor workers. This is an important finding because the traditionally strong support for the Alliance in the 1994–2004 period was to be found among industrial semi-skilled production workers.

Gender

The differentiation of dispositions and attitudes between women and men is marked, but it did not vary significantly from the 2008 survey. More women than men tended to avoid the disclosure of their voting preferences. The difference between men and women who disclosed their political differences is narrow. In the 2008 survey, 42.4 per cent of women indicated that they would vote for the ANC, down from 68.2 per cent in the 2004 survey. Importantly, the decline in support for the ANC did not seem to benefit other parties. Rather than vote against the ANC, 12 per cent of women indicated that they would not vote at all (see Tshoaedi 2012: 100). In the 2014 survey, 43 per cent of women indicated that they would vote for the ANC and an equal number would not state for whom they were going to vote.

Where differentiation begins to show is among women and skill, and women and education: the more skilled and educated women are, the less politically inclined they are. There is also a divergence where women are found to be responsible for more than one household and more than five dependents. Here, the unions concerned are the Southern African Clothing, Textiles and Allied Workers' Union (Sactwu), Sadtu, Nehawu and Denosa, where there are larger concentrations of women. Unfortunately, the number of women is too small for the survey to make defining statements: for example, if we take the stronger ANC-supporting unions like Sadtu and Nehawu, men tend to support the Alliance more than women (52 per cent as against 40 per cent). Such numbers, though, are statistically unreliable.

What is obvious, however, is that men and women hold divergent views about trade union priorities and this divergent trend needs further research. There are a number of gender-sensitive studies of a qualitative nature that speak to gender relations in black working-class life. S'thembiso Bhengu's (2014) PhD thesis, for example, shows that in one of Cosatu's most militant shop floors organised by Numsa, radical ideas cohabited with a strong masculine culture around the *amadoda*, with the attempt to introduce women on the shop floor a resounding failure. There was a sense that union work was a man's prerogative. Similarly, Nomkhosi Xulu's (2012) study of KwaMashu hostel-dwellers showed quite a bifurcation in political commitment between men and women across the political spectrum from Inkatha to the ANC.

What is not so obvious is the secular decline over years among women. There are two trends that provide a very partial answer: the increasing union membership of women in white-collar occupations with the concomitant decline of women in textile, clothing and leather manufacturing. That fact that such industries are still prevalent in the Western Cape, and that coloured people are disaffected and persistently hostile to the ANC, might add to this trend.

Migrancy

Migrancy plays an important role. During the apartheid past, being a migrant was a legally imposed category that strictly regulated life chances and contrasted the experience of such a cohort as opposed to Section 10 'urbans'. Now, it is a subjective self-definition, meaning that one's life trajectory is primarily concentrated around a rural household, and one's involvement in urban work is there to support that trajectory. In the survey only 29.6 per cent of respondents self-defined as migrants. They would in the main be involved in trade unions like the NUM (65 per cent), the Chemical, Energy, Paper, Printing, Wood and Allied Workers' Union (Ceppwawu) (50 per cent), Numsa (36 per cent) and the Food and Allied Workers' Union (Fawu) (30 per cent). A further complicating factor is that there is an obvious commonality of response around a range of issues that differentiates those migrants who still reside in single-sex hostels as against all others, but the figure is statistically trivial as only fifteen workers from our sample reside in hostels.

Support by migrants for the ANC and the Alliance is marginally stronger than by residents of urban areas (49 per cent and 47 per cent respectively). If one removes the Numsa migrant responses, the support becomes very strong indeed, at

55 per cent. Where they differ from 'urbans' is over issues of support for community involvement and in a range of issues about improvement of life's conditions, or service delivery. As this forms part of other chapters, I will only highlight the political aspect of migrancy – which is not surprising at all as the trade union movement from the 1980s onwards was built around very strong migrant labour support.

Ethnicity

Ethnicity as a variable, and especially in its interaction with provincial location, is particularly revealing. For example, the strongest support for the ANC and the Alliance is to be found in KwaZulu-Natal (57.4 per cent) and the lowest in the Western Cape (38 per cent). Fascinating also is that the Eastern Cape (47.2 per cent) and Gauteng (45.4 per cent) are below the survey's average of 47.5 per cent. There is no doubt that KwaZulu-Natal is the epicentre of the Alliance and there seems to be more confidence in the current post-Polokwane leadership.

The closest indicator of ethnicity in the survey was around first-language responses: isiXhosa was the largest at 33.1 per cent, isiZulu at 23.7 per cent (Sesotho 6.5 per cent, Sepedi 5.2 per cent, Setswana 4.8 per cent – together to add another 21.7 per cent of African language speakers), Afrikaans at 13.6 per cent and English at 7.9 per cent. The strongest support for the Alliance comes from isiZulu speakers at 61 per cent, followed by isiXhosa speakers at 50 per cent, and it declines to 32 per cent among English speakers (Indian, coloured) and to 30 per cent among Afrikaans speakers (mostly coloured). Among coloured workers, the strongest support of the Alliance is to be found among farm workers in the Western Cape. Among isiXhosa speakers, the support for the Alliance is stronger in the Western Cape (54 per cent) than the Eastern Cape (46 per cent), whereas among isiZulu speakers the support is high in both KwaZulu-Natal and Gauteng (63 per cent and 58 per cent respectively).

Religion

The overwhelming majority (74.9 per cent) of respondents, men and women, belong to faith-based communities, so its contrasting 'other' is small. The only insight that can be gleaned from the survey is that there is a higher correlation between such belonging and indices of depoliticisation. Higher proportions of respondents were to be found in the non-disclosure of voting preferences and/or non-voting intentions, whereas the opposite was correct for the non-belonging (20.3 per cent) whose higher concentrations were found in NUM and Numsa. Only further qualitative work could take us closer to whether religious congregations are supplanting associational and political life in the community and how robust these tentative insights might be. What the parallel of religion and working life shows is that religious congregations are powerful associational props for foreign migrant workers in South Africa (Tame 2017) and among unemployed and survivalist women's networks in the context of disappearing formal jobs (Mosoetsa 2012).

CONCLUDING REMARKS

The seven sociological variables provide markers of differentiation in the post-2008 period. They present a serious challenge to Cosatu and the Alliance. Despite the ANC's 62 per cent electoral victory, the leadership should be worried about its support among the members of the trade union movement. The signed-up membership of the ANC stands at 31.2 per cent (paid-up: 17.2 per cent) and the SACP is at 7.8 per cent (paid-up: 6.2 per cent), which shows resilience, but the reach of such membership is shrinking. This is well understood by the leadership for, as Gwede Mantashe, former NUM general secretary and secretary general of the ANC, said towards the end of 2014 and in the run-up to the special national congress that ratified the expulsion of Numsa from Cosatu, this would be bad for the Congress Alliance as a whole (as reported in *City Press*, 10 November 2014). In the meantime, generation, education, workplace experience, gender, migrancy, ethnicity and religion, singularly and in interaction, are gaining in relevance as regards differentiation. The year 2008 gave us the first inkling of the importance of the first two; the current survey has added the rest of the sociological variables under discussion.

BIBLIOGRAPHY

Anon. 2014. Weak Cosatu not good for ANC – Mantashe. *City Press*, 10 November. http://www.news24.com/Archives/City-Press/Weak-Cosatu-not-good-for-ANC-Mantashe-20150429 (accessed 29 November 2016).
Bell, Terry. 2013. Intriguing hints on future by shop stewards survey. *The Star*, 30 August.
Bhengu, S'thembiso. 2014. Wage income, migrant labour and livelihoods: Beyond the rural-urban divide in post-apartheid South Africa: A case of Dunlop Durban factory workers. PhD thesis, University of KwaZulu-Natal, Durban.
Blauner, Robert. 1964. *Alienation and Freedom: The Factory Worker and His Industry*. Chicago: University of Chicago Press.
Buhlungu, Sakhela and Malehoko Tshoaedi (eds). 2012. *Cosatu's Contested Legacy: South African Trade Unions in the Second Decade of Democracy*. Cape Town: HSRC Press.
Community Agency for Social Enquiry (Case). 2013. *Cosatu Shop Steward Survey Findings Report*. Commissioned by the Forum for Public Dialogue (FPD). Braamfontein: Case.

Ginsburg, David, Edward Webster, Roger Southall, Geoffrey Wood, Sakhela Buhlungu, Johann Maree, Janet Cherry, Richard Haines and Gilton Klerck. 1995. *Taking Democracy Seriously: Worker Expectations and Parliamentary Democracy in South Africa*. Durban: Indicator Press.

Hart, Gillian. 2002. *Disabling Globalization: Place of Power in Post-apartheid South Africa*. Pietermaritzburg: University of KwaZulu-Natal Press.

Hart, Gillian. 2013. *Rethinking the South African Crisis: Nationalism, Populism, Hegemony*. Pietermaritzburg: University of KwaZulu-Natal Press.

Laclau, Ernesto. 2015 [1978]. *Política e ideología en la teoría marxista. Capitalismo, fascismo, populismo*. Madrid: Siglo XXI.

Lane, Tony. 1974. *The Union Makes Us Strong: The British Working Class, Its Trade Unionism and Politics*. London: Arrow Books.

Mosoetsa, Sarah. 2012. *Eating from One Pot: The Dynamics of Survival in Poor South African Households*. Johannesburg: Wits University Press.

Pillay, Devan. 2015. Cosatu and the Alliance: Falling apart at the seams. In *Cosatu in Crisis: The Fragmentation of an African Trade Union Federation*, edited by Vishwas Satgar and Roger Southall. Johannesburg: KMMR Publishing.

Sitas, Ari. 1985. From grassroots control to democracy: A case study of the impact of trade unionism on migrant workers' cultural formations on the East Rand. *Social Dynamics* 11(1): 32–43.

Sitas, Ari. 2010. *The Mandela Decade: Labour, Culture and Politics in Post-apartheid South Africa*. Pretoria: Unisa Press.

Tame, Bianca. 2017. 'Comfortable others': The process of identity niching among female migrant domestic workers, private employment agencies and employers in Cape Town. Draft PhD thesis, University of Cape Town.

Tshoaedi, Malehoko. 2012. Making sense of unionised workers' political attitudes: The (un) representation of women's voices in Cosatu. In *Cosatu's Contested Legacy: South African Trade Unions in the Second Decade of Democracy*, edited by Sakhela Buhlungu and Malehoko Tshoaedi. Cape Town: HSRC Press.

Von Holdt, Karl. 2002. Social movement unionism: The case of South Africa. *Work, Employment and Society* 16(2): 283–304.

Xulu, Nomkhosi. 2012. Changing migrant spaces and livelihoods: Hostels as community residential units, KwaMashu, KwaZulu-Natal, South Africa. PhD thesis, University of Cape Town.

4

Is Cosatu Still a Working-Class Movement?

**Andries Bezuidenhout, Christine Bischoff
and Ntsehiseng Nthejane**

INTRODUCTION

Members of Cosatu unions in our survey earned an average monthly income of
R12 361.26, ranging from an individual who earned R45 000 a month to one who
earned just R1 086. Of the entire sample, 25 per cent earned less than R6 800 per
month and half earned less than R11 000 per month. There were also differences
between Cosatu members who were members of public sector unions (average
monthly income R14 108.58) and private sector unions (average monthly income
R10 760.92). The households of more than 80 per cent of these union members
were entirely dependent on wages for household incomes, with only 4.4 per cent
reporting receiving child-care grants and fewer than 1 per cent receiving either old-
age or disability grants. These wages supported on average 4.26 other household
members, including children, as dependents (members of private sector unions
supported more household members, an average of 4.39 dependents, whereas
members of public sector unions supported an average of 4.05 dependents).

These figures illustrate the income diversity among members of trade unions
historically affiliated to Cosatu. In an opinion piece in the *Mail & Guardian*, Loane
Sharp (2014), an economist associated with the Free Market Foundation, argued

that a 'class war' was behind the divisions in Cosatu that led to the expulsion of Numsa:

> The middle class has fundamentally different values to the working class, including upward job mobility (as opposed to the working-class value of job security); home ownership; saving for retirement; independence from government financial assistance; and high-quality government services in policing, schooling and healthcare. The Numsa-Cosatu split, then, is much more complex than it at first appears. It is a battle for the heart of the ANC. It involves the long wave of South Africa's economic history. It sets the working class against the middle class in an epic battle of interests.

In this reading of the situation, Numsa members have a more radical working-class approach, whereas Cosatu, dominated by public sector unions, would have more conservative – or possibly liberal – values based on their interests rooted in the experience of class mobility.

There are clearly a number of limitations to this analysis which relates a complex set of issues to a distinction between a working class and a middle class. First, the alignment of the trade unions in the conflict contradicts the argument. The NUM is one of Numsa's main opponents and it would be a stretch of the imagination to describe the NUM's members as middle class, even though the union has succeeded in organising the emerging layer of team leaders and junior managers into the union. Sactwu's members are as working class as Numsa's and this union has not supported the decision to leave the Alliance (this may be due to the influence of Ebrahim Patel, this union's former general secretary who left the union to become a minister in the Zuma cabinet). Still, the fact that Sactwu has not taken Numsa's position poses a challenge to Sharp's class analysis. Then, the Eastern Cape's structures in Sadtu have also come out in support of Numsa – yet another counter-example.

Nevertheless, the hypothesis that the rupture in Cosatu is at least in some way related to the changing composition of its membership base is worth interrogating both theoretically and empirically, as long as this analysis is seen as an exploration of one possible contributing factor, rather than an 'epic battle of interests', as Sharp argues. In this chapter, we analyse the changing class composition of Cosatu's membership based on the Taking Democracy Seriously survey data from 1994 to 2014, but we also draw on Cosatu's own household-based surveys of its membership conducted by Naledi in 2008 and 2012. The findings of our workplace-based survey correspond to a large extent to those of the Cosatu household-based survey.

NEOLIBERAL GLOBALISATION AND CLASS FRAGMENTATION

Rather than general claims about working-class values and interests versus those of the middle class, we draw on Guy Standing's (2011, 2014) work that explores how globalisation and increased labour market flexibility across the globe led to the emergence of new forms of labour market insecurity. Needless to say, neoliberal economists like Sharp would view increased flexibility in a positive light and would see this as a strategy that would lead to a more progressive atmosphere in terms of profit maximisation and economic gains for companies globally. However, as Standing argues (2011: 6), increased flexibility has been at the expense of workers who have since gone through a number of economic and social transitions. 'As flexible labour spread, inequalities grew, and the class structure that underpinned industrial society gave way to something more complex but certainly not less class based.'

It is within this context that we borrow from Standing's notion of class fragmentation under globalisation, in which he identifies different emerging class positions, namely (i) the elite, (ii) the salariat, (iii) proficians, (iv) the working class, (v) the precariat, and (vi) the unemployed. According to Standing, the elite primarily consists of a wealthy minority with economic capacity sufficient to afford them the ability to influence most of the government's undertakings. The salariat are those individuals who have stable full-time employment and aspire to move into the elite class and enjoy a number of social benefits that are subsidised by the government. The majority of this group is concentrated within large corporations, government agencies and public administration, including the civil service. The class of proficians is made up of a smaller group of individuals who possess a number of skills and can occupy more professional positions within the labour market, which automatically fits them into certain jobs that require their expertise, although they do not necessarily strive for long-term employment. When Standing refers to the working class, he means individuals who are mostly involved in skilled or unskilled routine and manual work, who are more economically challenged and who rely in part on state welfare programmes when they retire. Finally, the precariat consists of those who find themselves in more precarious class positions, with no sense of security or upward social mobility.

Standing (2011) argues that the precariat is diverse and fragmented, ranging from manual workers employed on non-standard contracts of employment and those who work in the informal economy, to undocumented migrants who eke out a living through piecemeal economic activities or in clandestine employment, and to graduate students who work in the emerging service sector, at times doing highly qualified work such as computer programming or social media-based marketing campaigns but under insecure conditions of employment. Standing argues that the precariat is the new 'dangerous class', since this is where many of the social movements in recent times have come from, from the role of unemployed graduates in the Arab Spring to immigrant rights organisations and the 'Occupy' movements around the globe. Traditional trade unions are mostly both marginal and marginalised in these kinds of struggles (for a number of critiques of Standing's work, see Chun 2016; Paret 2016; Scully 2016; Wright 2016; as well as a response to these in Standing 2016).

We show in this chapter how Cosatu's membership base has changed over time. Under apartheid, the black working class was less diverse because of class and race commonalities: thus the common recognition and realisation of the consciousness around which solidarities were built during this time. Apartheid legislation and active discrimination meant that there was little opportunity for career advancement. However, in post-apartheid South Africa, the lid on social mobility for the black working class has been lifted, and we see more and more workers moving across social classes, getting a better education and thus better jobs – which in turn renders them capable of moving up the social ranks. Cosatu members now straddle various class positions and fall within what Standing (2011) would describe as the salariat, proficians, the working class and the precariat. Former comrades have even moved into the elite, a process that creates contradictions of its own. This multifaceted change in class structure not only forms the core of our argument but also serves to reveal how the neoliberal strategy continues to further fragment the labour market that is in constant mobility between different class positions.

UNIONS AND THE WORKING CLASS

We situate our interrogation of Cosatu's changing class composition within a broader understanding of the changing structure of the South African labour market. For this we primarily draw on the Labour Force Survey data from 2014 and do so in order to provide for a more generalised picture as a point of comparison. South Africa has a population of 53 million, of which 35 million are of working age (16–64 years). According to the Labour Force Survey, at the end of 2014 15.4 million of these people were classified as in employment, of which 11 million were employed in the formal sector, 2.5 million in the informal sector, 700 000 in agriculture and 1.2 million in private households.

In terms of occupational levels, the Labour Force Survey classified those who were considered to be employed as follows:

Manager: 1.4m

Professional: 1m

Technician: 1.6m

Clerk: 1.6m

Sales and service: 2.6m

Skilled agriculture: 90 000

Crafts and trades: 1.8m

Plant and machine operators: 1.3m

Elementary workers: 3.2m

Domestic workers: 1m

An additional breakdown of those considered to be employed can be made as follows: 13 million are considered to be employees; a further 800 000 are employers; 1.2 million work as own account workers; 100 000 work as unpaid household members. Of those considered employees, 10.5 million have written contracts of employment but only 8.2 million of them are employed permanently. An additional 2 million are employed on contracts of limited duration (these can range from casual cashiers to university vice chancellors) and a further 2.8 million are on employment contracts of unspecified duration. Only 3.9 million employees are members of trade unions, and the wages and working conditions of roughly 2 million are covered by bargaining councils. The wages of others are set by collective bargaining (3 million), by employers unilaterally (6 million), and the rest by mutual agreement. The Labour Force Survey does not state how many of these employees are covered by sectoral determinations. Only 6.4 million employees make pension fund contributions, 7.9 million contribute to the Unemployment Insurance Fund (UIF) and 4.1 million have medical aid.

These figures provide for some context of the varying levels of permanence, inclusion and security that characterise the lives of South African employees. Thus far we have looked at those considered to be employed. The Labour Force Survey considers 5 million South Africans to be unemployed, of which 3.4 million suffer from long-term unemployment. It should be noted that those considered to be unemployed are those who are actively seeking work, and an additional 2.5 million so-called discouraged job seekers are counted as 'not economically active' because they have given up hope of finding work. We would argue that they should be counted with those considered to be unemployed, along the lines of what South African statisticians call the 'expanded definition of unemployment'. In addition to this large group of discouraged job seekers, there are 6.3 million students, 2.8

Table 4.1:   South Africa's labour market structure

Total population: 53m	Population of working age (16–64 years): 35m
Not economically active: 12.5m	Students: 6.3m Home-makers: 2.8m Disability, illness: 1.6m
Unemployed: 7.5m	Long-term unemployment: 3.4m Job losers: 1.7m New entrants: 2m Discouraged job seekers: 2.5m
Precariat: 6.8m	Informal sector: 2.5m Casual, outsourced, limited-duration contracts: 3.3m Domestic workers: 1m
Working class, salariat, proficians: 8.2m	Pension fund contributions: 6.4m; UIF: 7.9m; medical aid: 4.1m Trade union members: 3.9m Bargaining council: 2m; Collective bargaining: 3m Employer decides wages: 6m

Source: Compiled by the authors, based on Statistics South Africa (2012, 2014)

million people classified as 'home-makers', and 1.6 million who are disabled or ill and can therefore not work.

In the table above we present a graphic illustration of the structure of the South African labour market by drawing on these figures and Standing's conceptualisation of the changing class structure that results from economic restructuring under neoliberal globalisation.

FROM UNSKILLED, SEMI-SKILLED TO SKILLED, PROFESSIONAL ...

At its high point, Cosatu had a membership of 2.2 million. This was the result of three waves of unionisation. The first wave of members comprised workers who were organised into the initial manufacturing unions that grew out of the militancy of the 1973 strikes. The second wave was the NUM that became part of the movement when it joined up with the Federation of South African Trade Unions (Fosatu) and other formations in 1985. The third wave was that of the public sector unions which emerged after 1990 and benefited because the Labour Relations Act of 1995 brought public sector employees under the same dispensation as the private sector in terms of collective bargaining and organisational rights. Public sector unions were so marginal to Cosatu and to debates in labour studies that the researchers did not even include any unions from the public sector in the first Taking Democracy Seriously survey in 1994. The sample only included members from public sector unions in 2004.

From 1994, union members were asked to classify themselves as professional, clerical, supervisors, skilled, semi-skilled or unskilled. It is interesting to note that less than 1 per cent classified themselves as professional in 1994, 1998 or 2004. This is significant, since public sector unions were included in the 2004 survey. There is a major shift in the last two surveys, with 20 per cent of our sample classifying themselves as professional in 2008, and 19 per cent in 2014. This constitutes a fifth of Cosatu members, certainly a massive shift from the early 1990s. Those members who classified themselves as clerical remained more or less constant, with those classifying themselves as supervisors increasing slightly from 4 per cent in 1994 to 6 per cent in 2014. What is interesting, though, is an increase of those who classify themselves as skilled, rising from 21 per cent in 1994 to 37 per cent in 2014, and a decrease of those who classify themselves as unskilled, declining from 30 per cent in 1994 to a mere 8 per cent in 2014, almost equal to the members who are supervisors. This means that whereas 60 per cent of Cosatu members were semi-skilled and unskilled workers in 1994, by 2014 only 29 per cent classified themselves as unskilled or semi-skilled (see Table 4.2).

What explains this major transformation in Cosatu's membership composition? We explore three possible explanations. First, the fact that a number of public sector unions joined the federation may explain the increase in the number of

Table 4.2:   Skill level, 1994–2014 (all values as percentages)

	2014	2008	2004	1998	1994
Unskilled	8	6	12	18	30
Semi-skilled	21	16	26	35	30
Skilled	37	39	42	30	21
Supervisor	6	8	9	5	4
Clerical	7	8	8	8	10
Professional	19	20	–	–	–
Other	1	3	2	3	5
Don't know/Refuse to answer	1	–	–	–	–
Total	**100**	**100**	**100**	**100**	**100**

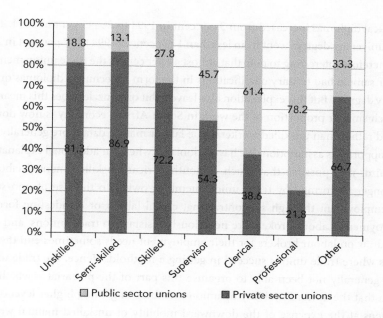

Figure 4.1: Skill category by private sector and public sector unions, 2014

professionals – mostly teachers and nurses who are members of Sadtu, Denosa and Nehawu. This is confirmed when one breaks down the levels of skill according to whether members belong to private sector or public sector unions for the 2014 survey. The data show that 78 per cent of union members who classify themselves as professionals are from public sector unions, whereas unskilled, semi-skilled and skilled members tend to come from private sector unions, with 81 per cent (unskilled), 87 per cent (semi-skilled) and 72 per cent (skilled) from private sector unions. Public sector unions joining Cosatu explains the increase in the number of professionals, but does not provide enough of an explanation for the decline in the number of unskilled members as an overall proportion of members. We have to look elsewhere for this.

Second, there may be the possibility that the post-apartheid regime has allowed for trade union members to upgrade their skills over time. The data over time seems to provide some support for these explanations. The proportion of members who had completed Grades 5–7 declined from 15 per cent in 1994 to a mere 2 per cent in 2014, and those who had completed Grades 8–10 went from 44 per cent in 1994 to a low 11 per cent in 2014. In contrast, those who had completed Grades 11–12 increased from 31 per cent in 1994 to 45 per cent in 2014, and members with technical diplomas increased from 3 per cent in 1994 to 20 per cent in 2014. Those with university degrees went from less than 1 per cent in 1994 to 17 per cent in 2014. It is therefore interesting to note that almost 40 per cent of the trade union members in our sample had tertiary qualifications in the form of technical diplomas or university degrees. But this explanation also leaves a bit of a puzzle. Does this mean that a much smaller proportion of the work in South Africa's economy is now done by skilled rather than unskilled workers? The labour market data more generally does not support this assumption. We have to look elsewhere for additional explanations.

Third, it is possible that much of South Africa's unskilled manual labour is no longer performed by trade union members owing to the rise of non-standard employment through subcontracting, casual labour or clandestine forms of employment. Labour brokers are notoriously resistant to trade unions, and firms that draw on labour brokers for their employment needs sometimes end the contracts where trade unions succeed in getting a foothold. Hence, the trade unions have generally not been able to organise this part of the precariat – which may mean that the upward mobility by union members in gaining higher level of skill happens at the expense of the downward mobility of unskilled manual workers who no longer form the heart of the union movement, and now form part of South Africa's growing precariat.

However, it may also be possible that our workplace-based sample is not able to pick up union members who work in less organised parts of the economy, such as construction sites or filling stations, the latter an example of a less typical part of the labour market that Numsa succeeded in organising in recent years. To test this point we turn to Cosatu's household-based survey. Here we should mention

Table 4.3:   Highest level of education, 1994–2014 (all values as percentages)

	2014	2008	2004	1998	1994
No formal education	–	–	–	3	2
Std 2 or lower/Grade 4 or lower	1	–	2	3	4
Std 3–5/Grades 5–7	2	3	6	11	15
Std 6–8/Grades 8–10	11	16	28	38	44
Std 9–10/Grades 11–12	45	44	38	37	31
Technical diploma	20	18	13	5	3
University degree	17	13	7	2	–
Other	3	7	6	1	1
Total	**100**	**100**	**100**	**100**	**100**

that this survey only selected union members with an income lower than R12 000 a month, so it has its own bias against upwardly mobile union members. In 2006, a quarter of Cosatu members counted as professionals – mostly teachers and nurses – while 21 per cent were semi-skilled production workers and 13 per cent were elementary workers. In contrast, skilled and clerical workers made up a larger share of members in other unions. Just 14 per cent of Cosatu members, and 10 per cent of other union members, had only primary education; most of the rest had some secondary, and about a quarter (mostly educators and nurses) had a tertiary degree.

In the 2012 Cosatu/Naledi survey, these occupational-level categories are somewhat altered. In this year, and quite tellingly, 2.7 per cent of Cosatu union members were classified as managers. A further 19 per cent were classified as professionals (including nurses and teachers); 26 per cent as skilled artisans, technicians or supervisors; and another 13 per cent as administrative workers, secretarial or clerical workers, or shop assistants. In this survey, the researchers did not distinguish between semi-skilled and unskilled workers and merely included a broad category termed 'labourer or general worker', with 37 per cent of the sample classified as such.

So, rather than contradicting our findings, the Cosatu/Naledi surveys seem to confirm that there seems to be a growing skilled and professional cohort of members and a declining proportion of unskilled manual workers who are union members. To be sure, both our survey and the Cosatu/Naledi surveys find that members of trade unions affiliated to Cosatu have higher levels of matric, as well as tertiary qualifications, than those employed in the labour market more generally. In the case of the Cosatu/Naledi survey, this is despite the fact that only union members with an income lower than R12 000 are included. We argue that this is explained, at least in part, by public sector unions with their teachers and nurses joining the Cosatu ranks; by the upward mobility of Cosatu members more generally (now including a number of managers); and by the casualisation of elementary work and the difficulty in organising the growing precariat – those in non-standard employment who are subjected to new forms of workplace despotism and informalisation.

Finally, before we conclude our argument, a note of caution: we recognise here that, owing to the devaluation of the teaching and nursing professions under apartheid and neoliberal post-apartheid restructuring, there may be a valid critique of our classifying teachers and nurses as professionals – and part-time teachers may even be classified as part of Standing's notion of the precariat. This point underscores the contradictory nature of class positions (Wright 1985).

Table 4.4: Occupational levels of Cosatu members compared to the Labour Force Survey of 2014 (all values as percentages)[1]

	Taking Democracy Seriously 1994	Taking Democracy Seriously 2014	Cosatu/Naledi Survey 2006	Cosatu/Naledi Survey 2012	Labour Force Survey 2014
Manager	0 (Professional)	19 (Professional)		2.7 (Manager)	9
Professional	4 (Supervisor)	6 (Supervisor)	25 (Professional) 3 (Semi-professional)	19 (Professional teacher or nurse)	6
Clerk	10	7	8	13 (Administrative worker, secretarial, clerical worker, shop assistant)	11
Sales and services	21 (Skilled)	37 (Skilled)	9 (Sales) 6 (Services)		15
Technician			9 (Skilled)	26 (Skilled worker, artisan, technician, supervisor)	10
Skilled agriculture					1
Craft and related trade					12
Plant and machine operator	30 (Semi-skilled)	21 (Semi-skilled)	21 (Semi-skilled)	37 (Labourer or general worker)	8
Elementary	30 (Unskilled)	8 (Unskilled)	13 (Elementary)		21
Domestic worker					6
Total	100 [5 (Other or no response)]	100	100 [6 (Other and no formal schooling)]	100 [3 (Other)]	100

Table 4.5: Levels of formal education of Cosatu members compared to the Labour Force Survey of 2014 (all values as percentages)[2]

	Taking Democracy Seriously 1994	Taking Democracy Seriously 2014	Cosatu/Naledi Survey 2006	Cosatu/Naledi Survey 2012	Labour Force Survey 2014
No schooling	2	0	14 (Less than primary)	8.6 (None, some primary or completed primary)	2.6
Less than primary completed	19 (Grade 7 or lower)	3 (Grade 7 or lower)			6.9
Primary completed					3.9
Secondary not completed	44 (Grades 8–10)	11 (Grades 8–10)	28 (Secondary without matric)	29.2 (Some secondary without matric)	33.4
Secondary completed	31 (Grades 11–12)	45 (Grades 11–12)	31 (Matric)	36.5 (Matric completed)	31.6
Tertiary	3 (Technical diploma) 0 (University degree)	20 (Technical diploma) 17 (University degree)	27 (Tertiary degree or diploma)	14.7 (Diploma after matric or FET diploma) 10.4 (University or technikon degree)	20.2
Other	3	3		0.6	1.2
Total	100	100	100	100 [3 [Other]]	100

CONCLUSION

Cosatu's membership has changed over time. Public sector unions joining the federation has had an impact on its class composition, the upward mobility of members has added another dimension, and the growing precarious nature of work has led to the emergence of a new cohort of insecure workers who are often not organised by existing unions. It is far from a 'class war' between a working class and a middle class – we have witnessed a complicated process of class restructuring, with the composition of Cosatu being altered accordingly. However, one should note that using an individual's position in the economy as a basis for class analysis is clearly problematic. People live in households and communities and have commitments to family members and others to whom they have obligations of social repricocity. The Marxist sociologist Erik Olin Wright (1985) has used the term 'contradictory class location' to describe the middle classes of the capitalist system in order to illustrate that values and political choices cannot be linked to a person's class position in a structural way. One might apply this notion of a contradictory class location to the old working class wedged between the salariat/proficians and the emerging precariat. Some employees may have permanent contracts of employment, but their positions are far from secure.

We do not wish to take a position here on whether the precariat is a class, or even a class-in-the-making. In this regard Wright (2016: 134–135) argues: 'The precariat, as a rapidly growing segment of the working class and the bearer of the sharpest grievances against capitalism, may have a particularly important role to play in struggles over the rules of capitalism and over capitalism itself, but it is not a class in its own right … The salience of precariousness as part of the condition of life for millions of people in the world today does not depend on whether people in such positions are viewed as being in a distinct class. What matters is the reality of the conditions they face and what can be done about it.' Hence, although Wright and others criticise Standing for relegating the working class to the past, there seems to be agreement that precarity matters. Presenting the divisions in the labour movement as a struggle between the working class and the middle class entirely ignores these divisions, however we may disagree over its classification and implications.

Acknowledging how the economy has altered the functioning of the labour market and how this has affected patterns of class inequality, as well as the implications this has for trade union organisation, all remain part of a challenge for the labour movement. In the next chapter of this volume we argue that one needs to consider household dynamics in addition to changes in the labour market and workplace in order to understand the class basis of changing solidarities and allegiances.

NOTES

1   Totals may not always add up to 100 per cent because of rounding.
2   Totals may not always add up to 100 per cent because of rounding.

BIBLIOGRAPHY

Alexander, Peter, Claire Ceruti, Keke Motseke, Mosa Phadi and Kim Wale. 2013. *Class in Soweto*. Pietermaritzburg: University of KwaZulu-Natal Press.

Chun, Jennifer Jihye. 2016. The affective politics of the precariat: Reconsidering alternative histories of grassroots worker organising. *Global Labour Journal* 7(2): 136–147.

Paret, Marcel. 2016. Towards a precarity agenda. *Global Labour Journal* 7(2): 111–122.

Scully, Ben. 2016. Precarity North and South: A Southern critique of Guy Standing. *Global Labour Journal* 7(2): 160–173.

Seekings, Jeremy and Nicoli Nattrass. 2005. *Class, Race, and Inequality in South Africa*. New Haven, CT: Yale University Press.

Sharp, Loane. 2014. Class war behind Cosatu-Numsa divide. *Mail & Guardian*, 21 November. http://mg.co.za/article/2014-11-21-class-war-behind-cosatu-numsa-divide (accessed 10 December 2014).

Standing, Guy. 2011. *The Precariat: The New Dangerous Class*. London: Bloomsbury.

Standing, Guy. 2014. *A Precariat Charter: From Denizens to Citizens*. London: Bloomsbury Academic.

Standing, Guy. 2016. The precariat, class and progressive politics: A response. *Global Labour Journal* 7(2): 189–200.

Statistics South Africa (StatsSA). 2012. *Census 2011*. Statistical Release P0301.4. Pretoria: StatsSA.

StatsSA. 2014. *Quarterly Labour Force Survey*. Statistical Release P0211. Pretoria: StatsSA.

Wright, Erik Olin. 1985. *Classes*. London and New York: Verso.

Wright, Erik Olin. 2016. Is the precariat a class? *Global Labour Journal* 7(2): 123–135.

5

Labour Aristocracy or Marginal Labour Elite? Cosatu members' income, other sources of livelihood and household support

Christine Bischoff and Bianca Tame

WORKERS, HOUSEHOLDS AND SOUTH AFRICA'S SOCIO-ECONOMIC ORDER

This chapter attempts to examine critically the view of Cosatu workers as a labour aristocracy or a 'self-interested' elite. It does so by examining wage data gathered from members of Cosatu affiliates in the fifth of a series of surveys of Cosatu membership which have been conducted since 1994, and it looks at the wage data through a number of other variables derived from questions in the 2014 survey of membership.

The notion of Cosatu members as a labour aristocracy can be related to the growing divisions in the labour market between permanent and temporary workers and high-income and low-income earners (see Forslund and Reddy 2015: 84–88). Our data suggests that Cosatu does not organise many temporary workers but it does organise workers who earn low wages. Importantly, those who support the labour aristocracy thesis often use labour market data as applied to individuals. In this chapter we take seriously the point that trade union members support dependents on their wages. Pnina Werbner's (2010) use of the notion of a 'marginal labour elite' provides a far more useful way of understanding Cosatu's membership. Werbner's 'marginal labour elite' locates trade union members outside of the workplace and in relation to their social reality by focusing specifically on their role in the household as a wage earner.

Twenty years into democracy, South African society is still marked by immense socio-economic problems such as chronic levels of unemployment and incessant levels of poverty and inequality. The number and intensity of strikes have increased in private and public sector workplaces. Globally, in the phase of information-technology-led capitalism, the number of workers employed as permanent workers is decreasing as the number employed as temporary, casual or part-time workers is increasing.

This trend is explained by Jan Theron's (2010) description of the interrelated processes of 'informalisation from above' and 'informalisation from below'. Whereas 'informalisation from below' refers to those who engage in survivalist activities or self-employment, 'informalisation from above' is a response to employers' efforts to restructure workplaces by externalising labour. This process fragments and differentiates the workforce by creating a layer of workers who, despite being located in the formal workplace, find themselves on the outside of labour legislation and collective bargaining because their employer, the service provider, determines their working conditions and is not legally bound to an employment relationship with the core business.

The increase in new types of employment can be attributed to particular global forces associated with neoliberal globalisation: employment that is not 'decent', is precarious and is comprised of unorganised (vulnerable) workers continues. Nevertheless, the majority of these workers are not organised by Cosatu. The challenge of adequately organising this growing stratum of workers has been aptly described by Ari Sitas (2008, 2010) as the 'crisis of representation'. While Cosatu has continued the campaign for decent work – calling for permanent status and social security benefits for all – the challenge of representing casual, part-time and informal workers remains. The need for labour to 'broaden its constituency and form alliances with groups outside of the traditional unions in the formal sector' is a key theme raised by many (Webster et al. 2008: 38; see also Hofmeyr 2012).

Even though South Africa's current 'social wage package' of free primary health-care, no-fee-paying schools, social grants such as old-age pensions and child support, RDP housing, and the provision of basic services (water, electricity and sanitation) to households has helped to reduce poverty in the country, it is still a fact that more than half (54 per cent) of black Africans live in poverty. Evidently the increase in the average welfare of citizens through the social grants system has become an important source of livelihood for a considerable segment of the population.

The dire situation of most households affected by unemployment and with no or limited access to work is reflected in the Oxfam report (Teka Tsegay et al. 2014) on hidden hunger in South Africa. It reveals that despite 15 million people having access to social grants, many run out of money to buy food. For those with low-paid or irregular work, food security is hindered because households are unable to sustain stable access to food – with many reporting that they reduce meal sizes or skip meals. Research conducted by Sarah Mosoetsa (2011) in Mpumalanga and Enhlalakahle confirms this finding as well.

In addition, exclusion and impoverishment for the majority of the population persists. Various poverty alleviation strategies by the government have had an impact on the poorest section of the population, but inequality in income as measured by the Gini coefficient has increased in post-apartheid South Africa, rising to an epic 0.685. South African society is one of the most unequal societies in the world.

A South African Commercial, Catering and Allied Workers' Union (Saccawu) official shares his sentiments regarding the low wages and income disparities within his sector:

> ... It [the working class movement] does not address the question of inequality, poverty in our case. If you look at the CEO of Shoprite Checkers for example, he earned himself R52 million as a bonus for one year whereas ... for part-timers, they earning for example R2 000, R2 500 a month which is a huge wage ... gap between the directors and your senior managers and with the ordinary workers. There's a huge gap in terms of the wages. There's a lot of disparities of course within our sectors (interview, Saccawu official, 2014).

In South Africa, the incidence of protracted strikes in many industries is indicative of organised workers who have become increasingly frustrated with their low pay, with their companies reneging on their promises to improve their working (and living) conditions and with their own trade unions for failing to protect and advance their interests.

COSATU MEMBERSHIP: A LABOUR ARISTOCRACY?

Peter Waterman (1975) contends that the historical use of the concept 'labour aristocracy' relates to the highly skilled and unionised section of the working class who were affiliated with the middle class economically, socially and politically in mid- and late-nineteenth-century Britain. Friedrich Engels argued in 1858 that the English proletariat were 'becoming more and more bourgeois'. Lenin used the concept during the First World War to argue that a 'privileged upper stratum of the proletariat in the imperialist countries lives partly at the expense of hundreds of millions of members of uncivilised nations'. The concept, therefore, could be used to describe the entire working class or just a part of it (such as skilled artisans or clerical workers, or members of trade unions, or certain unions, or trade union leaders). In addition the concept was used to describe the conservative position of a working class or within a working class, particularly in European and American contexts.

The concept has also been applied to the working class of the African conti-nent when explaining the conservatism among 'third world workers' (Harris 1973 cited in Waterman 1975). The African debate is that the regularly employed are also unionised wage earners but are a small proportion in comparison to the labouring population of Africa. This small group tends to be employed in the private sector, working for large multinational corporations, or they are in government employ-ment. As the majority of the labouring population work in the informal sector or in agriculture and are not members of a trade union, they are less likely to exert the same pressure that the unionised workers can exert on bargaining for wage increases. However, the acceptance and relevance of the application of the labour aristocracy concept to the African context has been debated and has given rise to several theses by Marxist scholars (Jack Woddis, Giovanni Arrighi, John Saul and Chris Allen, to name a few). They concur that there are conservative and privi-leged constituents among the African working class, but refer to different groupings when discussing the labour aristocracy. In particular, Saul and Arrighi's distinction between an urban proletariat and rural proletariat, referred to as the 'proper pro-letariat', denies the rural-urban connection and heterogeneity of the working class (Waterman 1975; Werbner 2010). Waterman calls for more empirical work to be done in order to refine the theoretical concept within Marxist class theory.

Some are of the view that Cosatu represents a 'labour aristocracy' against the massive sea of socio-economic problems (Buhlungu et al. 2006). Others do not endorse this view. Instead, they acknowledge that while Cosatu members display similar characteristics to the traditional description of the 'labour aristocracy' – that they are better skilled and educated, have access to stable and secure employ-ment with benefits, and represent working-class conservatism – research findings suggest otherwise (Buhlungu et al. 2006; Pillay 2006). The two key contributions that discredit the labour aristocracy thesis are provided by Devan Pillay's (2006) account of how organised workers continue to participate in community and industrial action despite their 'privileged status' as organised members. This particular theme is revisited in Chapter 7 in this book.

Werbner (2010: 693) proposes the notion of a 'marginal labour elite', similar to the idea of organised workers representing a 'privileged minority', to 'theorise the crucial differences between permanently employed, unionised African wage earners and the "ever-increasing" number of casualised workers in the informal economy'. By focusing on the personal finances of female industrial-class workers, she describes them as representing the 'marginal labour elite' because of their access to certain privileges. For example, access to mortgages, plots of land, private health and burial insurance as well as stable full-time employment in the public sector are outlined in her case studies. What is especially striking in Werbner's research is that, despite having access to these privileges, female trade unionists engage in full-time paid work, voluntary union activism and multiple livelihood strategies to offset their low earnings to sustain multiple and growing households.

In this respect, Werbner (2010) situates the 'marginal labour elite' outside of the workplace and in relation to their social reality by focusing specifically on their role in the household as a wage earner. This is important because the issue of precarious work, even among those who are organised, is juxtaposed with their privileged status as a labour elite.

Like our previous survey results, our findings in 2014 indicate that there is a high percentage of Cosatu members in permanent employment (87.7 per cent in 2004; 92.2 per cent in 2008; and 90 per cent in 2014). However, we added two new questions to our previous survey questionnaire to consider workers' access to other sources of income in their household, and the number of households and dependents they support. Recent scholarship on household dynamics in South Africa has shed light on how trade union members (irrespective of employment status) are pressured to pool resources to survive, so our need to include these questions was most relevant.

Mosoetsa's (2011) work, for example, illustrates the significance of redistributive networks in the context of formal wage labour decline. Her work draws our attention to the various livelihood strategies adopted by households in two KwaZulu-Natal townships, Mpumalanga and Enhlalakahle, as a response to high unemployment levels. Her findings indicate that women play a central role in ensuring the day-to-day survival of households, through their social grants, subsistence production or income from working in the informal economy. These household livelihood strategies are sometimes supplemented with income generated from illegal shebeens and the sexual economy (Mosoetsa 2011; Sitas 2010; Xulu 2012).

As with most of the recent literature on the decline of the wage earner, our attention is drawn to how households adapt to the shift from access to wage labour to other forms of livelihoods (see, for example, Sitas 2010; Xulu 2012). One consequence of this shift is the growing household – referred to as 'clustering' by Mosoetsa (2011: 26) – which 'is influenced by the need to secure income and food' but 'often results in greater income insecurity and overcrowding'.

Our survey results indicate that the number of dependents organised workers have per household averages four, and that more women than men said that they are part of these redistributive networks. With gender and intergenerational dynamics concerning forms of labour (paid or unpaid), unemployment and resource allocation, recent literature demonstrates that the household represents a 'site of bargaining and conflict' (Kabeer 1994; Mosoetsa 2011). As Sitas (2010) notes in his book *The Mandela Decade*, wage earners experience the pressure of this social reality because they feel responsible for their families' livelihood strategies. However, at the same time, while wages gradually increase, the pressure of this socio-economic reality often limits their purchasing power.

Nicholas Pons-Vignon (2015) makes the argument that the (racially) unequal apartheid wage structure has not been significantly altered in South Africa, and whereas some have 'benefited' by receiving rising incomes and greater security, 'the suggestion that they are overpaid seems odd'. His reasoning is that most black workers were grossly underpaid during apartheid, so when this was rectified legally there was a low base to work from for wage increases. In addition, recent data suggests that the wage share of national income has gradually dropped, especially in the private business sector, which, he argues, suggests that profits, not wages, represent the biggest proportion of the share. Dale McKinley (2015) points out that in the last fifteen years the overall share of revenue (with wages included) accruing to workers in the platinum mining industry has decreased by over 50 per cent. Those who are paid low wages are not necessarily happy, but workers have little choice in light of the fact that there are insufficient alternatives to wage employment for people's survival in South Africa because of high unemployment coupled with the scarcity of jobs for certain skill sets, as Pons-Vignon (2015) concludes.

Based on these broader contextual issues, a Cosatu official criticises the idea that members are a 'labour elite' by situating workers in relation to their social reality:

> Well, there's always been the claims by sections of business and government who want to undermine organised workers as a labour elite and or separation between workers and the unemployed, but 60 per cent of the membership

of Cosatu earns less than R3 500. By no stretch of the imagination can that be defined as a labour elite. The reality also is nearly 20 per cent of the workers' wages is paid in remittance to family members. So they [are] sharing their wages, that's the only way the other family members are able to survive. So that may be the argument from the business sector to try and discredit unions, but workers in the working class generally know that workers are low-paid in their aggregate and that workers share their salaries with other unemployed workers, so they are not seen out there among the working class as a labour elite (interview, Cosatu official, 2015).

WAGES IN SOUTH AFRICA

Taking into account recent statistics, out of a working population in 2014 of 35.5 million (aged between fifteen and sixty-four) just 20.3 million form the labour force. Of this labour force, only 15.1 million are actually working on a regular basis, either in the formal or informal sector. The minimum living level (MLL) is calculated at approximately R4 500 to R5 000 per month (Coleman 2014), and the divisions between the top wage earners and those at the bottom of the wage structure are increasing. Neil Coleman (2014) states that over half of South African workers earn below the estimated MLL and they can be thought of as the 'working poor'. Only mining, manufacturing and the public sector pay workers above the MLL (more than R4 000). In 2013, the median wage was R3 033 and this means that half of all workers earn below R3 033, with approximately half of 'African' workers earning below R2 600 in 2013 (Coleman 2014).

As of July 2014, in the formal sector there are 8 123 000 (or 63 per cent) typical, or permanent, full-time workers and 4 872 000 or 37 per cent atypical, or temporary, part-time workers – or 'unspecified' and 'temporary' contracts – with a total of 12 995 000 workers in the formal sector in South Africa (StatsSA 2014b). Approximately one-third of these formal sector employees have a stable income, a salary of R11 800 per month, pension and paid leave. About 70 per cent of formal sector employees receive a salary of R3 240 per month (the National Income Dynamics Survey estimates the median income for South African households to be R3 100 per month and the minimum wage for workers in core industrial and manufacturing sectors is around R2 700 per month). It is often the lower-paid workers who embark on strikes to earn more – these workers also support many children and adults who are dependent on their wages. In fact, the South African Institute of Race Relations (SAIRR) (2013) found that on average every worker in South Africa has to support themselves and three additional unemployed people. Households headed by women earn less than 50 per cent of households headed by men.

This socio-economic reality is recognised and acknowledged by union leaders. For example, at a collective bargaining meeting between Sactwu and an employer, the union official was taken by surprise when the company presented its findings on how many dependents its employees support. She explains:

> It seems that women are sort of now keeping up the households and have the extended families that they need to see to. And then the company came with a survey and [it] was quite interesting to hear their presentation on that, which was quite genuine in our opinion, we could relate to it. And we were actually glad that the management took the time to run a survey on their own employees. It's a big company ... what they've discovered [from] their own calculations ... one employee ... had eight, seven or five dependents that is dependable upon their salary (interview, Sactwu official, 2014).

The SAIRR found that around 30 per cent of all those employed are working in temporary, part-time and contract positions, and of unemployed black people 67 per cent are in long-term unemployment, while the figure for unemployed whites is 50 per cent. The overall share of wages as a percentage of gross domestic product (GDP) declined from 57 per cent in 1994 to 50 per cent in 2012. For those working in the private sector, the wage share dropped from 48 per cent to 42 per cent.

Cosatu is still composed of the majority of organised workers in unions affiliated to, and formerly affiliated to, the federation. The types of new jobs created mirror the divisions not only in the labour market but also within Cosatu and among its own affiliates. In South Africa there has been a decline in industrial production as well as employment in manufacturing, whereas there has been an increase in employment in the service sector and a significant rise in public sector employment. The ANC government has introduced an expanded public works programme (EPWP) to address the high levels of unemployment among unskilled and semi-skilled labour.

In terms of the development of new forms of employment (atypical work), the dominant response in Cosatu has been to rely on the state to restrict these. The strike in the postal services is evidence of this approach. At the heart of the 2014 strike by the CWU (a Cosatu affiliate), which organises postal workers, was the demand made on management to turn temporary workers into permanent workers.

Cosatu has continued its decent work campaign so that temporary workers can be afforded the right to decent work. In particular, the call for labour brokers to be banned across all sectors has been high on its agenda. Cosatu has argued that labour brokers do not create jobs; they deskill workers; they 'trade human beings like commodities'; they undermine collective bargaining rights; and they pay low wages to cut costs for clients (Vavi 2011).

As intermediaries offering flexible labour – a global trend that has gained prominence – labour brokers are seen to play a significant role in the labour market. Instead of banning labour brokers, the state has opted to regulate the industry. Some view this positively, especially as the infamous 'bakkie brigade' are targeted. Others are cynical of regulation because unregistered brokers can easily pop up elsewhere and continue with their unscrupulous practices that disregard workers' rights. However, not all labour brokers operate in the same way as the 'bakkie brigade' type. John Botha, a member of the Confederation of Associations in the Private Employment Sector (Capes), has made a distinction between these unregistered brokers and 'reputable businesses' (Anon. 2011). Reputable labour brokers comply with labour legislation by providing workers with employment contracts, UIF and annual leave.

Cosatu's call to ban labour brokers has raised considerable debate among reluctant employers who benefit from the triangular employment relationship of Adcorp, the Capes and economists. Jan Hofmeyr (2012), for example, has referred to the banning of labour brokers as a 'high-risk strategy for employment' since employers would have to permanently employ casual or part-time workers. Reluctant to do so and wary of government regulation, companies started to move away from engaging labour brokers – with as many as 550 closing down in 2012 (Anderson 2012).

The banning attempt has not been successful. Patrick Phelane, Cosatu's market policy commentator, said, 'I think that battle [against labour broking] has been lost. All we can do is to agitate against the worst forms of abuse and to try to eventually strengthen regulation in favour of workers' (Benjamin 2015). While it has not succeeded in banning labour brokers, Cosatu has played an important role in drawing attention to them and encouraging decent work for part-time/contract workers.

More recently, the amendments to the Labour Relations Act which came into effect on 1 April 2015 state that labour-broker workers who have been employed for three months must become permanent employees. The aim of the Act is to give contract workers job security. However, employers and labour brokers have already started to react defensively by not renewing contracts and dismissing workers. For example, 2 000 workers at the University of South Africa (Unisa) were dismissed by the temporary employment service provider that placed them. Jacqui Ford, the president of the African Professional Staffing Organisation (Apso), has indicated that since April 2015 only 23 per cent of 4 546 contract workers have become permanent employees, 30 per cent have received longer contracts and the remaining 47 per cent have had their contracts terminated (Maswanganyi 2015).

The Free Market Foundation economist Loane Sharp has argued that with changes to the Labour Relations Act as many as 254 000 retrenchments will take place, mainly in the manufacturing and finance sectors (Maswanganyi 2015). These statistics are not encouraging, given that more than 1 million people are employed through labour brokers on a short-term basis. Cosatu's main contention all along has been that these jobs will not be lost because employers still need the work to be done. But the challenge of the impact of labour market policies on employment remains.

A Saccawu official explains this union's dilemma and stance regarding part-time workers in the retail industry:

> … in our retail sector where you'll find atypical forms of employment like the part-timers which are earning peanuts if I may put it that way and also working reduced hours, earning meagre salary … I think over 60 per cent of workers are part-timers in both retailers … we have taken steps as a union. When we put demands for negotiations, we are saying also those part-timers and or atypical forms must also benefit from the outcomes or whatever we have agreed to with the employers in terms of the increase with the wages and working conditions. Again I must welcome the amendments in the labour law … (interview, Saccawu official, 2014).

Only one in four workers is unionised (24.4 per cent union members as a percentage of workers in the private sector as of 2013) and this has provided fertile ground for the emergence of rival trade unions, sometimes with breakaway groups from a dominant trade union within a sector taking advantage of the representation gap among workers. Rival unions have emerged most noticeably in the mining, manufacturing, healthcare, teaching and transport sectors.

Within the labour market, the lower-end service jobs are marked by low wages and few if any benefits, and the work is temporary. Atypical workers (workers employed on a part time, temporary, casual basis) have minimal structural power, whether in the workplace or in the labour market. Permanent workers feel that their security of tenure is undermined by increasing flexibility in the labour market, and that employers use contract labour to create divisions among the workforce. The current strategy of many Cosatu affiliates is to extend the existing forms of representation to atypical workers by bringing these workers into the existing form of representation – for example, the bargaining council system or through a ministerial determination – and, as far as they can, secure for them the protections enjoyed by other workers.

Thus, very few Cosatu affiliates represent non-standard workers or organise workers on the periphery, and they have not met the challenge of organising workers in new forms of employment. This has increasingly become a major source of tension within the federation.

Cosatu is still part of the ruling Alliance with the ANC and SACP, and leadership positions in Cosatu affiliates have opened up paths to upward social mobility, albeit for a minority. In its own September commission report, Cosatu (2012) warned of the impact that the upward mobility of shop stewards would have on its organisational structure, stating that 'there are worrying organisational trends – lack of service, lack of skills, lack of discipline, lack of commitment – that could generate a crisis if not addressed.' Cosatu itself is concerned at the outcome of this phenomenon of social mobility and has termed it a problem of 'social distance', which means that there is a growing distance developing between shop stewards and ordinary workers or between leaders and their base (see Masondo 2012). A South African Transport and Allied Workers' Union (Satawu) official comments in the following way on social distance:

> There is ... [social distance] in a sense that structures are not functioning. In an organisation we have got structures from top down. If those structures are not properly in place, social distance will be created. But if the structures are in place we do not expect national leadership to be visible to workers every day, but workers they lead themselves at the local level, regional level, provincial level to the national level ... proper communications, they are structures of the constitution that assist the organisation to be able to run smoothly ... but if those structures are not in place for one reason or the other obviously social distance will be there. But if those structures are in place, they are in good standing and the leaders of those structures are working according to their mandate, then there will be no social distance. So it depends because each and every affiliate of Cosatu has its own constitution and that constitution talks to that but it's a question of whether those structures are in place or not (interview, Satawu official, 2015).

From our in-depth interviews a recurring theme that emerges from the affiliate officials is that there is social distance between leaders and ordinary members. Leaders were described as a self-interested elite. Their failure to prioritise workers' interests over political or economic aspirations is central to the discourse on the internal divisions that are emerging within the federation. For example, a Satawu official elaborates:

> The leaders of the trade unions are manipulating the powers that are vested to them by the congress. One, to do what serves their interests. Two, to make sure that those not supporting them or challenging them or contesting them ideologically, they get rid of them. So that perpetrates divisions and cliques within the trade union [and] as a result the focus of the leadership is not on what the workers need to be addressed (interview, Satawu official, 2015).

Simply put, ordinary members want 'to fight labour brokers, get rid of them. They want us to fight e-tolling. They want us to improve NDP because NDP is not serving the interests of workers entirely' (interview, Satawu official, 2015). A Cosatu official (interview, 2015) adds that this division between leaders and workers is a form of social distancing which 'is also created by huge disparities in the salaries of trade unionists … each and every meeting they go into they speak about these differences in salary disparities [but] for them to fix them, in their own organisations, it's another thing.'

These sentiments are shared by officials who try to account for the tensions within the union movement. Their dissatisfaction with agenda items that seem to prioritise other issues over workers' interest compounds their frustration. For example, with reference to the CEC structure, an official notes:

> The main point is there is a separation between the leaders. Like in the CEC of Cosatu, main discussions there don't focus on the interest of workers, they focus on the interest of leaders. Like in the CEC of many unions, the focus is not on the shop-floor issues, the focus is on the issues which concern the leaders. I have attended many CECs in Samwu [South African Municipal Workers' Union]. It's all about what interests them, what will benefit them. Leaders will spend few hours discussing issues that concern workers (interview, Samwu official, 2015).

Like others, he adds that leaders' interests are often informed by both personal and ideological motivations. A Cosatu official explains that ideology has emerged as a result of a sharpening contradiction within Cosatu '… about those who think that the Alliance is still relevant and those who think that the Alliance is no longer relevant, those who think that the National Democratic Revolution is on course and those who think that there is [a] neoliberal policy trajectory that has been pursued by the leading ruling party'.

The danger of this, as noted by a Satawu official, is that 'Cosatu is competing with Fedusa and Nactu. But if you look at a level of how [we are] improving our capacity in terms of servicing our members as compared to our competitors, we are far below.' This gives rise to the appeal of rival unions. Irrespective of whether these interests stem from ideological or personal endeavours or both, what is clear is that ordinary members and leaders perceive a self-interested elite among their ranks who are undermining workers' interests.

COSATU MEMBERSHIP AS A MARGINAL LABOUR ELITE – THE EVIDENCE

For the first time in the longitudinal study of Cosatu workers, the 2014 survey included questions on income and on other types of support in the household. We used the income data and cross-tabulated it against variables of gender, education level, security of tenure, type of dwelling, migrant labour and the number of dependents supported. We also looked at Cosatu workers' involvement in community protest action and on service delivery issues.

First, we describe the general findings. In the 2014 survey, we interviewed 619 Cosatu members. In our sample of Cosatu members, 32 per cent were women and 67 per cent were men. There were 148 shop stewards interviewed, 72 per cent of them men and 24 per cent women. Over a third of women had a matric qualification (37 per cent), but more women (25 per cent) than men (13 per cent) had a university degree. There is no difference between men and women in terms of full-time employment (it is 90 per cent for both groups) and in terms of part-time or temporary employment (it is 10 per cent for both groups). Cosatu members classified themselves as skilled (37 per cent) and as professional (29 per cent). More men (36 per cent) than women (20 per cent) in our sample said that they were migrant workers; more migrant women (90 per cent) than men (85 per cent) supported a household. When women indicated that they were migrant workers and that they supported a household, the number of households supported by women was greater than the number supported by men. More women (49 per cent) than men (38 per cent) supported one household. More men (54 per cent) than women (46 per cent) supported two households, but more women (14 per cent) than men (9 per cent) supported three households and more women (6 per cent) than men (5 per cent) supported four and more households. Women carry the burden of supporting many households when they are migrant workers. Most women (53 per cent) in our sample lived in a family house that is owned or has a mortgage, followed by 11 per cent who lived in rented flats.

For example, women who earn R19 271 per month support four and more households and 5.5 dependents. This is a logical finding, as these women in our sample of Cosatu members were more likely to earn a stable income: they were professionals (29 per cent) and they had a university degree, so were less likely to have income instability. We also asked the Cosatu members whether there were other sources of income in their household, such as social grants or an income from renting out a room. The majority (81 per cent) indicated that there was no other source of income, but more women than men depended on a child grant and meant, when they stated 'other', that they had their own business. The analysis of data also revealed that as income earned increases, the number of households supported and the number of dependents supported also increases.

Wages of Cosatu members

When looking specifically at wage data, we decided to re-categorise the continuous data on income into discrete categories, based on the fact that 30 per cent of wage earners earn a median wage of R11 800 per month and 70 per cent earn a median wage of between R11 800 and R3 100 or less per month, as stated above. We developed the same categories of income in our data set so that we could further analyse some of the key variables. It should be noted that we only asked the Cosatu members to indicate what their actual wage or salary is per month, so the figures below are actual, not median, wages.

Table 5.1 shows that the most frequent wage category the members fall into (at over a third or 36.7 per cent of the sample) are those who earn between R11 801 and R20 000 per month.

Table 5.1: Wage categories of Cosatu members

	Number	Per cent
R3 100 or less per month	23	5.7
R3 101 – R6 000 per month	66	16.3
R6 001 – R9 000 per month	71	17.5
R9 001 – R11 800 per month	51	12.6
R11 801 – R20 000 per month	149	36.7
R20 001 or more per month	46	11.3
Total	**406**	**100**

No answer: 213 respondents

We ran cross-tabulations of the three income categories (namely a wage of R3 100 or less per month, wage of between R3 100 and R11 800 per month, and wage of R11 801 or more per month) by other key variables. We indicate where the analysis reveals that there is a relationship between the variables. We do not analyse the strength of the relationship between the variables as one that is strong or may be statistically significant as we did not conduct inferential statistical tests. All we do is describe the relationship between the two variables and conclude with some tentative statements.

A quarter of our sample indicated that they are shop stewards. Of those, 53.2 per cent earned a wage of R11 801 or more per month; 46.3 per cent of those who indicated they were not a shop steward earned in the same wage category. Therefore, shop stewards do not earn much more than ordinary members and it can be argued that there is no relationship between level of income and leadership in the union.

From the cross-tabulation of income categories in Table 5.1 by other variables, the analysis reveals that in the category of the wage of R11 801 or more per month, men earn more than women. In the category of the wage between R3 100 and R11 801 per month, men also earn more than women. In the wage category of R11 801 or more per month, over a third (36.7 per cent) have a university degree and 30.1 per cent have a technical diploma. Almost two-thirds of the sample of Cosatu members earning between R3 100 and R11 800 per month have a Grade 11–12 qualification. Just under two-fifths (39.1 per cent) of Cosatu members earning a wage of R3 100 or less per month have a Grade 8–10 qualification. There is clearly a relationship between median-wage levels and gender and level of education in our data.

Within the wage category of R11 801 or more per month, 39.3 per cent of Cosatu members fall into the professional occupational category, and 33.2 per cent fall into the skilled occupational category. Within the wage category of between R3 100 and R11 800 per month fall 33.5 per cent of Cosatu members who are skilled, and 32.4 per cent who are semi-skilled. Within the wage category of R3 100 or less per month fall 39.1 per cent of Cosatu members who are skilled and 30.4 per cent who are unskilled. There is clearly a relationship between the skill level and median-wage levels in our data.

Most Cosatu members are employed on a permanent basis (92.4 per cent). Even though the sample is small, there are some Cosatu members who earn a wage of R3 100 or less per month employed on a temporary full-time fixed-contract basis. Most Cosatu members, across all the wage categories, indicated that they do not have any other income in their households, but those within the wage category of R3 100 or less per month indicated that they have a child grant as income in their household. Therefore, household members rely on the Cosatu member's income, and not only household members – there is also the issue of the costs of migrancy and the support of other households that are covered by the Cosatu member's income.

Of those Cosatu members who earn a wage of between R3 100 and R11 800 per month, 41 per cent say they are migrant workers, and 24 per cent who earn a wage of R11 801 or more per month say they are migrant workers. Cosatu members across all three wage categories who are migrant workers support a household. Of those who earn R3 100 or less, 75 per cent support one household. Of those migrant members earning between R3 100 and R11 800, 61.2 per cent support two households. Over half of Cosatu members who earn a wage of R11 801 or more per month support two households. There is an association between the median-wage levels and the number of households supported. Our data seems to suggest that the higher-income earners have to support more households than those in the lower-income categories.

Over two-thirds (69.4 per cent) of Cosatu members who earn a wage of R11 801 or more per month state that they live in their own family home, whereas 39.4 per cent of those earning between R3 100 and R11 800 live in their own family home, and 21.7 per cent earning R3 100 or less live in an RDP house.

Within the wage category of R3 100 or less per month, an astounding 70 per cent of Cosatu members state that workers in their workplace have been involved in industrial action since 2009. This supports the assertion made above that it is mostly lower-paid workers who embark on strikes to improve their wages. However, our data reveals that just over half of Cosatu members in the wage category of between R3 100 and R11 800 per month say the same. Just under half of those who earn a wage of R11 801 or more per month report that their workplace has been involved in industrial action. This finding can be linked to the overall increase in strike activity post-apartheid. According to the Department of Labour's strike information database, there were far more work stoppages in 2013 than in the previous four years (Department of Labour 2013a). There were also some significant and protracted strikes in the community, in the social and personal industry (for example, in the hospitals, in the hospitality and university sectors, by technicians from South African Airways (SAA), by bus drivers), and in the mining and manufacturing industries. Over a third (34.8 per cent) of Cosatu members who earn a wage of R3 100 or less per month have participated in community protest action since the last national elections in 2009. When asked whether the statement that local government service delivery in their area was satisfactory, almost two-thirds of Cosatu members who earn a monthly wage of between R3 100 and R11 800 strongly disagreed. Just over half of those earning R11 800 or more per month disagreed with this statement. The other half agreed that local government service delivery in their area was satisfactory and effective.

Overall, analysis of the data reveals that the high levels of protest action among Cosatu members do not support the notion of this group of organised labour as a self-interested elite. The analysis of the income category variable by all the other variables above seems to suggest that within Cosatu there are differences between members in terms of what they earn per month and their levels of education and skill, the kind of job they hold, the kind of dwelling they live in, whether they are a migrant worker, the number of households they support if they are a migrant worker, the other sources of income they receive, whether there has been industrial action in their workplace, whether they have participated in community action, and their attitudes towards service delivery in their area.

Next, we analysed the data on how this internal division is playing itself out among the affiliates (and former affiliates) of Cosatu. Table 5.2 illustrates the answer to this.

Table 5.2 shows that the high-income earners (a wage of R20 001 or more) are members of Nehawu (15.2 per cent), followed by the NUM (13.0 per cent) and then Police and Prisons Civil Rights Union (Popcru) (10.9 per cent). Those who earn a wage of R11 801 to R20 000 per month are also concentrated in the public sector trade unions: Sadtu (21.5 per cent), Popcru (16.8 per cent), Nehawu (12.8 per cent). In the R6 001 to R9 000 wage range, members from Ceppwawu (29.6 per cent) and from NUM (21.1 per cent) fall into this category. Of those who earn between R3 101 and R6 000 per month, 27.3 per cent are Nehawu members, 22.7 per cent Saccawu members and 21.2 per cent NUM members. The low-income earners are concentrated in manufacturing: Fawu (52.2 per cent), Saccawu (21.7 per cent). We can tentatively conclude that these results relate to problems among some of the affiliates. In 2002, Fawu members were unfairly dismissed by their company. These members took Fawu to court for not representing them, and won damages in the high court. There is a growing gap internally within some affiliates between the top and bottom wage earners, and a growing crisis in representation.

The divisions between low- and higher-income earners have an effect on the solidarity among Cosatu members. For example, a Saccawu official explains:

> Like in the Spar strike, we called the federation to support that strike but none of the affiliates of Cosatu supported [it] despite the call we made. So it has got a negative impact of course ... Again, let me refer you to, for example, in one strike of Shoprite Checkers about six years ago we called a consumer boycott to support the strike but then we also saw the picketing lines, we saw comrades from public sectors, I am not going to mention the union, crossing the picket line, going and buying at Shoprite Checkers as we made a call not to cross the picket line (interview, Saccawu official, 2015).

Table 5.2: Income categories by trade union affiliate

	R3 100 or less per month	R3 101 – R6 000 per month	R6 001 – R9 000 per month	R9 001 – R11 800 per month	R11 801 – R20 000 per month	R20 001 or more per month	Total % among Cosatu affiliates
NUM	4.3%	21.2%	21.1%	7.8%	5.4%	13.0%	11.8%
Numsa		4.5%	5.6%	11.8%	6.7%	13%	7.1%
Ceppwawu	4.3%	7.6%	29.6%	5.9%	3.4%	2.2%	8.9%
Sactwu		1.5%					0.2%
Popcru		1.5%	4.2%	33.3%	16.8%	10.9%	12.6%
Samwu			11.3%	9.8%	10.1%	6.5%	7.6%
Satawu	13%	4.5%	1.4%		0.7%	8.7%	3.0%
Denosa			1.4%	9.8%	1.3%	6.5%	2.7%
Sasbo				3.9%	14.1%	10.9%	6.9%
Sadtu				2%	21.5%	10.9%	9.4%
CWU				3.9%	5.4%	2.2%	2.7%
Saccawu	21.7%	22.7%	7%				6.2%
Nehawu	4.3%	27.3%	7%	9.8%	12.8%	15.2%	13.5%
Fawu	52.2%	6.1%	9.9%				5.7%
Pawusa		3%	1.4%	2%	2%		1.7%
Total	**100%**	**100%**	**100%**	**100%**	**100%**	**100%**	**100%**

To fully test the notion of Cosatu membership as a self-interested elite, we cross-tabulated the income categories by whether the Cosatu members know and support the Employment Tax Incentive Bill (more popularly known as the youth wage subsidy). Tables 5.3 and 5.4 below reveal the results.

Table 5.3 reveals that although most Cosatu members do not know about the youth wage subsidy in aggregate, more Cosatu members in the highest wage category (R11 801 or more per month) know about the youth wage subsidy (at 43.9 per cent) than those in the lowest income category of R3 100 or less per month (at 8.7 per cent).

Table 5.4 shows that at an aggregate level more Cosatu members support the youth wage subsidy than not. In fact, support for the youth wage subsidy is higher (at 60 per cent) among the top income category of a wage of R11 801 or more per month.

Our tentative statement is that our data suggests that within Cosatu membership itself there is a growing internal division between members who are top income earners and those who are not improving their low wages, and that Cosatu members who earn top wages may be the labour aristocracy. However, once the focus is on the Cosatu member outside of the workplace, and the focus moves to their role

Table 5.3: Income categories by level of knowledge of the youth wage subsidy among Cosatu members

Know about the youth wage subsidy	Wage of R3 100 or less per month	Wage between R3 100 and R11 800 per month	Wage of R11 801 or more per month
Yes	8.7 %	28.2 %	43.9 %
No	91.3 %	69.7 %	52.6 %
Question not asked/ Don't know		2.1 %	3.6 %
Total	100 %	100 %	100 %

Tabel 5.4: Income categories by support among Cosatu members for the youth wage subsidy

Support the youth wage subsidy	Monthly wage categories		
	Wage of R3 100 or less per month	Wage between R3 100 and R11 800 per month	Wage of R11 801 or more per month
Yes	50.0 %	58.5 %	60.0 %
No	50.0 %	41.5 %	40.0 %

in the household as a wage earner, then the notion of any Cosatu members representing the labour aristocracy can be debunked.

COSATU MEMBERSHIP AS A MARGINAL LABOUR ELITE: CRITICAL REFLECTION ON THE DATA

While our survey's objective has remained constant over the years, we realise that the sociological variables that we have included in our research design are important for a broader understanding of workers' conception of democracy. Our intention is not to replicate existing surveys, especially those that have examined the household dynamics among wage earners, but to supplement and reflect on our research findings alongside the issues that leading scholars have begun to problematise. By doing so, we are able to reflect critically on why reference to organised labour representing a 'labour elite' is problematic. At the same time, however, we reflect on gaps in our research design and where we could integrate questions to disaggregate further differences among organised workers. For example, with reference to other sources of livelihoods in the household, we do not know whether the workers pool their income with other family members who are permanently employed wage earners, or whether those who have access to a house engage in subsistence farming. We think that questions like this should be included in future surveys of Cosatu membership.

While our data continues to reflect a group of workers who represent a marginal labour elite mainly owing to their relative privileges, our sampling strategy does not adequately reflect the wage disparities between the different affiliates. Because access to workplaces through unions and managers was seriously affected by the mistrust and ambivalence regarding our research intentions, more workers belonging to a particular affiliate (especially those who earn above the minimal living level) are captured in our sample than those who form part of the low-income wage category. This is an important point to consider if we take into account the above argument of the Cosatu official that many of their members actually fall into the low-income category.

Some have argued for or criticised the notion of Cosatu membership as a labour aristocracy or a self-interested elite. The reasons for this criticism can be related to the growing divisions in the labour market between permanent and temporary workers and between high- and low-income earners. The lower-end service jobs are marked by low wages and few if any benefits – and the work is temporary. The dominant response in Cosatu has been to rely on the state to restrict the development of new forms of employment but not to organise these workers.

We have also demonstrated that affiliates of Cosatu are not homogeneous. The internal division within Cosatu is between members of these affiliates on their support for the ANC/SACP/Cosatu Alliance and members of affiliates who have a high income. There are clearly two dominant groups, and we suggest that there is a labour elite within the federation itself, where one group tends to exhibit the characteristics of a labour aristocracy. However, Cosatu members as a whole support the youth wage subsidy, which somewhat problematises labelling them as a labour aristocracy. We thus conclude that continual reference to organised labour representing a 'labour elite' is problematic, as workers are not a homogenous group, and live with and among those who are unemployed and who depend on the Cosatu worker's income.

Our findings from the in-depth interviews with union officials indicate that there is an ongoing tension between leaders, who appear to be the 'self-interested elite', and ordinary members. Our data set also reflects a group of workers who represent a 'marginal labour elite' because although they have access to a set of privileges (the most notable from our findings being access to a house, permanent employment and an income above the minimal living level), their income is used to support dependents. As our sampling strategy does not adequately reflect the wage disparities between the different affiliates, this may be something to reflect on in future surveys.

BIBLIOGRAPHY

Anderson, Alistair. 2012. Hundreds of labour brokers close shop. *Business Day Live*, 24 August. http://www.bdlive.co.za/national/labour/2012/08/24/hundreds-of-labour-brokers-close-shop (accessed 4 July 2015).

Anon. 2011. Bakkie brigade brokers may crash. *City Press*, 3 December. http://www.news24.com/Archives/City-Press/Bakkie-brigade-brokers-may-crash-20150430 (accessed 4 July 2015).

Benjamin, Chantelle. 2015. PIC's stake in labour broker Adcorp irks Cosatu. *Business Times*, 21 June. http://www.timeslive.co.za/sundaytimes/businesstimes/2015/06/21/PICs-labour-broker-stake-irks-Cosatu (accessed 4 July 2015).

Buhlungu, Sakhela. 2010. *A Paradox of Victory: Cosatu and the Democratic Transition in South Africa*. Pietermaritzburg: University of KwaZulu-Natal Press.

Buhlungu, Sakhela. 2014. Has the giant fallen? The split within South Africa's largest trade union federation, Cosatu. *The Frantz Fanon Blog*, 12 November. http://readingfanon.blogspot.co.za/2014/11/has-giant-fallen-split-within-south.html (accessed 13 November 2014).

Buhlungu, Sakhela, Roger Southall and Edward Webster. 2006. Conclusion: Cosatu and the democratic transformation of South Africa. In *Trade Unions and Democracy: Cosatu Workers' Political Attitudes in South Africa*, edited by Sakhela Buhlungu. Cape Town: HSRC Press.

Coleman, Neil. 2014. A national minimum wage for South Africa. Presentation at the 27th Annual Labour Law Conference, Sandton, South Africa, 5–7 August. http://www.cosatu.org.za/docs/misc/2014/neilcoleman_llcnmw.pdf (accessed 13 November 2014).

Congress of South African Trade Unions (Cosatu). 2012. *The 11th Cosatu Congress Secretariat Report*. http://www.COSATU.org.za/eventslist.php?eid=31 (accessed 30 November 2014).

Department of Labour. 2013a. *Annual Industrial Action Report 2013*. Pretoria: Department of Labour.

Department of Labour. 2013b. *Annual Labour Market Bulletin, April 2011 – March 2012*. Pretoria: Department of Labour.

Fogel, Benjamin, Sakhela Buhlungu, Paul Dwyer, Steven Friedman and Alex Lichenstein. 2014. Debate: The future of the workers' movement in South Africa. *Africa Is a Country*, 20 February. http://africasacountry.com/debate-the-future-of-the-workers-movement-in-south-africa/ (accessed 14 November 2014).

Forslund, Dick and Niall Reddy. 2015. Wages and the struggle against income inequality. In *Cosatu in Crisis: The Fragmentation of an African Trade Union Federation*, edited by Vishwas Satgar and Roger Southall. Johannesburg: KMMR Publishing.

Hofmeyr, Jan. 2012. *Transformation Audit 2011: From Inequality to Inclusive Growth*. Cape Town: Institute for Justice and Reconciliation.

International Labour Organization (ILO), Organisation for Economic Co-operation and Development (OECD), International Monetary Fund (IMF) and the World Bank. 2012. *Boosting Jobs and Living Standards in G20 Countries: A Joint Report by the ILO, OECD, IMF and the World Bank*. http://www.oecd.org/g20/topics/framework-strong-sustainable-balanced-growth/Boosting%20jobs%20and%20living%20standards%20in%20G20%20countries.pdf (accessed 30 November 2014).

Kabeer, Naila. 1994. *Reversed Realities: Gender Hierarchies in Development Thought*. London: Verso.

Masondo, Themba. 2012. The sociology of upward mobility among Cosatu shop stewards. In *Cosatu's Contested Legacy: South African Trade Unions in the Second Decade of Democracy*, edited by Sakhela Buhlungu and Malehoko Tshoaedi. Cape Town: HSRC Press.

Maswanganyi, Ntsakisi. 2015. Bid to curb labour broking 'negates job creation efforts'. *Business Day Live*, 30 March. http://www.bdlive.co.za/national/labour/2015/03/30/bid-to-curb-labour-broking-negates-job-creation-efforts (accessed 4 July 2015).

McKinley, Dale. 2014. The political significance of Numsa's expulsion from Cosatu. *South African Civil Society Information Service*, 10 November. http://www.sacsis.org.za/s/story.php/s/2193 (accessed 13 November 2014).

McKinley, Dale. 2015. South Africa's freedom journey fatally undermined by continuing crises of poverty, unemployment and inequality. *South African Civil Society Information Service*, 13 January. http://www.sacsis.org.za/site/article/2242 (accessed 13 January 2015).

Mosoetsa, Sarah. 2011. *Eating from One Pot: The Dynamics of Survival in Poor South African Households*. Johannesburg: Wits University Press.

Pillay, Devan. 2006. Cosatu, alliances and working class politics. In *Trade Unions and Democracy: Cosatu Workers' Political Attitudes in South Africa*, edited by Sakhela Buhlungu. Cape Town: HSRC Press.

Pons-Vignon, Nicolas. 2015. Are workers overpaid in South Africa? *South African Civil Society Information Service*, 21 January. http://sacsis.org.za/site/article/2254 (accessed 21 January 2015).

Sitas, Ari. 2008. The road to Polokwane? Politics and populism in KwaZulu-Natal. *Transformation* 68: 87–98.

Sitas, Ari. 2010. *The Mandela Decade, 1990–2000: Labour, Culture and Society in Post-apartheid South Africa*. Pretoria: Unisa Press.

Sitas, Ari. 2012. Cosatu, the '2010 Class Project' and the contest for the 'soul' of the ANC. In *Cosatu's Contested Legacy: South African Trade Unions in the Second Decade of Democracy*, edited by Sakhela Buhlungu and Malehoko Tshoaedi. Cape Town: HSRC Press.

South African Institute of Race Relations (SAIRR). 2013. *Race Relations in South Africa, 2012*. Johannesburg: SAIRR.

Standing, Guy. 2009. Inequality, class and the precariat. In *Work after Globalisation: Building Occupational Citizenship*. Cheltenham: Edward Elgar.

Statistics South Africa (StatsSA). 2010. *Monthly Earnings of South Africans*. Report PO211.2. Pretoria: StatsSA.

StatsSA. 2012. *Labour Market Dynamics in South Africa, 2012*. Pretoria: StatsSA.

StatsSA. 2013. *National and Provincial Labour Market Trends 2003–2013*. Report PO211.4. Pretoria: StatsSA.

StatsSA. 2014a. *Poverty Trends in South Africa: An Examination of Absolute Poverty between 2006 and 2011*. Report 03-10-96. Pretoria: StatsSA.

StatsSA. 2014b. *Quarterly Labour Force Survey, Q1, 2014*. Report PO211. Pretoria: StatsSA.

Teka Tsegay, Yared, Masiiwa Rusare and Rashmi Mistry. 2014. *Hidden Hunger in South Africa: The Faces of Hunger and Malnutrition in a Food-Secure Nation*. London: Oxfam. http://policy-practice.oxfam.org.uk/publications/hidden-hunger-in-south-africa-the-faces-of-hunger-and-malnutrition-in-a-food-se-332126b (accessed 10 December 2014).

Theron, Jan. 2010. Informalization from above, informalization from below: Options for organization. *African Studies Quarterly* 11(2&3): 87–105.

Vavi, Zwelinzima. 2011. Why have we decided to embark on this campaign programme? *Campaigns Bulletin*, October. http://www.cosatu.org.za/docs/campbul/2011/october.pdf (accessed 1 July 2015).

Vavi, Zwelinzima. 2012. General Secretary Address to Cosatu 11th National Congress. 18 September, Johannesburg.

Waterman, Peter. 1975. The 'labour aristocracy' in Africa: Introduction to a debate. *Development and Change* 6(9): 57–74.

Webster, Edward. 2006. Trade unions and the challenge of the informalisation of work. In *Trade Unions and Democracy: Cosatu Workers' Political Attitudes in South Africa*, edited by Sakhela Buhlungu. Cape Town: HSRC Press.

Webster, Edward, Rob Lambert and Andries Bezuidenhout. 2008. *Grounding Globalization: Labour in the Age of Insecurity*. Oxford: Blackwell.

Werbner, Pnina. 2010. Appropriating social citizenship: Women's labour, poverty, and entrepreneurship in the Manual Workers Union of Botswana. *Journal of Southern African Studies* 36(3): 693–710.

Xulu, Nomkhosi. 2012. Changing migrant spaces and livelihoods: Hostels as community residential units, Kwa-Mashu, KwaZulu-Natal, South Africa. PhD thesis, University of Cape Town.

6

The Politics of Alliance and the 2014 Elections

Janet Cherry, Nkosinathi Jikeka and Boitumelo Malope

INTRODUCTION

Dramatic events since the 2014 national elections have seen the Tripartite Alliance come under increasing strain. Contestation around policies – most recently the Tax Administration Laws Amendment Act – and around political processes has seen the tensions between the three parties to the Alliance testing it to the limit. However, in the last months of 2015, when it seemed that the days of the historic Alliance were numbered, it was brought back from the brink of collapse. Cosatu lost its strongest affiliate, but the federation retained its cohesion – at least formally – and the Alliance was declared to be alive and well.

Although analysts and activists on the left anticipated a fundamental break between Cosatu and the ANC, and looked to extra-parliamentary movements for a new progressive alignment in South African politics, this was not reflected in the views of ordinary workers. That the majority of delegates to the Cosatu special congress of July 2015, and again at the national congress of November 2015, voted to ratify the expulsion of Numsa and of Zwelinzima Vavi and to reaffirm commitment to the Tripartite Alliance should not have come as a surprise. If the voice of ordinary workers (rather than worker or political leadership) is carefully listened to, the reason for the maintenance of the Alliance, despite its deep divisions along policy lines, can be better understood.

This chapter reflects on the key debates and divisions around policy issues within the Alliance, how ordinary workers understand these debates, and what influence they have on policy making. The chapter will show that increasing tension in the Alliance is clearly reflected in the Taking Democracy Seriously survey and in interviews with Cosatu leaders. As with previous surveys, the 2014 survey was conducted before an election, primarily to test the relationship of the organised labour movement to the institutions of representative democracy in South Africa. In this chapter, that relationship can be assessed through worker participation on two levels: the election of representatives in government (at various levels) and the participation in policy formulation by those representatives.

The main institutional reflection of this relationship is the Tripartite Alliance between the ANC, the SACP and Cosatu. This chapter will show us that the relationship has changed, and is strained. The chapter will discuss the change with four interlinked points: how the relationship has changed, what influence Cosatu has within the Alliance, how workers understand their interests to be represented in Parliament, and what the future of the Alliance may be. Some questions will be answered. If the 'socialist axis' within the Alliance has been broken, as some claim, what implications does this have for Cosatu and for organised labour? What is the explanation for the rupture within Cosatu? What do workers and worker leaders say about the Alliance?

THE TRIPARTITE ALLIANCE UNDER STRAIN

In October 2014, as the Alliance came increasingly under strain, suspended Sadtu leader Mncekeleli Ndongeni quoted Oliver Tambo as saying, 'No unity can be built on the shifting sands of evasions.'[1] He elaborated:

> Now what is causing the strain mainly revolves around the policy evolution and policy direction that government has to take, different from what has cemented the unity of the Alliance over the decades – the common understanding that the NDR [National Democratic Revolution] is the direct route to socialism by the SACP, and all of them agreeing [on] the Freedom Charter being the Programme of Action that unites the Alliance. That everybody

understood, and we had no difference on what is to be done, after the 1994 breakthrough ... it became clear that now the ANC is in government and tends to want to enforce a kind of unity that is not based on the principles that the Alliance had been based on, to enforce a position where by other Alliance parties must play the role of supporting the ANC because it is government in power, and any differences expressed by the leadership of the other two parties in the Alliance would be seen as an attack on the ANC government. For some time the SACP and Cosatu have been on the same side, seeing the deviation from the side of government on the policy direction that was expected to have evolved, to have been involved by the leading party once it was in government; so there was a dwindling ... of involvement of Alliance partners in policy formulation. Those that would have been fought for and agreed at an Alliance summit level would not be implemented; they would be ignored after the Alliance summit, and government would proceed as if there's not been a summit (interview, Sadtu official, 2014).

From the leadership side, then, the tensions in the Alliance are due to policy differences between the radical left within the Alliance, and the ruling party and its allies. The Sadtu official continued:

Looking at what is taking place now, it is clear that people agree that there is a rupture ... We are of the view that the rupture is between those who want to preserve the status quo and do not want radical change – in terms of policy formulation there is nothing that indicates that there is really a commitment or political will for a radical change in the country – and those who do want radical change.

Expelled Sadtu president Thobile Ntola did not mince his words about the nature of the 'rupture' which he described as between 'those who want Cosatu to be the labour desk of the ANC versus those who want Cosatu to be independent and militant' (interview, Thobile Ntola, 2014).

However, such statements by leaders of particular unions, which represent the 'left' position in Cosatu, are not necessarily an accurate reflection of how ordinary workers understand the Alliance and the current tensions within it. One of the important purposes of the Taking Democracy Seriously survey is to reflect the voice of ordinary workers, and test it against the publicly articulated views of trade union leaders.

THE POLITICS OF POLICIES

Cosatu leaders interviewed were broadly in agreement that the tensions within the Tripartite Alliance are based on deep divisions around policies, which in turn are based on ideological commitments. For example, when a Cosatu local official in the Nelson Mandela Bay municipality was asked whether the divisions in Cosatu were based on personality clashes or on ideological differences, he stated:

> I agree one hundred percent the difference is ideological. The problem with the federation [is that] even comrades who are ideologically linked to the right wing, they don't pronounce on that ... for those [workers] that are politically immature, they are not able to differentiate between those [leaders] that are standing on behalf of the working class and the poor, and those that are not leading on behalf of the working class and the poor but on behalf of capital, for example (interview, Cosatu local official, 2014).

The crude version of the argument is that the ANC and SACP have 'sold out' the socialist agenda to capitalism. A more sophisticated argument is that even the essentially social-democratic demands of the National Democratic Revolution – as contained in the Freedom Charter – have been compromised by the ANC's adoption of neoliberal policies. These tensions have been reflected in struggles around particular policies and legislation which have played out in the period between the 2009 and 2014 elections.

The implementation of Growth, Employment and Redistribution (Gear) in 1996; the passing of the Employment Tax Incentive Act (youth wage subsidy) without its being endorsed in Nedlac; and contestation over the economic chapter of the NDP – these developments, and others which will be documented, have weakened Cosatu's influence on policy direction. The origins of this contestation over policy can be traced back to the pre-transition era. A good starting point is the 1990 Harare meeting where Cosatu, the ANC and a group of researchers first sat together to formulate an economic plan for a democratic South Africa. Pulling in one direction, Cosatu and the ANC came up with an opaque economic plan. They envisaged a democratic state's commitment 'to the development of a high employment, high wage, high productivity economy' with space 'for organised labour in the formulation and implementation of all economic policy' (ANC 1990: 12). This space for Cosatu to participate in policy formulation allowed for organised labour to make an important contribution to, and to influence, the RDP, the first macroeconomic policy for a democratic South Africa. The space was further institutionalised with the formation in 1995 of Nedlac, where government, labour and business would come together to iron out policy differences.

The first time this space was undermined was with the introduction of the Gear policy without its going through Nedlac, just two years after the RDP was introduced. Cosatu warned that Gear would wreak havoc; however, they wanted to judge it on 'its impact on the working class and the poor, job creation and job retention, impact wage levels, workers' rights, provision of infrastructure, role of the state in the productive sector of the economy and labour market policy' (Shilowa 1997). As they had anticipated, their predictions were spot on. The space created by Nedlac was further undermined when AsgiSA, a policy/plan thought to be a modified version of Gear, was introduced.

With Cosatu being slowly and systematically alienated, President Mbeki was seen to be causing a rift within the Alliance, and occasionally reminded the SACP that just as the party has its socialist priorities, so too does the ANC have its own, and different, priorities. The battle for the soul of the ANC was to begin with Cosatu and the SACP aiming to exert pressure to reclaim the space that was being eroded – a space that afforded Cosatu and the SACP the opportunity to be involved in policy processes and, more importantly, to determine policy content. An opportunity presented itself with the Polokwane conference for Cosatu and the SACP to oust President Mbeki and position Jacob Zuma, who was seen to be representing workers' interests, as president.

After Polokwane, with Zuma in office and the euphoria still high, it was time for the ANC to deliver the space that labour badly needed in order to express its policy interests through some Alliance leaders occupying positions on the ANC list to Parliament and to provincial and local government – the most notable being SACP leaders Jeremy Cronin and Blade Nzimande. Cosatu leaders added to the ANC's parliamentary list during President Zuma's second term were Thulas Nxesi and Fezeka Loliwe (Sadtu); Senzeni Zokwana (NUM); and Fikile Majola, Joe Mpisi, Thozama Mantashe and Pulani Mogotsi (all of Nehawu). The problem with such a move meant that many leaders were simultaneously in influential bodies of the ANC, SACP and Cosatu, thus placing themselves in contorting positions. With some members in Cosatu feeling that the space created was not being used, voices of dissent started to express this frustration more loudly. When asked if President Zuma had outmanoeuvred Cosatu, the expelled Sadtu leader responded: 'We are going to outmanoeuvre him, and set the revolution on track' (Thobile Ntola, interview, 2014).

That high levels of poverty, inequality and unemployment are still not being adequately addressed is widely recognised by social movements and opposition parties in South Africa, and is reflected in the response by workers to the question 'What needs to be addressed before the next election?' Two of the key policies that have been developed by the ANC to tackle these challenges are the NDP and the Employment Tax Incentive Act (youth wage subsidy). The Alliance has been deeply divided over both policies, the strongest voice of disapproval coming from Cosatu, especially in relation to the youth wage subsidy and the economic chapter of the NDP. Increasing public pressure from Cosatu on the ANC causes some officials within Cosatu to repeatedly alter their positions or to appear apologetic. On the one hand, the president of Cosatu, Sdumo Dlamini, has not publicly criticised the youth wage subsidy with the same venom as the former secretary general Zwelinzima Vavi. On the other hand, he has criticised those who attack the ANC, and asked members to close ranks – which have indeed been closed by systematically silencing the most vocal voices, those of the secretary general of Cosatu and his closest Numsa allies. When it appeared that the NUM's hegemony within Cosatu was being challenged, the expulsion of Numsa and Zwelinzima Vavi repositioned the NUM as dominant in the federation. The tensions within Cosatu became public, and the 2014 survey supports the analysis that the divisions within Cosatu which strain its relationship with the ANC are not due to personality clashes within the federation but are a reflection of a number of factors: policy disagreements with the ANC, and within Cosatu itself, and a disconnect between the Cosatu leadership and the workers they represent.

The National Development Plan

As an example of this disconnect on issues of policy, Cosatu leadership has been opposed to the NDP and the youth wage subsidy. However, the survey results indicate that members either do not know what these policies are, or do not really understand them. When asked if they knew what the NDP was, only a third of workers (34.2 per cent) said that they did. Of those who claimed to know the policy, three-quarters of the workers (74 per cent) supported it, despite Cosatu's vehement opposition to it. Complicating this response further is that only half of the workers surveyed (52 per cent) actually knew the federation's position on the NDP. An overwhelming 64.7 per cent of the workers did not know what the NDP was.

Although the 'Numsa faction' have been quick to point out that the NDP's economic chapter is firmly situated within a neoliberal economic framework, SACP leaders in government have played down the adoption of the NDP by the ANC in the face of Cosatu and broader civil society criticism. Jeremy Cronin, for example, has called on people not to 'monumentalise the NDP', and Blade Nzimande has indicated that it still open for discussion: 'Let us continue to engage on the NDP.' The Numsa left understand this to be the 'nationalist faction within SACP' which has become an 'instrument of containment' of working-class demands. A different interpretation of the SACP's statements is simply that if the NDP is to have any chance of working it has to be inclusive and have broad acceptance within society. It appears from the survey that the promotion of the NDP as an inclusive plan has been successful, at least at a superficial level, in that the majority of workers do support it.

The youth wage subsidy and Nedlac

The youth wage subsidy is also one of the policies that the federation has vehemently opposed, to a point where they had to 'defend' their position when the DA marched to their head office in Braamfontein in May 2012. The policy, which is intended to stimulate job growth, is viewed by the federation as having undesired consequences. When workers were asked if they knew what the youth wage subsidy was, 35 per cent claimed to know and 63 per cent said they did not know. Of those who know, 52 per cent support it and know Cosatu's position on it. How is this 'disconnect' between Cosatu members and the leadership's position on policies to be understood? The answer may lie in the functioning of Nedlac, as well as the institution of political education in Cosatu and its affiliates.

The youth wage subsidy is an important illustration of this disconnect, as seen by Cosatu's three-year long opposition in Nedlac to the proposed legislation. The fight was lost when the Bill was passed through Parliament without its having been agreed upon in Nedlac. A somewhat cynical view is that the ANC used the moment when Cosatu was in turmoil due to the suspension of Zwelinzima Vavi to 'push through' the Bill in October 2013 (it was signed into law by President Zuma in December of that year). This is an indication of the weakness of Nedlac as an institution, as well as a weakness of Cosatu in utilising the space that this institution provides. Workers were asked if they knew what Nedlac was. Again, two-thirds (66 per cent) of workers did not know. Only 32.5 per cent knew. Of those who knew, 61 per cent had not been at a union meeting where there had been a report-back on Nedlac. Despite this lack of information, 74 per cent of workers still believe that Nedlac is 'an important body through which your union federation can influence policy which is of direct importance to workers'.

In addition to the weakness of Nedlac as an institution, it is also acknowledged that political education in Cosatu is stagnant. Weaknesses in Cosatu's own processes of reporting back to shop stewards and consulting them on policy issues are also highlighted by the survey. The criticism was raised that Cosatu head office is increasingly dominated by 'technocrats' and that there are very low levels of consultation and participation by ordinary workers.

The Pension Act and Nedlac

The passing of the Tax Administration Laws Amendment Act, which came into effect in March 2016, is the most recent instance of organised labour being excluded from government decision making. For a brief moment the rejection of the Act brought Cosatu and Numsa together, with both the federation and Numsa applying under Section 77 for permission to strike on socio-economic grounds. The government argues that the Act is in the interests of workers, as it ensures that they retain adequate funds from their pensions to support them in old age. The substance of Cosatu's objection to the Act is that workers will be 'forced to buy annuities from a private insurance industry' (Nehawu 2016a). Cosatu argued that it is the right of employees to decide on how their pension money is stored. In addition – and surely a valid point in South Africa – is Cosatu's argument that 'there must be a fundamental change in the private retirement insurance industry' (Nehawu 2016b).

Behind the substantive objection to the Act lies the problematic process of adoption of the change. Cosatu's accusation that the government 'sneaked in' the clause dealing with retirement annuities without consulting organised labour was refuted. President Zuma issued a statement on 27 January 2016 refuting the allegations by outlining the lengthy process of consultation through Nedlac (Government of South Africa 2016). In a statement, Cosatu responded that the president was lying (Cosatu 2016).

Given the above policy conflicts between Cosatu and the ANC government – which are both substantive and procedural in most instances – it is perhaps surprising that there has not been a decisive break-up of the Alliance. In order to understand how the Alliance has held together for twenty years, despite the tensions which go back to 1996, it is useful to explore how workers understand the democratic process and their relationship to the government.

THE POLITICS OF ELECTIONS

The key institution of the national democratic process is the national elections, by means of which individual workers, as citizens, participate in the election of the government. In every election since 1994, Cosatu has aligned itself with the ruling ANC,

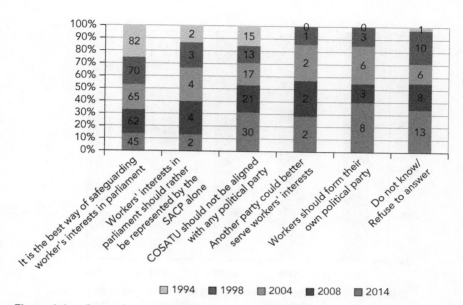

Figure 6.1: Cosatu has entered into an alliance with the ANC and SACP to contest the 2014/1998/1994 elections. What do you think of this arrangement?

as part of the Tripartite Alliance. Despite the tensions around policy issues outlined above, the same electoral alliance was maintained in 2014. Workers were asked the following question: 'Cosatu has entered into an alliance with the ANC and SACP to contest the 2014/1998/1994 elections. What do you think of this arrangement?'

The workers' response, as illustrated in Figure 6.1, shows a significant drop in support for the Alliance among Cosatu members, from 82 per cent in 1994 to 45 per cent in 2014. This can be understood to be reflecting their disillusionment with the ANC government in implementing policies which are openly rejected by Cosatu, including the NDP and the youth wage subsidy – although, as shown above, workers sometimes support the policies that their leadership has rejected.

Workers and worker leaders are aware that their influence in Parliament is limited, and that the ANC effectively coerces its MPs to pass legislation unpopular with other members of the Alliance. This is reflected in the views of leaders of Cosatu affiliates who feel that they are ignored by the ANC in the policy process and that the SACP has 'taken sides' with the ANC in accepting neoliberal policies. The strategy to advance a working-class agenda by ensuring that the SACP takes more of a leadership role within the Alliance is thus compromised:

> … the Communist Party for example is the one that will take you to the socialist dispensation. But if the Communist Party policies and the programmes

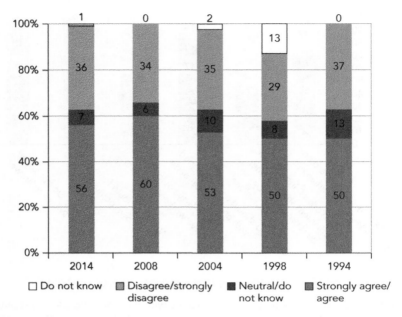

Figure 6.2: Workers cannot rely on political parties to protect their interests

echoes that of the ANC then we are going to have a problem, even if the Communist Party will become a leader, because it will be a national liberation movement, you know that it is 'cloned' into a national organisation … (interview, Cosatu Nelson Mandela Bay local official, 2015).

This is reflected in the responses to the following statement, which is a corollary to the above question: 'Workers cannot rely on political parties to protect their interests.'

As seen in Figure 6.2 above, Cosatu workers are divided on this issue: consistently half or more than half agree or strongly agree with the statement, indicating the fiercely independent tradition of some Cosatu affiliates and their scepticism towards being represented by political parties. However, a substantial minority disagree, which is consistent with workers' support for the Alliance in the previous figure and with their expressed intention to vote for the ANC.

While trade union leaders feel that they have been excluded by the ANC and the SACP when it comes to policy formulation, it is hard for ordinary workers to participate in these processes, even under normal circumstances, without political conflict or tension. We asked the question 'Do you agree with the following statement? The ANC should only pass legislation or policy that is supported by the Alliance' (Question 97). Most Cosatu members (68 per cent) feel strongly that the ANC should only pass legislation or policy that is supported by the Alliance, while 20 per cent disagree. Whether they understand the content of the policy, or support a particular policy, is not the issue here: it seems that it is the democratic principle that Cosatu members are concerned about – that their voices are heard, that they have given a mandate to the ANC to represent them in Parliament, and that the ANC has reneged on its mandate by adopting policies and laws which are 'anti-worker'.

This brings us to move from the substantive issues of policy content and class interest to the procedural issue of democracy – how workers' interests are represented, and how they understand the democratic process in South Africa.

REPRESENTATION IN PARLIAMENT AND IN OTHER STRUCTURES OF GOVERNMENT

The importance of democratic mandates for Cosatu workers is borne out in the survey questions dealing with workers' concept of political democracy and representation in Parliament. When asked (Question 82) whether they thought that Cosatu and its affiliates should send representatives on the ANC list to national Parliament (as they did in 1994), 58 per cent said yes and 33 per cent said no – an almost two-thirds–one-third split, as for some other questions. In response to the same question regarding sending worker representatives to provincial and local government (Questions 83 and 84), there was no significant difference from the national Parliament, with 60 per cent saying yes and one-third saying no.

These responses may, however, change in future regarding local government, where independent worker candidates may contest ANC seats in contravention of the Alliance. An interesting example of the sophisticated use of electoral policies by Cosatu workers is the unexpected and dramatic election of an independent candidate in Ward 42 of the Nelson Mandela Metro, as recounted in Chapter 7 (on community politics) of this volume.

The possibility of worker candidates standing for local government is also reflected in the divided response to Question 86, 'Should elected union office bearers be allowed to simultaneously serve as local government councillors?' It was asked for the first time in 2014, with 36 per cent of workers saying yes and the majority of 57 per cent saying no.

Cosatu workers believe strongly in the principle of recall of leadership if they do not implement their mandate, as was understood by the workers. In response to the question 'Do you think that if Cosatu representatives on elected political institutions do not do what workers want, they should be recalled/removed?', an overwhelming 93 per cent of workers responded in the affirmative. How is such recall to be effected when worker representatives are elected through the ANC? A third said this would be done through elections (they will not re-elect them); 41 per cent said through Cosatu internal processes (although this is not possible in the current electoral system); and the remainder said through mass action, although it is hard to see how this would be possible. What this indicates is what could be called a 'democratic impulse' from workers – to try to 'correct' the current unsatisfactory arrangement through recalling representatives. That this is not possible within the current electoral system is not reflected or understood by workers.

There is a corresponding increase in support for the idea that the labour move-ment should be independent of political parties, which can be interpreted as a reclaiming of the old Fosatu independent left position. There is also increased sup-port – although still very limited – for a workers' party. The idea that the SACP should represent working-class interests in government is not taken seriously, with only 2 per cent of Cosatu workers (fifteen individuals in 2014) supporting this idea consistently since 1994. This reponse is consistent with the view expressed above that the SACP is not capable of advancing working-class interests in Parliament as its policies and programmes have been subordinated to those of the ANC.

More interestingly, the option that another party could better serve worker inter-ests was supported by even fewer Cosatu members, indicating that workers, even if disillusioned with the ANC, are not changing their vote to the EFF or the Workers and Socialist Party (Wasp). This finding is somewhat contradicted by the finding of Question 105 in which workers are asked what they would do if things did not change: 30 per cent responded that they would vote for another party if government failed to deliver and 19 per cent said they would continue trying to put pressure on unionists in Parliament (a significant drop from the earlier years of the Alliance), while the largest category opted for extra-parliamentary means of pressure/mass action and a further 30 per cent felt helpless and said they would do nothing.

OVERLAPPING LOYALTIES: COSATU, ANC AND SACP

Whether workers will be willing to vote for a party other than the ANC, or to align themselves with a new formation of the left, depends on their loyalty to the

ANC and the SACP. Fifteen per cent of Cosatu members surveyed were SACP members, while over half (54 per cent) of Cosatu members surveyed were ANC members (Questions 95 and 96). SACP membership is concentrated in NUM and Numsa, with a significant SACP membership (over 10 per cent) in Samwu and the Police and Prisons Civil Rights Union (Popcru). SACP membership is also higher among shop stewards, as could be expected, with higher levels of political education concentrated here: 27 per cent of the shop stewards were SACP members, whereas 12 per cent of those who were not shop stewards were SACP members.

The 54 per cent of Cosatu workers who are ANC members correlates roughly with the consistent 55 per cent to 60 per cent of workers who support the Alliance, and who think that Cosatu should continue to send worker representatives to Parliament and to provincial and local government through the Alliance, as ANC representatives. Other questions tested whether Cosatu members are members of the political party they intend voting for, and whether they are active members of a political party. Unsurprisingly, roughly the same 60 per cent (who support the Alliance and are ANC members) are members of the party they intend to vote for; perhaps more surprisingly, 45 per cent of workers claimed to have attended a branch meeting of a political party in the past year – quite a high level of political participation by ordinary workers.

WORKERS' UNDERSTANDING OF POLITICAL DEMOCRACY

How do workers understand the electoral process and the way in which their interests, as citizens and as workers, are represented? Nearly two-thirds (73 per cent) of Cosatu workers think that the party they intend voting for has worker interests at heart (Question 92); despite the assertion of leadership that the ANC is following a neoliberal or capitalist route, ordinary workers have confidence that their interests are still at the heart of the national liberation movement.

Having elected their chosen party to Parliament, how are workers to hold these political representatives to account? Workers apply the principles of trade union democracy to the national political arena, even where it is hard to see how this can practically be carried out; hence the majority (74 per cent) of Cosatu workers said that when they vote for a political party in an election that party must consult with its supporters on all issues (Question 87). The same 75 per cent of workers believe that when the party makes decisions in Parliament that affect its supporters, it must report back to the people who voted for it 'every time' (Question 88).

Table 6.1: If the majority of people who vote for a party in an election are workers, then that party …

	1994	1998	2004	2008	2014
… must represent only the interests of workers	32	54	40	85	75
… must represent the interests of all supporters, including those who aren't workers	399	392	378	360	395
… must represent the interests of all South Africans even if worker interests have to be sacrificed	206	191	233	178	230

While this somewhat idealistic notion of representative democracy reflects the union's internal democratic culture, as indicated in Chapter 9, workers are more pragmatic when it comes to understanding how parties actually represent the interests of the voters in Parliament.

Table 6.1 indicates a clear understanding among workers that Parliament is a body representing the citizens of the country, and that any political party that stands for election must represent all the citizens who vote for it. Integral to this understanding is the view that the ANC – which is the party the majority of workers voted for – is a party which emerged from the national liberation movement, a multi-class movement representing a broad spectrum of society.

Workers also indicated a sophisticated understanding of electoral politics, and did not overemphasise the 'politics of personality' in their choice of party, as is reflected in the answer to Question 90: 'When you decide to vote for a particular party, which is the most important factor behind your decision?' The actual performance of the party (31 per cent), closely followed by its stated intentions in the form of policies (28 per cent), was the primary basis for most workers' electoral choice. Although some workers did judge the party on the basis of their loyalty to the tradition (20 per cent) or their assessment of the leadership (16 per cent), these answers were less significant than policies and the delivery of promises.

Regarding the electoral system (Question 91 asked, 'Would you prefer to be represented by members in Parliament elected through a … ?'), there is no difference between the numbers who would retain the existing system of proportional representation using a list of party candidates (31 per cent), and those who would prefer a change to a constituency-based or 'first past the post' system (31 per cent). Another group of nearly the same size (24 per cent) expressed their preference for the mixed system, as currently used in local government elections, to be extended to national level.

In general, workers accept the institutions of representative democracy and participate actively in the electoral system. Only 4 per cent of survey respondents said they did not intend to vote in the 2014 election (Question 98), even though expectations of representation of their interests in Parliament are not always met.

Given this acceptance of the system of representative democracy, and the decline in support for the Alliance, together with diminishing confidence in the SACP, who will workers vote for? Is there potential for realignment of the left behind Numsa, and how will this be expressed in the political arena?

THE 'NUMSA MOMENT'

As will be clear from the previous section, the level of tension in the Alliance which led to the rupture in 2014 had been rising for some time. Numsa is the union at the centre of the rupture, and Cosatu leadership know from long experience that Numsa is likely to be at the forefront of criticism of government policies. In 2014, as the ANC celebrated twenty years of democracy, with emphasis laid on its achievements of twenty years in government, Numsa did a more critical appraisal of the gains and losses made by the labour movement. The unhappy conclusion that more losses than gains had been made laid the basis for the rupture within the Alliance and within Cosatu itself.

'The Communist Party is in the belly of the state': The role of the SACP

At the centre of the rupture in the Alliance is the role of the SACP, understood by the 'Numsa bloc' to have relinquished its historically self-defined role as the vanguard of the working class. The SACP is understood to have changed from the Mbeki era (when it was critical of the ANC's shift to the right) to uncritical support for the Zuma administration – to the extent that SACP leaders not only implement unpopular policies such as the Gauteng e-tolls, against Cosatu's wishes, but went as far as to openly side with the South African Police Service in the Marikana massacre of mineworkers. Cosatu leaders understand this to be the result of the SACP's failed strategy of placing members in key positions in the state, which has not succeeded in advancing the interests of the working class – in the process of pursuing this strategy, senior SACP members have developed a vested interest in maintaining their positions in government as career politicians.

Some trade union leaders argue that the problems of Cosatu started with problems within the Alliance, in particular the falling-out between Numsa and the

SACP. As Numsa leaders became more confident in asserting their criticism of the SACP, the SACP response was combative, attacking Numsa for 'business unionism', and defending Cosatu. The ANC, on the other hand, attempted to be conciliatory, sending former Cosatu leaders such as Sydney Mufamadi to mediate.

As the rift between Numsa and the SACP widened, the SACP drew closer to NUM; the influence of office bearers of NUM in structures of the party bears this out. For example, Senzeni Zokwana, the former national president of NUM, is also both the minister of agriculture and the national chairperson of the SACP. The former general secretary of NUM is in the Central Committee of SACP; and the provincial secretary of North West Province of the SACP is also a senior officer bearer in NUM.

The outcome of this shift in influence is that while the SACP still has a strong influence on Cosatu at the national Central Executive Committee level – hence the attempt at the 'containment' of Numsa which resulted in its expulsion – this influence is waning at the lower levels, and in certain provinces.

At national government level, however, SACP leaders retain key positions in the cabinet, and so have to deal on a daily basis with the contradictions of being in the ANC government and implementing policies unpopular with the working class, as well as other contradictions which manifest in a society of extreme inequality. The most notable recent example is that of SACP leader Blade Nzimande, as minister of higher education, having to deal with the unexpected revolt of university students and workers in November 2015 and 2016. Some worker leaders blame the SACP for not providing a stronger policy direction within the state:

> … you'll find the Communist Party is piggybacking on the back of the Alliance. Whatever the ANC implements as … legislation, you don't find now the SACP being vocal to say those policies are … detrimental to the future of the working class, they will always nod and agree and what the government implements is an attempt to improve the lives of workers, but still people are living in squalor, people are still languishing in poverty, there's lots of unemployment. The Alliance which now at this point should be giving guidance, the Communist Party is in the belly of the state … they could shape the government in the direction that could benefit people … (interview, Numsa official, 2014).

The Eastern Cape dynamic

In the Eastern Cape, where Numsa is understood to have significant sympathy from other Cosatu affiliates and from workers on the ground, there have been warning signs over the past two or three years that the rupture was imminent.

The Eastern Cape, in particular the industrial centres of Buffalo City and Nelson Mandela Bay, are understood to be strongholds of the ANC and of a militant and highly politicised labour movement. Up until fairly recently, Cosatu and the SACP used to take the same position on policy debates, and used to engage with the ANC through Tripartite Alliance structures as the 'socialist axis'. As the SACP has moved closer to the ANC, the argument goes, the socialist axis has broken. This dynamic is illustrated by a few accounts of events in Nelson Mandela Bay:

- Cosatu cutting ties with the ANC

This event occurred in the context of allegations of corruption within the Nelson Mandela Bay municipality, and the demand for the release of the Kabuso Report dealing with these allegations. Nceba Faku, former mayor of Nelson Mandela Bay, was chairman of the regional ANC at the time. The Cosatu Port Elizabeth local sub-mitted a list of demands to the ANC. At a meeting of the shop-stewards council, a resolution was passed by shop stewards to cut all ties with the ANC until the ANC responded to those demands. It should be noted that this was a council of shop stewards from all Cosatu affiliates; and that the Cosatu Provincial Executive Com-mittee accepted the resolution of the local.

This was a forerunner of the Numsa decision not to support the ANC in the 2014 elections. Following the 2013 special congress of Cosatu, where Numsa had argued that Cosatu should leave the Alliance, Numsa indicated its position on the elections: it would not support the ANC. Although it would not encourage workers to vote for any particular party, it would not commit its considerable resources to the ANC election campaign.

In Nelson Mandela Bay, where in previous elections Numsa had run the elec-tion command centre, mobilising workers for the elections through factory vis-its and using its extensive organisational resources to support the ANC election campaign, this was withheld in the run-up to the 2014 poll. The ANC had to go it alone, few other unions having the capacity to support it actively in election campaign work. Whether this had a direct effect on ANC election results is not certain, as the survey indicated that 84 per cent of workers in the Eastern Cape who intended to vote would vote for the ANC; as noted elsewhere, the loyalty of Cosatu members to the ANC remains strong, an enduring solidarity. Never-theless, the ANC was right to be worried: as in the 2016 local government elec-tions, the Nelson Mandela Bay Metro was lost by the ANC, and a coalition of the Democratic Alliance (DA), Economic Freedom Fighters (EFF), Congress of the People (Cope) and other councillors now controls the city. The ANC secretary general, Gwede Mantashe, in response to these concerns, visited ANC branches in the metro, as well as Numsa-organised motor factories including Volkswagen, to convince workers to remain loyal to the ANC. Jacob Zuma led a high-powered ANC delegation to Nelson Mandela Bay in December, and ANC provincial secretary Oscar Mabuyane named the Nelson Mandela Bay region as the 'hottest of hot spots' in the ANC (George 2014).

- Cosatu tension with the SACP

Reflecting the tensions between the SACP and the Numsa bloc leadership, at the SACP provincial congress in October 2014 the SACP did not elect the Cosatu provincial chairman David 'Stix' Toyisi onto its Provincial Executive Committee. While Cosatu had elected a new provincial executive at a special congress in June 2014, the divisions were already playing themselves out in the contested election of provincial secretary Macvicar Dyasopu, who died tragically in January 2017. Although Toyisi's election as Cosatu chairperson was not contested, the SACP did not elect the prominent labour leader into its provincial leadership – something that it would almost certainly have done prior to the tensions within the Alliance and the SACP itself.

- Tension within Cosatu

Reflecting the tension within Cosatu after the suspension of Zwelinzima Vavi in August 2013, the Eastern Cape Cosatu shop-stewards council held in December 2013 supported the call for a special national congress. The Eastern Cape shop stewards voted in favour of Vavi's reinstatement, and publicly rejected Cosatu president Sdumo Dlamini by drowning him out with song and not allowing him to finish his speech.

In 2015, ANC secretary general Gwede Mantashe noted that Samwu, Nehawu, Popcru and NUM were 'the only unions working with the ANC in the metro'. He went on to describe a situation where relations in the Tripartite Alliance were so bad that 'both Cosatu and SACP [are] refusing to participate in Alliance meetings and activities ... the influence of Numsa in the region [is] putting an additional strain on the Alliance relations' (Ndamase 2015).

The evidence of such growing tension in the Eastern Cape gave analysts a clear warning of the rupture to come. How these divisions translate into political action in the future and, in particular, how they would manifest in the local elections of 2016 is the question that organised labour and its allies were asking. This is explored in the final section below: what is the future of the Alliance, and is there potential for a new socialist or workers' party, or a broad movement of the progressive left?

THE COSATU RUPTURE AND THE FUTURE OF THE ALLIANCE

When workers were asked whether they think the Alliance should continue and contest the next election, the response was consistent – a drop to 46 per cent in support for the continuation of the Alliance; and just under 30 per cent supporting the independence of the labour movement.

The moment of rupture can also be linked to the changing composition of Cosatu (see Chapters 3 and 4 in this volume). In brief, contestation within the mining sector saw the weakening of NUM, and consequently the loss of its historic dominance within Cosatu nationally. Numsa tried to replace it and to become the new hegemon but, as expected, this did not go uncontested by other Alliance members, in particular the SACP, which took upon itself the mantle of containing the left dissidents. This led to the controversial expulsion of Numsa from Cosatu and the subsequent support by the seven unions – referred to here together with Numsa as the Numsa bloc, as distinct from the NUM bloc.

The survey findings on particular unions' support for the Alliance correlate quite closely with the Cosatu rupture. The unions with the highest level of support for

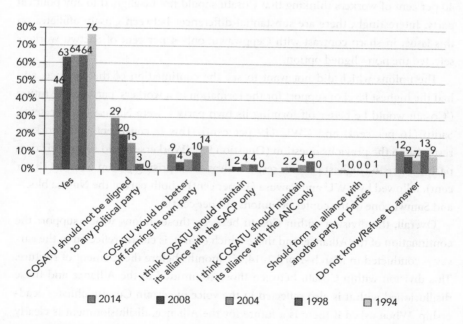

Figure 6.3: Do you think that this Alliance should continue and contest the election after 2014?

the Alliance in the May elections (Question 93) were NUM (80 per cent) followed by Popcru and Samwu (48 per cent) and Sadtu (45 per cent). Samwu and Sadtu, although still in the NUM bloc in Cosatu, are both suffering from deep divisions around the current crisis and the expulsion of Numsa. Similarly, on whether the Alliance should continue (Question 94), there were substantial differences between Cosatu affiliates, with 82 per cent of NUM members supporting the continuation of the Alliance, compared to only 31 per cent of Numsa members. Sactwu and Samwu (part of the NUM bloc) saw two-thirds of workers supporting the continuation of the Alliance, with Nehawu and Popcru (also part of the NUM bloc) having over 50 per cent of workers supporting the continuation of the Alliance. The other unions all had less than 50 per cent support for the Alliance continuing, the lowest being the Finance Union (Sasbo) (17 per cent). Denosa (21 per cent) and the Public and Allied Workers' Union of South Africa (Pawusa) and CWU (25 per cent), three of the 'Numsa bloc' unions, were the next lowest.

The unions which did not want to see the continuation of the Alliance, and had the highest level of support for Cosatu not to be aligned to any political party, were Sasbo (60 per cent), Ceppwawu (40 per cent) and Numsa (39 per cent). Ceppwawu, although not part of the Numsa bloc, retains a scepticism of Alliance politics, with 40 per cent of workers thinking that Cosatu should not be aligned to any political party. Interestingly, there are substantial differences between Cosatu affiliates on this issue; in sharp contrast with Ceppwawu, only 4 per cent of Sactwu workers selected the non-aligned option.

The unions which did not want to see the continuation of the Alliance, and had the highest level of support for the formation of a workers' party in the future ('Cosatu would be better off forming its own party'), were Numsa (16 per cent), Sadtu (16 per cent) and CWU (19 per cent). This is consistent with workers' response to the previous question (Question 93), 'Workers should form their own party', where the highest positive response was unsurprisingly from Numsa (18 per cent), followed by CWU and Pawusa (13 per cent) – both part of the Numsa bloc – and Samwu, one of the contested unions (14 per cent).

Overall, the division within Cosatu between those unions which support the continuation of the Alliance, and those which do not, is clearly reflected in the survey – conducted in March–April 2014, six months before the moment of rupture. This division within Cosatu between those committed to the Alliance and those disillusioned with it is also reflected in the voice of certain Cosatu affiliates' leadership. When asked if there is a future for the Alliance, disillusionment is clearly expressed by a Nehawu official:

I don't think it will be a good thing to say maybe the Alliance must end. But this a democratic country and we are the affiliates of Cosatu. If there are people who think that this Alliance is not assisting us, we cannot say they are wrong or right, we need to discuss these things in the congresses of Cosatu. Currently the only time where we see Alliance works together is when we go to the elections, but after the elections you don't see any programmes and it's a concern to me, because the Alliance is supposed to work 24/7 if we have elections or not. Currently it's just an 'alliance of convenience', that is the only term I can use … this Alliance was built by blood you know, so we cannot just underestimate that, but we need to be realistic when we deal with these things. We need to work very hard, because it's not the Alliance we used to know that we are having currently (interview, Nehawu official, 2015).

Nehawu, although a loyal Cosatu affiliate, is critical of how the Alliance seems to work only to assist the ANC in election campaigns. Sadtu, one of the unions which remained inside Cosatu despite internal divisions, is also divided about the future of the Alliance:

Having seen what has been taking place, it's clear that the Alliance in the form in which it is cannot have a future … unless – I do not know what can suddenly come on the minds of the leadership, but it doesn't look like leaders are prepared to come down and confront the real issues that are causing differences … and when it's like that there can't be a future based on the shifting sand of evasions, as Oliver Tambo once said that 'no unity can be built on the shifting sands of evasions'. Unity of the Alliance has to be based on honesty amongst ourselves to confront reality, so that we may be able to move forward. Other than that there can't be a future (interview, Sadtu official, 2014).

For one Cosatu Eastern Cape official interviewed, the future of the Alliance comes down to policy: his understanding is that while the government has to act in the national interest, it is apparent that the ANC government is now adopting policies which are not in the interests of the majority of workers:

The Alliance is still relevant, but gradually over time we have seen real changes … there was a general understanding historically in Cosatu that the

Alliance is the political centre which must advance transformation in the country ... but the reality is that post-1994 with the introduction of neoliberal policies which have been viewed by Cosatu as an attack on the position of workers, the Alliance has not been able to be instrumental as it was prior 1994. Because of limitations on government ... in the global environment in which it exists, the leadership of the Alliance has been under strain, because of differences in perspective and approach. The government has to develop policies which in its view respond to all interests of all people in the country; we are a revolutionary and transformative trade union, we do feel the policy discourse is not what we want as workers at the end of the day (interview, Cosatu Eastern Cape official, 2015).

This takes us back to the beginning of this chapter, where the emerging policy differences between the ANC and Cosatu were outlined. The final question which our survey put to Cosatu members was related to this critical issue: if the government cannot meet worker expectations, what will workers do?

The rupture in the working-class movement is also reflected in the response of workers to the question of what they will do if the government does not deliver on its promises. As can be seen in Table 6.2, the response in 2014 was quite spread out, with the highest numbers of workers either following the 'pluralist parliamentary' route and intending to vote for another party, or intending the 'extra-parliamentary' route of mass action. A significant minority – though still a minority – favours the formation of a new party which will act in the interests of the working class.

Table 6.2: If the government elected in the next election fails to deliver most of these benefits, workers will ... (more than one response possible)

	1994 (%)	1998 (%)	2004 (%)	2008 (%)	2014 (%)
... put pressure on unionists in Parliament	67	89	86	23	19
... vote for another party in the next election	40	68	43	20	30
... form an alternative party that will provide these benefits to workers	39	65	39	6	10
... participate in ongoing mass action to force the government to deliver on its promises	70	75	71	39	30
... do nothing	4	20	7	4	5

CONCLUSION: LEFT REALIGNMENT, THE UNITED FRONT AND THE FUTURE OF THE ALLIANCE

Some analysts and activists of the left have seen the moment of rupture as a positive indicator of the potential for realignment of the left. Devan Pillay (2015: 133), for example, argues somewhat optimistically that the 'Numsa moment, along with the United Front process, opens up the possibility of the emergence of a new democratic left politics'.

Following its expulsion, Numsa took a decision not only to break decisively with the Alliance, but to organise outside the federation, across the sectoral spectrum, disrespecting the 'one sector, one union' principle of Cosatu. For the new unions, the organisational principle is based on the value chain rather than on the sector. Zwelinzima Vavi, based in the Numsa national office building, has begun the laborious process of building a new trade union federation. The new federation hopes to capture the majority of as yet unorganised workers; in addition, the possibility exists of Nactu, as well as Amcu and other small independent unions, amalgamating into a new labour federation. Even braver talk is of a new socialist workers' party, a powerful left-wing labour federation spearheading a new progressive politics which will pose a serious challenge to the Alliance and, in particular, to the ruling ANC.

Numsa has also taken the lead in the formation of the United Front, which has been given impetus by the expulsion of Numsa from Cosatu. The idea had been percolating for some time; the Numsa special national congress of December 2013 gave a mandate for the Numsa national leadership 'to unite trade unions, rural and urban social movements, faith-based organisations, women's and youth organisations and other popular formations in action to fight rising unemployment, deepening inequality and poverty' (Numsa 2014).

As the invitation to the Preparatory Assembly, which was held on 13–14 December 2014, stated:

> This assembly will be representative of several constituencies, organisations and stakeholders who are part of struggles against all forms of neoliberal policies in our country that have placed an onerous burden on the poor and the working class.

The Assembly did adopt the guiding principles that framed the formation of the United Front, and elected an interim steering committee to oversee preparations for the launch; however, the launch, initially scheduled for April 2015, and later for early 2016, had not yet taken place at the time of writing.

Prior to the 2016 municipal elections, the United Front registered as a political party, but only to contest elections in municipalities in the Eastern Cape as the United Front of the Eastern Cape; simultaneously Numsa was finalising plans to form a workers' party. While some considered the United Front to be a greater threat than the DA, it was the EFF that obtained a small but significant percentage of the township vote, and it was the DA that gained overall control of the metro. The United Front Eastern Cape managed to obtain only one seat in the Nelson Mandela Metro council in the 2016 election, and no seats in Buffalo City.

It would seem that the foundations of the United Front are somewhat shaky. On the one hand, the labour component (Numsa and its allies) is not as strong as it appears to be. Worker leaders are struggling to convince workers of the idea of the United Front, perceived as an opposition to the ANC in a constituency which has strong political loyalties, as indicated by the election results. The unions in Cosatu which support Numsa, with the exception of Fawu and Saccawu, are some of the weakest affiliates. Despite their support for Numsa, the unions which attempted to take up the issue at the special congress in July 2015 were outvoted, and now remain within the federation in a politically weak position. Samwu and Sadtu have suffered divisions but have remained within the federation. Denosa supported Vavi, but did not support the United Front or the break with the Alliance and, together with Sadtu, remains within the federation. Only Numsa and Denosa have held special or consultative congresses to update their mandate on current political issues. Other unions, such as Ceppwawu, have not even held national meetings to obtain that mandate. This has led to the situation where a press conference of provincial leaders was called to condemn their national leadership for acting outside its mandate.

Other political party allies of the United Front – the Azanian People's Organisation (Azapo) and the PAC, as the old black consciousness and Africanist 'left' – have little support and even less organisational capacity. At the same time, the civil society partners in the United Front are not strong either. The new social movements of the unemployed, the landless and the shack-dwellers have a limited organised grass-roots constituency, little organisational capacity and few material resources to draw on. The South African National Civics Organisation (Sanco) is dependent on the ANC, and independent residents' associations are as yet unorganised, although this is on the cards. The burden is on Numsa, which despite its organisational strength has weaknesses in its political leadership. And as one local activist asked: 'The United Front needs worker participation and leadership – but do workers need the United Front?'

Does this indicate that the time has come for a decisive break between the progressive labour movement and its old ally the ANC? The left leaders who, in some cases, have been suspended from Cosatu – or expelled, as in the case of Sadtu president Thobile Ntola – feel that the time has come to 'liberate ourselves from the liberation movement' (interview, Thobile Ntola, 2014). In order to do so, argues Ntola, it is necessary to 'forget the symbols [of the liberation movement] and move forward with our historic mission. If we achieve the mission, then we can remarry it with the symbols.'

The reality, though, is that the Alliance is not about to collapse, and nor is the ANC likely to give many concessions to labour, whether inside or outside Cosatu. With the dramatic downturn in the South African economy in 2015, and the loss of jobs in manufacturing, even the strongest unions such as Numsa are on the defensive. Some of the unions in the Numsa bloc – Denosa, Samwu and Sactwu – have remained inside Cosatu, cautiously hedging their bets by remaining in the safe haven of the Alliance. Satawu remains in Cosatu but is significantly weakened. The majority of Cosatu workers – in particular those in the public sector unions – support them in this.

However, Fawu and Saccawu have indicated that they are going to go with Numsa and join the new federation. The reasons for Fawu and Saccawu leaving Cosatu are based in issues of process and constitutionality, rather than in policy differences as articulated by Numsa. Fawu reacted, in particular, to the consolidation of power by the Central Executive Committee and the lack of democracy within Cosatu, indicating its unhappiness with the voting process in the special congress and the national congress. Splinter unions from existing affiliates – Sadtu, Samwu and Ceppwawu – have also indicated identification with the new federation. The new federation, which is due to launch in April 2017, has also got Amcu on board, and thus will organise a significant proportion of the mining, heavy industry and transport workers. If Nactu amalgamates with the new federation, there will be a 'super-union' of metal and transport workers; together with mineworkers, the constituency of the new federation will constitute the powerful strategic manual-labour backbone of the working class. The bringing in of Nactu has been made possible by Numsa's breaking of the alliance with the ANC, which was a stumbling block to any prospects of unity, despite agreement between Cosatu and Nactu on substantive policy issues in Nedlac. It remains to be seen how unions such as Amcu – coming from a very different political tradition and culture – will gel with the deeply embedded democratic tradition and processes of unions such as Numsa.

NOTE

1   The quote 'No true alliance can be built on the shifting sands of evasions, illusions and opportunism' was contained in the 8 January 1980 speech of Oliver Tambo, on the 68th anniversary of the ANC. He was in turn quoting from an article written by Nelson Mandela in 1953. See http://www.anc.org.za/show.php?id=4361. This phrase was used by suspended Sadtu leader Ndongeni in an interview with Nkosinathi Jikeka in October 2014.

BIBLIOGRAPHY

African National Congress (ANC). 1990. Recommendations on post-apartheid economic policy: Workshop on economic policy for a post-apartheid South Africa, Harare, 28th April to 1st May 1990. *Transformation* 12: 2–15.

Congress of South African Trade Unions (Cosatu). 2016. Cosatu rejects and denounces the fallacious claims by Treasury and the Presidency. Press statement, 28 January. http://www.cosatu.org.za/show.php?ID=11304#sthash.FhA0KdTv.dpuf (accessed 20 April 2017).

George, Zine. 2014. Zuma turns his focus on metro. *Daily Dispatch*, 11 December.

Government of South Africa. 2016. Presidency on consultation with labour on tax law. Statement of the Presidency, 27 January. http://www.gov.za/speeches/update-consultations-labour-tax-law-occurred-over-period-27-jan-2016-0000 (accessed 20 March 2017).

Ndamase, Mkhululi. 2015. ANC fears losing metro. *The Herald*, 14 October.

Nehawu (National Education Health and Allied Workers' Union). 2016a. Nehawu statement on the developments in higher education, the new tax laws, national health insurance and collective bargaining, 25 January. http://www.nehawu.org.za/files/ (accessed 20 March 2017).

Nehawu. 2016b. Retirement insurance reforms. Pamphlet, January.

Numsa (National Union of Metalworkers of South Africa). 2014. United Front People's Assembly. Press release, 12 December. http://www.numsa.org.za/article/united-front-peoples-assembly/ (accessed 20 March 2017).

Pillay, Devan. 2015. Cosatu and the Alliance: Falling apart at the seams. In *Cosatu in Crisis: The Fragmentation of an African Trade Union Federation*, edited by Vishwas Satgar and Roger Southall. Johannesburg: KMMR Publishing.

Shilowa, Mbhazima. 1997. Employment creation. Address to Cosatu Policy Conference. 15–17 May 1997. http://www.cosatu.org.za/show.php?ID=1457 (accessed 20 April 2017).

7

Cosatu, Service Delivery, Civil Society and the Politics of Community

Janet Cherry

INTRODUCTION

South Africa has seen an explosion of protest in recent years – protests in the poor, working-class townships and informal settlements in every city, and in many small towns across the provinces. These protests, termed 'service delivery protests' as many (although by no means all) of them are demanding the provision of services, are usually targeting the local authorities or municipal councillors responsible for such services in the townships where the protestors live.

How do organised workers, who are members of the same working class, respond to or interact with these protests? Do they share the demands of the protestors? Do they perhaps provide leadership – organisational or strategic – to these protests, based on their trade union experience? This chapter explores the relationship of Cosatu members to 'the community' – and whether there are in reality two working classes: those in formal employment, living in formal townships, and those who are at the margins of the economy and society, without jobs or services.

The 'service delivery protest' phenomenon has drawn a significant amount of academic attention, and a range of explanations: see Karl von Holdt et al. (2011), *The Smoke that Calls*; Peter Alexander (2010), *The Rebellion of the Poor*; and Doreen

Atkinson (2007); among others. Von Holdt and his colleagues have reflected on how the protests are integrally related to local power dynamics within the African National Congress (ANC), and that the ANC itself is 'the locus of many of these struggles and contestations' (Von Holdt et al. 2011: 7). Many of the protests are led by ANC activists or activists from other members of the Alliance, notably the South African Communist Party (SACP). In one of the case studies documented in *The Smoke that Calls*, a trade union leader was also among the leadership of the protests. However, there has been little reflection on the relationship of members of Cosatu affiliates to these protests. As the protests are in the main residentially based – in that people who are resident in a particular locality have a grievance related to that locality, whether it be a demand for housing or for toilets or clean water – it could be expected that workers living in these areas might share the demands and participate in the protests. The 2014 Taking Democracy Seriously survey enables an exploration of where organised workers are living and what their living conditions are like – and how they relate to the protests.

The Cosatu leadership is of course acutely aware of these protests, and addressed the issue at its 2011 Central Committee meeting, to which the secretariat reported as follows:

> There is a wave of community service delivery protests, which are about spe-
> cific local grievances, but are also related to the structural problems in the
> economy. The patience of increasing numbers of poor working-class com-
> munities seemingly is running thin. They are facing a huge squeeze in the
> former black only residential areas, as well as the former bantustans. They are
> living with massive unemployment and grinding and humiliating poverty
> in places such as Alexandra, while across the road they see that the grass is
> green in the flashy buildings in Sandton. At times we have come to appreciate
> that there are also opportunistic agendas around elections to fuel 'service
> delivery protests' to promote individual careers. Behind these opportunistic
> tendencies are members of all the components of the Alliance. Cosatu, SACP,
> Sanco and even ANC cadres pursuing careers in the ANC and failing to
> achieve this and suddenly stoke anger and mobilise communities for violent
> community 'service delivery protests'. This goes back to what all have pointed
> out that the biggest enemy of the ANC is the ANC itself (Cosatu 2011: 49).

The secretariat's response to this complex relationship between community grievances and Alliance politics was to urge 'locals of Cosatu to link up with communities so that we can take up their issues with relevant authorities. The CEC wanted

Cosatu to not only champion community struggles but to build a strong relationship between organised workers and mushrooming issue-based social movements' (Cosatu 2011: 49).

The secretariat acknowledged, however, that '[t]his has not happened except in a few isolated cases' (Cosatu 2011: 49). Cosatu members are in overwhelming agreement that unions should have 'active links with community organisations/civil society organisations/social movements'. Over 80 per cent of workers have consistently agreed or strongly agreed with this statement in all surveys since 2004.

However, perhaps the above survey question – which puts community organisations, civil society organisations and social movements together – requires some breaking down, as different meanings can be ascribed to each of these terms, and the terms themselves do not mean the same thing.

SOCIAL MOVEMENTS AND CIVIL SOCIETY MOBILISATION

On the leadership level, Cosatu, as a national federation, has maintained active links to social movements and civil society pressure groups at national and provincial level. The Opposition to Urban Tolling Alliance in Gauteng is perhaps the most recent and interesting example. This campaign united an extraordinarily broad alliance against the government's introduction of toll roads, including the official opposition (the DA), business interests, taxi drivers and workers. Some of the most impressive mass action campaigns in recent years saw thousands of drivers blocking the roads and effectively rendering the toll roads unworkable for a day.

Other national social movements, including the Treatment Action Campaign (TAC), have worked successfully with Cosatu over many years to bring pressure to bear on government – in the case of the TAC, to provide antiretroviral treatment to HIV-positive people. There are also many national campaigns which do not constitute a movement or an organisation, but in which Cosatu has worked in close alliance with civil society groupings. These include the Anti-Privatisation Campaign, the One Million Climate Jobs campaign, the People's Budget, the Basic Income Grant Campaign and campaigns against high food prices and high electricity tariffs. Cosatu has in many cases been the initiator of these campaigns, playing the role as the leading progressive civil society formation, attempting to influence government around broader issues of social justice and policy implementation. Cosatu's strategic alliance with other elements of civil society over particular policy issues is thus often in tension with its formal alliance with the ruling party (see Ballard et al. 2006).

Cosatu has also formed alliances with Equal Education around ensuring the functionality of public schools, and with Streetnet International and local street vendors' associations concerning the informal economy and the rights of informal sector workers. The Cosatu affiliate Saccawu, in alliance with other civil society organisations, led the campaign against WalMart's buying out South African companies. International solidarity campaigns with the people of Palestine and of Swaziland have also seen Cosatu playing a leading role in coalitions with other civil society organisations.

This very broad range of issues and campaigns does not amount to a coherent movement. It is only in the past few years that the alliances between various issue-based movements have started to come together, often under the leadership of Cosatu, to form a more coherent civil society 'position' and strategy. In line with its mandate from national congresses, Cosatu has attempted to work more closely with other civil society formations. Civil society mobilisation around the Jobs and Poverty Campaign led to the first major Civil Society Conference in October 2010. This conference signified the beginnings of open tension between the governing ANC and its Alliance partners:

> The ANC NWC [National Working Committee] chose to launch a harsh attack on Cosatu and the Conference, objecting to the fact that it hadn't been invited to the Conference, and making a range of allegations, including that it was an attempt 'to put a wedge between civil society formations, some unions, the ANC and its government'; that civil society found the government 'guilty in abstentia of inactivity in fighting corruption' etc. Most surprisingly the statement alleged that this initiative could be 'interpreted as initial steps for regime change in South Africa', and suggesting that unnamed international forces were funding the initiative aimed at weakening, dividing and ultimately dividing the ANC and the Alliance, and setting up an opposition party (Cosatu 2011: 47).

More recent events have seen this tension continue to be reflected in the divisions within Cosatu and the fracturing of the Tripartite Alliance (both dealt with elsewhere in this volume). In addition, the mobilisation of civil society and coalitions with a range of social movements led to the formation of the United Front – led by Numsa and some other Cosatu affiliates – which aims to bring together various social movements into a coherent challenge to the neoliberal policies of the government (see Paret 2015: 54–56).

COSATU MEMBERS, SERVICE DELIVERY AND COMMUNITY STRUGGLE

When it comes down to the grass roots, however, the picture is somewhat different. Despite Cosatu's commitment to 'active links' with community organisations, there is little incentive for workers to be actively involved in struggles for service delivery. Alexander (2010: 31) notes that the service delivery protests are in the main carried out by the unemployed youth and concentrated in informal settlements, whereas the profile of the Cosatu worker in the survey is of employed workers living in formal housing. Half of the workers live in a privately owned house, 10 per cent in Reconstruction and Development (RDP) houses and another 30 per cent in rented formal accommodation; only 4 per cent live in a shack.

While this does not indicate where the houses are (in the suburbs or in the older townships, where municipal housing has been transferred into the residents' ownership), it does give a strong indication that there is a separation between Cosatu members, who are employed and who live in formal housing, and the residents of informal settlements, considered to be a 'subaltern class' or 'underclass' on the margins of the formal settlements and the formal economy, excluded and struggling for inclusion.

This is corroborated by the survey question 'Have any of the following services been provided or improved since the 1998/2004/2009 elections in your area?'

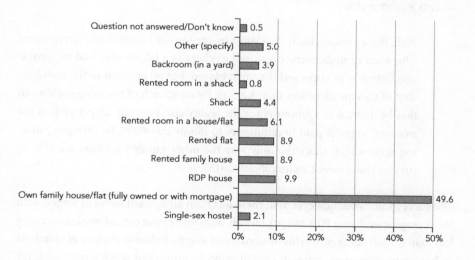

Figure 7.1: Where do you live during the times that you work? (2014 data)

followed by the question 'In which of the following areas would you like to see improvements after elections?' These questions were asked to ascertain levels of service delivery to the workers in their places of residence, and to find out what their needs or demands are, and the responses indicate that workers have seen improvements in service provision (specifically access to electricity and water) and better access to education and healthcare (in particular HIV/AIDS treatment). Wages, jobs and – interestingly – food access were named as the areas in which they would have liked to see improvements after the election. The problem of food access can be understood to be related to its relatively high cost and to the problem of low wages, as workers understand well that a high proportion of their wage is spent on food, together with transport and fuel.

The responses indicate that organised workers are relatively well-off; they are living in formal housing, and can afford to buy electricity and to send their children to school. Services (sanitation, water and energy) and the meeting of basic needs such as shelter are not their highest priority. Can it be assumed, then, that workers are not providing leadership to the community struggles of shack-dwellers around service delivery, the demands for housing and toilets? They are not the 'large underclass of unemployed' (Von Holdt et al. 2011: 6) who are struggling for inclusion.

This does not mean that the majority of workers are affluent or have changed class position. As one Cosatu official noted, dismissing the claims that Cosatu represents a 'labour elite':

> Well, there's always been the claims by sections of business and government who want to undermine organised workers as a labour elite and or separation between workers and the unemployed, but 60 per cent of the membership of Cosatu earns less than R3 500. By no stretch of the imagination can that be defined as a labour elite. The reality also is nearly 20 per cent of the workers' wages is paid in remittance to family members. So they [are] sharing their wages, that's the only way the other family members are able to survive (interview, Cosatu official, 2015).

The survey indicated, however, that there has been an upward trend in wages, with the average wage being R12 360 per month, and only 25 per cent of workers earning less than R6 800 per month. This upward trend may be linked to the loss of members in low-wage categories, through casualisation in municipal service provision, for example. It may also be related to the overall shift in Cosatu membership towards public sector unions representing professionals and middle-income workers.

Members of Cosatu unions in general identify improvements in education, health and service provision. The overriding problems they face are economic – the low wages of the employed. Unemployment is identified as the biggest problem for the 'other half' of the working class (the economically active population). The high level of unemployment offsets the wage gains made by organised labour, as the income from one wage or salary is inevitably redistributed among a number of family members or households (see Chapter 5 in this volume).

The areas which union members identified as having improved least – in their areas of residence – were policing and crime prevention, fighting corruption, and preventing drug and alcohol abuse. A comparative study (see Cherry and Prevost forthcoming 2017) of the old working-class township of Kwazakhele in Nelson Mandela Metro, conducted in the month after the 2014 election, corroborates this. Most residents of Kwazakhele are living in formal housing, with toilets, water and electricity provided, and access to education and healthcare much improved since 1994. Their concerns are poverty and unemployment – the economic exclusion of the 50 per cent of the economically active population who are unemployed – as well as the social problems of crime, violence and drug abuse.

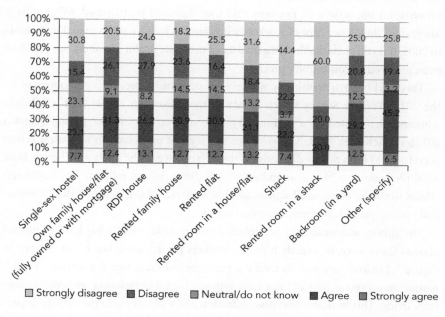

Figure 7.2: 'Local government service delivery in my area is satisfactory and effective'[1]

How do these concerns of workers relate to the politics of service delivery protests? Another question in the survey asked workers whether they agreed with the statement 'Local government service delivery in my area is satisfactory and effective' (asked in 2004, 2008 and 2014). This question elicited a clearly divided response between those workers who were satisfied with service delivery in their area and those who were not.

Although those workers who felt most strongly that service delivery is unsatisfactory were, understandably, those who were living in shacks, there is no obvious correlation between dissatisfaction with service delivery and type of residence – of the Cosatu members who live in their own houses, 47 per cent disagreed that service delivery is effective. Of Cosatu members living in RDP houses, 53 per cent were dissatisfied with service delivery. In other words, even among those Cosatu members living in formal housing with services, more were dissatisfied with service delivery than were satisfied.

If there is a high degree of unhappiness with local service delivery in the areas where Cosatu members live, do they participate in protests to demand better services – and perhaps even provide leadership to these protests? The survey asked the question 'Have you participated in community protest action since 2009?' and found that although the majority of workers had not participated in community protests, an impressive 27 per cent said that they had participated. While this is lower than the 45 per cent of workers who claimed to have participated in protests in 2008, it is still remarkable that a quarter of the trade union members sampled had been involved in community protest.

This level of participation by workers in community protest is corroborated by the 2012 Workers Survey which indicated that 'less than 25 per cent' of Cosatu workers participated in a community protest over a four-year period (Cosatu 2012b in McKinley 2014: 32). Whether this level of participation in protest action is considered high or low depends on the perspective of the analyst. Whereas Dale McKinley might see this as an indicator of declining labour militancy, in most societies it would be considered significant that a quarter of organised workers consistently participate in community protest action.

The survey was unable to get detailed information about what kind of protest actions these were, or exactly how the workers participated, but it can be seen in Figure 7.3 below, consistently with the previous question, that the workers' participation in protest action did not have any significant correlation with where they were living. This indicates that dissatisfaction and willingness to participate in protest action may be linked to local political factors in addition to material factors.

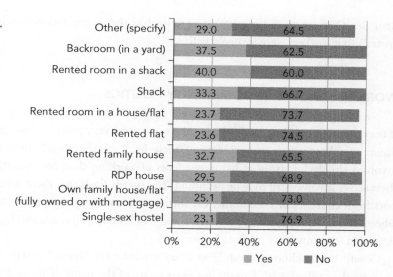

Figure 7.3: Where Cosatu members live cross-tabulated by whether they have participated in community protest action since the last election (in 2009)[2]

If the protests are being carried out by the unemployed youth, could we expect to find that older employed workers are more conservative in their attitude to such protests – particularly violent protests – and actually disapprove of them? The survey tried to dig a bit deeper into the service delivery protest phenomenon by asking workers about the violent nature of the protests. Of those workers who had participated in community protest action, 23 per cent said that the protests were violent (this is a decline from 2008). Further, in 60 per cent of these cases, workers indicated that the community or youth of that community had initiated the violence. This does not give an accurate reflection of whether workers approved of the violent protest, but it can be assumed that those who participated did support the protests. It is also a rather remarkable admission that in most cases it is the community which initiated the violence, rather than the authorities or the security forces.

However, community organisation is not the same as service delivery protest, and, indeed, there is some debate as to precisely how organised the protests are and whether the lack of effective community organisation at grass-roots level is perhaps one of the reasons for the protests often being spontaneous and/or violent. Then there is the absence of experienced trade union members playing a leadership role in these protests. So, while it is unlikely that Cosatu members are providing leadership in the protests of shack-dwellers, they may be doing so in other community struggles. Our survey did not enable us to analyse the nature and demands of the protests that workers were involved with.

WORKER LEADERS IN COMMUNITY POLITICS

If they are not providing leadership to the service delivery protests, how are trade union members active as residents of their local communities? They may be involved simply by virtue of being residents of working-class communities, and their active involvement may be declining. The survey finds that there is little support from churches or community organisations for unions engaged in strikes or labour action (Question 49); similarly, there is declining (although still high) participation in community protests by workers.

Cosatu itself acknowledged: 'Too often township/residential based stayaway from work is called, with Cosatu not even aware of the plans' (Cosatu 2011: 49). Yet there is evidence of a fairly high level of worker involvement in the 'formal politics' of the township. As could be expected, organised workers, who in many cases have experience as shop stewards or in other organisational capacities in the union, may play a leadership role within township structures such as ward committees or parents' committees. In 2014, the survey asked the question 'Are you involved in local government or community-based development initiatives (e.g. ward committees)?'

Table 7.1: Are you involved in local government or community-based development initiatives (e.g. ward committees)? (2014)

Yes, as elected councillor	4	0.6%
Yes, as elected delegate	8	1.3%
Yes, as elected councillor and elected delegate	14	2.3%
Yes, as community member	111	17.9%
Yes, as elected councillor and as community member	3	0.5%
Yes, as member of political party	31	5%
Yes, as elected councillor and as member of political party	1	0.2%
Yes, as community member and as member of political party	5	0.8%
Yes, as elected councillor, delegate, community member and member of political party	1	0.2%
No	441	71.2%
Total	**619**	**100%**

While there was an overall decrease in the number of respondents active in community politics – reflected in a rise in those who said they are 'not involved at all' from 60 per cent in 2008 to 71 per cent in 2014 – there were four elected councillors in the sample of trade union members, and a further eight trade unionists who were elected delegates to another structure such as a ward committee. In addition, a significant number of Cosatu members (31) are active as members of a political party in their area – in most cases, the ANC. By far the largest group, however, were those who responded that they are active 'as a community member' – nearly 20 per cent and over a hundred individuals. While there may be a decrease in involvement from previous years, the indication is that trade union members remain among the more active citizens in their communities. Of note is that a slightly higher percentage of Cosatu members are involved in 'formal politics' (29 per cent) compared with those who participated in service delivery protests or 'informal politics' (27 per cent), although these may be the same individuals – in other words, the one-quarter to one-third of workers who are 'activists' and politically involved in various ways. It is unlikely that Cosatu workers are sharply divided into two groups: those who participate in the 'formal politics' of local government, and those who participate in the 'informal politics' of protesting against it.

The involvement referred to in Table 7.1 may be with the Integrated Development Plan (IDP) process, or with other development initiatives of the ward councillor or the municipality. In addition, there is a range of initiatives at local level to address specific developmental or community concerns – from xenophobia to shopping centres to violence against women. Cosatu's female members are among the most vocal advocates of gender equality at local level. There are also examples of trade union members – specifically teachers – uniting with parents and pupils in action to solve teacher shortages, or engaging in protest action to resolve local education conflicts. This is explained by a Cosatu leader in relation to the militancy of the teachers under Sadtu – a militancy which is now causing some division within the teachers' union:

> South African Democratic Teachers Union … is able to take its own struggles on the streets, you will then understand that if some are not happy you will find that Sadtu is now badly divided because Sadtu is to be redirected to another direction which is not the one that Sadtu is traditionally known for … we think that they remain militant, but at times it depends on a character of a leadership at a particular point in time, otherwise at [sic] their own they remain militant (interview, Cosatu Nelson Mandela Bay local official, 2014).

121

Lastly, worker leaders are certainly involved in political conflicts at local level – through their involvement in an ANC branch, or an SACP branch, or another political organisation; or through being a union representative in a specific committee or campaign to deal with a particular issue. In some cases, worker leaders are encouraged by their community or their ANC or SACP branch to stand as ward councillor. The identity of an individual activist often blurs the boundaries between different organisational affiliations. This dynamic is captured below in a particularly interesting by-election held for the ward councillor of Ward 42 in Nelson Mandela Bay.

Cosatu workers were divided on the question of whether elected office bearers of a union should be allowed simultaneously to serve as local government councillors. Fifty-five per cent said 'no', 35 per cent said 'yes' and 10 per cent said 'do not know'. The understanding by the (slim) majority of workers that it is not ethical for a union official to also serve as a councillor, thus earning two salaries, is reflected here, rather than the idea that union officials should not be political representatives. However, this understanding does not prevent worker leaders who are no longer office bearers from standing for election.

The potential for worker leaders to challenge the ANC in local government is highlighted by the election of a Numsa and SACP leader as an independent candidate in the by-election in Ward 42 of Nelson Mandela Bay. This Uitenhage ward is an African working-class community, considered a loyal ANC constituency. The councillor, Andile Gqabi, was a former Volkswagen shop steward and at one point local secretary of both Numsa and Cosatu, and was national gender chairman of Cosatu as well as an SACP district leader. Following the contested local government elections of 2011, where forty-seven out of sixty ANC branches in the metro rejected the ANC's choice of councillors for election, the ANC singled out Ward 42 from the report of Nkosazana Zuma, and eventually expelled Gqabi from the ANC in August 2014. As his council seat became open, the ANC and its allies within the SACP put forward their own candidate for election. Gqabi took the brave decision, with the support of Numsa and its own allies within the SACP, to stand as an independent in the by-election of 6 November 2014 – something tried without much success by South African National Civics Organisation (Sanco) members in previous local elections in the metro. Gqabi gained 61 per cent of the vote, while the ANC gained 36 per cent, and had to share the minority vote with candidates from the Democratic Alliance (DA), Congress of the People (Cope) and the United Democratic Movement (UDM). While in the neighbouring Ward 46 by-election the ANC continued to gain its traditional 81 per cent of the vote, the Ward 42 results were described as an 'embarrassing' and 'humiliating' loss for the ANC (George 2014). However, residents of the ward made it clear that they were ANC supporters and that it was the local politics and the ANC's treatment of their community leader that had driven them to vote for an independent candidate. As Gqabi was a known worker and community leader, he had the confidence of the residents.

Additionally of interest is that the by-election reflects a sophisticated understanding of democracy in this typical African working-class community. While the ANC put considerable resources into the by-election, providing T-shirts and transport to the polls, the residents of Ward 42 used the secrecy of the ballot effectively: wearing the ANC T-shirts, they went to the polls and voted for 'their' councillor, Gqabi. This by-election has stimulated speculation on whether this strategy could be replicated in thousands of similar wards around the country. As the CWU (Eastern Cape) official explains:

> The worker works at the factory floor and when he leaves at his or her knock-off time he goes to his location and then when he gets to his location … now he deals with the high electricity, with roads, with high petrol price, so he have [sic] to join the political organisation whether you like it or not (interview, CWU official, 2014).

WORKER SOLIDARITY WITH COMMUNITY STRUGGLES

The official above was articulating Cosatu's 'old' position on the Alliance and how it is expressed at grass-roots level – a 'social unionism' position that the interests of the working class are not expressed only in the factory, but also in the community. The concept of social unionism embraces the idea that unions are not there solely for advancing the interests of worker members (hence it is counterposed to the concept of 'business unionism') but are a vehicle for social justice and for the empowerment of the working class as a whole (see Ross 2007; also see the discussion on social movement unionism versus economic unionism in Chapter 12). This is the idea that underlies Cosatu's involvement in, and sometimes leadership of, the campaigns outlined at the beginning of this article.

This kind of involvement in community politics is not the same as engaging in protest action, however. In a recent study of labour-community alliances, Dale McKinley argues that unions have 'failed to forge any kind of serious and longer term strategy to relate to, organise and support informal/casualised workers and the unemployed who dominate the membership of community organisations' (2014: 32). This analysis supports the idea of an emerging separation between the formal sector workers living in formal townships and the marginalised informal sector living in informal settlements. McKinley argues that they do not 'see' each other:

> When those communities protest over a lack of basic public services, for the most part they do not 'see' the public sector workers who deliver those services; and when union members go on strike to defend their jobs or improve their conditions of work, they largely fail to 'see' the mass of people who have no jobs or whose conditions are often much worse. The combined consequence is like two ships passing in the dark (2014: 32).

While this is vivid imagery, it is not borne out by our survey results, which indicate that workers' involvement with protest does not depend on their living in informal settlements. On the contrary, it is Numsa workers who participate most in community protest. Over 25 per cent of Samwu workers were involved in community protest. Nearly 30 per cent of Cosatu workers were involved 'as community members' in politics in some way. And over 80 per cent of Cosatu workers supported the idea of labour-community alliances.

Alexander (2010: 36) notes that the reasons for lack of involvement may not be a lack of sympathy for the protestors, but more practical reasons including insufficient time, and a spatial separation from the protests:

> On the ground, workers are generally (though not always) residents of townships, and easily sympathise with other members of their communities. However, as workers they tend to organise at work and in unions, which involves a spatial separation from the township. Time is taken up with work itself, and sometimes union activism, rather than township mobilisation. Arguably, while there are class interests that can unite workers and non-working or underemployed township residents, there are also divisions, especially in terms of use of time and organisation.

An additional reason for the weakness of more lasting and strategic alliances may be the lack of leadership from Cosatu at local level. A Denosa official reflects that the lack of political education in Cosatu has resulted in a failure of trade unionists to provide leadership to community struggles:

> Nobody is coming down to teach Cosatu members the politics, nobody is teaching us the social issues of community and [to] lead the community

now. So that is why we see these people are leading themselves, no one is guiding themselves, it destroys at the moment because *kaloku* (the thing is) there is no leader (interview, Denosa official, 2014).

In returning to the initial discussion on the service delivery protest phenomenon, it is worth reflecting on the position taken by Cosatu as a federation, and by particular affiliates. Alexander (2010: 35–36) notes that the Cosatu leadership has been 'rather quiet' about service delivery protests, although Zwelinzima Vavi addressed Samwu in November 2009 on the issue. Vavi linked the protests to the failures of the (Mbeki) government, and the policies of that government with which Cosatu has taken issue, notably the privatisation of basic services (in addition to 'cadre deployment' of unqualified people, presumably resulting in incompetent municipal management).

Samwu, as the union directly involved in service delivery at municipal level, is perhaps the logical union to look to regarding solidarity with, or direct involvement in, community protests. McKinley claims (2014: 27) that the last several years 'have been relatively barren when it comes to labour-community alliances for public services, especially at the national level and involving Cosatu'. However, Samwu – unlike Cosatu nationally – has publicly expressed open support for service delivery protests:

Our members on the ground know and experience the frustration of the poor. It is entirely consistent with the ideals of a democratic society for the poor to protest and collectively raise their demands. That is why Samwu supports those campaigning for an increase in services, and will continue to urge the government to make good on its promises to deliver them. Scores of perfectly legal protests on the question of service delivery have been met with hostile and unnecessary police violence (Samwu 2009 quoted in Alexander 2010: 36).

Nearly 30 per cent of Samwu members interviewed said that they had taken part in community protest action – raising further questions about whether they did so as residents of their community or whether they were somehow involved in their role as municipal employees in solidarity action with residents, and whether there was any conflict of interests between these two roles. Samwu members were not the most active in protest, however, with 41 per cent of Numsa members claiming to have taken part in community protests, and over 30 per cent of NUM and Nehawu members doing likewise. This may be related to the level of politicisation in the union, rather than the sector represented – in other words, it is not clear that municipal workers are more involved in community struggles because they are at the 'service delivery coalface'.

It has been posited that there is an emerging gap between community struggles and labour struggles, and that the social unionism preached by Cosatu is no longer practised 'on the ground'. McKinley, for example, has argued recently that 'there are very few formal and sustained labour-community alliances in South Africa' (2014: 6). His analysis is that by 2002 the 'momentum for further union action as well as labour-community alliances was effectively buried' as a result of the failure of Cosatu leadership to 'follow through' after the anti-privatisation strike of that year. McKinley argued that the Cosatu leadership 'adopted a de-politicised and individualistic approach, attributing the privatisation problem to technocrats within government …' An analysis of another longitudinal survey, but of Cosatu shop stewards, found a significant decline in community involvement by shop stewards from 1991 to 2012 (Paret 2015: 58).

While the Cosatu survey did not enable in-depth case studies of community protests, there have been some examples of trade union solidarity with specific community actions. Alexander (2010: 36) cites a 'remarkable' example of a Standerton community showing solidarity with striking workers from a poultry farm (however, the majority union in this case was a Fedusa affiliate). McKinley (2014) examines three cases of recent and more substantial labour-community alliances, involving Samwu in the Cape Town Housing Assembly, Denosa in the Eastern Cape Health Crisis Action Coalition and a number of Cosatu affiliates in particular programmes with the South Durban Community Environmental Alliance. The most successful direct actions involved Samwu and Streetnet in preventing the closure of the Durban market, and involved Satawu in the prevention of a Chinese shipment of arms from offloading in the Durban harbour.

McKinley is looking for the instances where such alliances are formed independently of the Tripartite Alliance and reflect an independent and local initiative around specific issues. He quotes Mzwanele Mayekiso, who observes that one of the hindrances to such alliances is the fear of being 'out of line' and labelled as 'defectors' from the Tripartite Alliance. 'More specifically, this has translated into a majority of unions and their members being "scared" to ally with, practically support or even regularly communicate with, non ANC-Alliance community structures' (McKinley 2014: 30).

However, McKinley is not examining the participation of Cosatu members as members of their community or their political party, whether in local government structures or other ward-based activities. As can be seen from the survey results above, the separation of union and community is not as clear as it is represented in McKinley's analysis. A high number of Cosatu union members participate in both forms of community politics: the formal politics of ward committees, clinic committees, and IDPs; and the informal politics of service delivery protests. There is also a third kind of community-labour alliance which is more structured around particular campaigns and issues, as illustrated by McKinley – but this is not yet at the point where it can be termed a social movement. Whether initiatives such as the United Front, or Democracy from Below, can lead to such a movement remains to be seen.

CONCLUDING REMARKS

Some challenging questions arise from this analysis of community struggles and service delivery protests. Is there a 'new syndicalism' emerging, whereby the labour movement builds its own political centre and challenges state power in isolation from 'the masses'? Is there a 'rebellion of the poor' (Alexander's term) or an 'insurgent citizenship' (Von Holdt's term) coming from the other half of the working class – the 'precariat', the unemployed, marginalised, excluded shack-dwellers? And where do these two movements intersect or come together?

Cosatu leadership is acutely aware of the danger of a divided working class, represented by two movements which do not cooperate – hence its urging that Cosatu should play a leadership role in community struggles:

> The danger of this is that a gulf may start to emerge between organised workers who in the context of the grinding crisis of unemployment, poverty and inequalities represent a privileged group, and the issue based social movements (Cosatu 2011: 49).

There are also implications for the United Front strategy being pursued by Numsa. If disaffection by the precariat/marginalised/shack-dwellers/casual workers is understood to be the driving force of the new movement, then this will not mesh easily with the concerns of organised labour, as most Cosatu members are living in formal townships and participate in formal politics. The United Front may struggle to find a common agenda between organised labour and the precariat. Moreover, while organised labour is in a vulnerable and defensive position, struggling to maintain strong and united affiliates and struggling to organise the unorganised, it is less likely to be able to provide strong and strategic leadership to a new social movement.

NOTES

1   Totals may not always add up to 100 per cent because of rounding.
2   Proportion may not add up to 100 per cent due to rounding or missing values.

BIBLIOGRAPHY

Alexander, Peter. 2010. Rebellion of the poor: South Africa's service delivery protests – a preliminary analysis. *Review of African Political Economy* 37(123): 25–40.

Atkinson, Doreen. 2007. Taking to the streets: Has developmental local government failed in South Africa? In *State of the Nation: South Africa 2007*, edited by Sakhela Buhlungu, John Daniel, Roger Southall and Jessica Lutchman. Cape Town: HSRC Press.

Ballard, Richard, Adam Habib and Imraan Valodia. 2006. *Voices of Protest: Social Movements in Post-apartheid South Africa*. Pietermaritzburg: University of KwaZulu-Natal Press.

Cherry, Janet and Gary Prevost. Forthcoming 2017. Kwazakhele after twenty years of democracy: The contradictory development of political pluralism and political alienation. *Transformation: Critical Perspectives on Southern Africa* 94.

Congress of South African Trade Unions (Cosatu). 2011. *Secretariat Report to 5th Central Committee, 2011*. Johannesburg: Cosatu.

McKinley, Dale. 2014. *Labour and Community in Transition: Alliances for Public Services in South Africa*. Municipal Services Project, Occasional Paper Number 24, June.

Ndamase, Mkhululi. 2014. ANC thrashed by former member in by-election. *The Herald*, 7 November. http://www.heraldlive.co.za/news/top-news/2014/11/07/anc-thrashed-former-member-election/ (accessed 19 April 2017).

Paret, Marcel. 2015. Cosatu and community struggles: Assessing the prospects for solidarity. In *Cosatu in Crisis: The Fragmentation of an African Trade Union Federation*, edited by Vishwas Satgar and Roger Southall. Johannesburg: KMMR Publishing.

Ross, Stephanie. 2007. Varieties of social unionism: Towards a framework for comparison. *Just Labour: A Canadian Journal of Work and Society* 11: 16–34.

Von Holdt, Karl, Malose Langa, Sepetla Molapo, Nomfundo Mogapi, Kindize Ngubeni, Jacob Dlamini and Adele Kirsten. 2011. *The Smoke that Calls: Insurgent Citizenship, Collective Violence and the Struggle for a Place in the New South Africa*. Johannesburg: Centre for the Study of Violence and Reconciliation and the Society, Work and Development Institute.

The Politics of Male Power and Privilege in Trade Unions: Understanding sexual harassment in Cosatu

Malehoko Tshoaedi

INTRODUCTION

In July 2013 the general secretary of Cosatu, Zwelinzima Vavi, was accused of rape and sexual harassment by a junior female colleague who was employed in an administrative position by Vavi himself. Vavi was suspended, but was later reinstated after the court declared the suspension to be unprocedural. Investigations into the allegations of sexual harassment and a charge of misconduct (engaging in a sexual act within the organisation's premises) were conducted by the federation. However, both allegations were later withdrawn by the accused, and Cosatu failed to proceed with the charge of misconduct against Vavi. Although Vavi was eventually dismissed from his position as the general secretary of Cosatu, the reasons for his dismissal largely focused on organisational politics and his failure to comply with organisational decisions.

In a television interview for the programme *Carte Blanche*, Vavi explained that he met the 26-year-old Jacqueline Phooko 'as one of the workers at SAA [South African Airways] and she was very efficient, very helpful and I was genuinely impressed' (cited in Seale 2013). It was after this that Vavi took the details of the woman and later offered her a job as one of the administrators at Cosatu head office in Braamfontein, where he was based. According to Phooko's account, there was no interview for the job, but Vavi claims that an interview was conducted by himself and an administrative secretary. Further explaining the nature of her employment, Vavi indicated that 'she was to do a trial run. When the six-month [contract] ended, we hired her. We call that headhunting' (cited in Seale 2013).

The aim of this chapter is to reflect on this sexual harassment saga and its implications for the politics of gender in Cosatu and its affiliates. I argue that sexual harassment is a broader social problem in South Africa and is not confined to trade unions. It reflects on the patriarchal nature of our society that promotes a misogynistic culture degrading women and sexualises their presence in the public space. Sexual harassment is an issue of gendered inequalities between women and men, with the latter in positions of power due to the 'privilege' of being heterosexual men. The gendered hierarchical leadership and occupational structure in the unions places men in strategic positions, with decision-making powers on hiring, promotion, salaries and work benefits (Acker 1990). I further argue that it is critical to problematise the privileges that men enjoy in a patriarchal system which gives them access to power and economic resources, thus enabling them to gatekeep women's access to economic/employment opportunities (see Connell 2005a). Often, these positions entitle men to control women's bodies and sexuality, with minimal or no consequences for their abuse of power as their sexual behaviour is often seen as part of the expected gender performance within a masculine organisational culture.

According to Harriet Bradley (1999: 34), gendered power enables those with access (often men) to have control over the behaviour of those who do not have access (often women). Women are often employed as support staff, mostly in administrative positions where they are expected to serve men (Acker 1990). The sexualisation of women is often inscribed in the description or definition of their job titles. And therefore, 'the willingness to tolerate sexual harassment is often a condition of the job, both a consequence and a cause of gender hierarchy' (Acker 1990: 152).

Access to power and economic resources privileges heterosexual men and permits them to make decisions about women's bodies and sexuality. Often, these decisions rest on the assumption that all women are heterosexual and also available for sexual relationships in the workplace. In her article on gendered organisations, Joan Acker argues that women's bodies are often policed through certain controls that reinforce masculinities and, thus, compulsory heterosexuality. Sexual harassment is understood as one mechanism through which power is enacted between individuals to create and maintain control of sexuality, and specifically to mandate women's performance of appropriately feminine heterosexuality (Brunner and Dever 2014: 461). We are also reminded by Linda Eyre (2000: 296) that sexual harassment is not merely an exercise of exerting power, but it also reinforces 'hetero-patriarchy'. Sexual harassment is integral to the performance of hegemonic masculinity and is a critical expression of the converging power regimes of gender and heterosexist oppression.

Raewyn Connell (2005b: 77) defines hegemonic masculinity as the configuration of gender practice which embodies the currently accepted 'answer to the problem' of the legitimacy of patriarchy – which guarantees (or is taken to guarantee) the dominant position of men and the subordination of women. Hegemonic masculinity is not just the form of masculinity that is culturally dominant, signifying a position of authority, leadership, success and being in control, but it is the expression of privilege (add power) men collectively have over women (Connell 1996 cited in Robinson 2005: 22).

The concept refers to performances ('patterned practices') by men in public and private spaces which are in accordance with the dominant discourses on hegemonic masculinity and manhood. Such performances are often rewarded or applauded, and those that are not are shamed and marginalised. Men can adopt hegemonic masculinity when it is desirable, but can at the same time distance themselves strategically from hegemonic masculinity at other moments (Connell and Messerschmidt 2005: 841).

This chapter further demonstrates how the issue of sexual harassment, which the unions have often considered as 'personal' and therefore not central to the core business of the unions, was used as a powerful political weapon in leadership battles of the federation. The Vavi incident, of course, took place at a time when the federation was undergoing an internal political crisis which divided it into two camps: the Vavi supporters versus the Sdumo Dlamini supporters. This division resulted in the two camps making public allegations against each other, further exposing the nature of the problem of abuse of power by senior union officials. These public allegations of sexual harassment against leaders of Cosatu have not, however, been useful in problematising the abuse of male power or challenging the hegemonic masculine culture in the unions. Instead, they have been used by various factions within Cosatu to strengthen their political battles.

I argue that Vavi's sexual harassment raises questions about gender equality and the role of trade unions in advancing this struggle. It gives us an opportunity to critically evaluate the continued inequalities in our society, where power continues to be a privilege for certain heterosexual men. Transformation has meant that some (black) men have gained power and are in significant positions of influence. But it is how they use their positions of power to further entrench the subordination and sexual objectification of (black) women in the workplace and in trade unions that is of concern. The failure of (black) men in trade union organisations to champion women's rights to gender equality and to fight against the violation of their sexual rights reflects on the lack of transformation in Cosatu unions.

This chapter is based on the Taking Democracy Seriously workers' survey (621 interviews) conducted in 2014 with Cosatu affiliates in Gauteng, North West, Eastern Cape, KwaZulu-Natal and Western Cape. It also draws from in-depth interviews that were conducted as part of the Taking Democracy Seriously research project, as well as earlier research conducted by the author (in 1997, 2003 to 2005, and most recently 2014) and on analyses of newspaper and media reports of the responses of Cosatu affiliates to the allegations of sexual harassment against the Cosatu general secretary.

SEXUAL HARASSMENT AS A BROADER SOCIETAL ISSUE

Sexual harassment is a major problem that cuts across all sectors of South African society. It is a problem not only for the trade unions, but also in various public spaces including universities, political organisations and workplaces. Recently, with the Fees Must Fall campaigns and the deployment of private security companies in the universities, scores of female students have raised their concerns and, ironically, have highlighted feeling insecure on campus as they have been sexually harassed by security personnel entrusted with their safety. On most campuses such complaints have been dismissed and female students have been asked to provide evidence.

Incidents of sexual harassment within the major political organisations the EFF, the DA and the ANC have also been in the spotlight in the past year. In the first case, EFF member of the Mpumalanga provincial legislature Ayanda Shabalala resigned from the party in 2015 after accusing the EFF of failing to protect women against sexual harassment perpetrated by some senior party leaders. In her address to the media, she stated:

> I requested that leadership rise up to protect women in the organisation, that women must be held with the same regard and respect that men are afforded and not to be seen as sexual objects before being recognised as independent powerful contributors to the organisation ... To this day, I have heard of no perpetrator being brought to book about such conduct (News24 correspondent 2015).

In the second case, a DA member of Parliament, Archibald Figlan, was accused by a staff member of sexual harassment during a protest march in Cape Town ahead of President Zuma's State of the Nation Address in 2015. According to the complainant, the DA MP 'took my hand and put it on his privates' during the march (as cited in Meyer 2015). The disciplinary investigation found Figlan guilty of contravening the party's constitution and he was then given a suspended sentence, allowing him to stay in his position as an MP and a leader of one of the standing committees for the DA.

In the third case, which involves the ruling political party that is largely credited for most of the progressive policies on gender equality, a senior provincial leader in the Western Cape, Marius Fransman, was accused by a 21-year-old woman whom he had recently hired as a personal assistant. Fransman was accused of sexually harassing the woman, insisting that she share a bed with him 'if she wants to make a success out of her career' (News24 Correspondent 2016). The resolution of the case took some time, Fransman (supported by some in the ANC) claiming the whole incident was a 'political conspiracy' against him by those opposed to his leadership in the Western Cape. Eventually, in November 2016, the ANC disciplinary committee found him guilty of misconduct and suspended his membership for five years. Indeed, judging by the history of the organisation in dealing with sexual harassment (see Hassim 2006), the ANC in this instance handed out a strong judgement against Fransman.

The manner in which public universities, political organisations and influential public figures respond to cases of sexual harassment has not been useful in alleviating the problem. Often, the responses perpetuate the perceptions of women as liars, crying foul while they cannot produce evidence, and they present women as objects of sexual desire which men cannot resist, and therefore sexual harassment cases are treated as just a once-off 'slip-up' and 'it won't happen again'. Such responses contribute to the continued discrimination and violation of women's bodies and sexuality in the workplace and in society more broadly.

RAISING SEXUAL HARASSMENT IN COSATU UNIONS

The battle over sexual harassment in unions has a long history, going back to the formation of Cosatu in 1985, when women demanded that the federation adopt a resolution to address sexual harassment in the workplace, although it was not publicly challenged by women until 1989 at the Cosatu national congress. The challenge was met with hostility, as men questioned the appropriateness of such a discussion (former Saccawu organiser cited in Tshoaedi 2008). 'There was a lot of resistance against it. There were questions like 'why?', '*singasanibizi dudlu*?'; 'are we no longer supposed to touch you?' (former Satawu organiser cited in Tshoaedi 2012: 102).

Many of the male delegates at the conference perceived sexual harassment as a personal or private matter that certainly did not exist in the trade unions. It was felt that the women who raised such matters in union forums or structures were bringing private matters into the public arena. Women were told that the congress was concerned with 'serious' political issues which deserved the full attention of the congress (Tshoaedi 2012). The code on sexual harassment was only adopted in 1994, five years after women had made the initial demand. This came as a result of serious allegations of misconduct by male delegates during one of the national congresses (Tshoaedi 1999).

The majority male leadership in Cosatu has consistently utilised dominant masculine identities within the unions to define politics that are relevant for the labour movement, silencing women on issues such as sexual harassment (Tshoaedi 2012: 102). Cosatu has been indifferent to the issue and has not encouraged public debates about it within its male-dominated structures. Sexual harassment in the unions has not been fully examined to reflect on the unequal power relations between women and men and the impact of these imbalances on the struggles for gender equality in the unions.

SEXUAL HARASSMENT AS AN ABUSE OF POWER BY MALE UNIONISTS

Research conducted across various trade unions has shown that sexual harassment is a persistent problem (Benya 2013; Briskin and McDermott 1993; Cobble and Michal 2002; Franzway 2002; Ledwith 2006, 2012; Tshoaedi 1999, 2002 and 2012). Suzanne Franzway (2002) observes that sexual harassment in Australian unions has persisted despite various attempts by gender activists within the unions to raise awareness through campaigns, seminars and informative discussions. In reference to her research with women in the unions, she further argues that sexual harassment names women's lack of safety at work as domestic violence names women's experience of sexual violence in the home (Franzway 2002: 284).

According to women employed in the unions, sexual harassment exists in each and every workplace, and unions are no exception. The gendered hierarchy in union leadership, where men are often senior and in powerful positions, puts women in positions of marginality and vulnerability to abuse of power by some male officials who have decision-making powers to approve employment contracts, promotions and benefits of staff members.

Research with women administrators and some women officials in Cosatu unions, and senior male officials, shows that not only ordinary officials but also senior officials, who had the power to decide women administrators' future in the unions, were involved. Women argued that sexual harassment in the unions was related to 'power and powerlessness' and that 'there is a fine line between sexual harassment and abuse of power. The issue is more of abuse of power than sexual harassment.' 'Most of the girls in the region do it. To be where they are [referring to senior administrative positions] they either had to sleep with someone or be someone's girlfriend and that is job security for them' (Numsa regional administrator cited in Tshoaedi 1999: 78).

Women perceive sexual harassment in the unions as a symbol of male domination and control over women by men (Tshoaedi 1999). Women who had experienced sexual harassment reported their fears of talking about it – let alone laying charges against the perpetrators – for fear of reprisals. One administrator reported: 'I have this fear that if you do you are out of the job. So it is some kind of a job security again … you cannot do anything about them' (Numsa administrator cited in Tshoaedi 1999: 78).

Although Cosatu adopted a code of conduct on sexual harassment, most of the women interviewed felt that the code of conduct was not effective. In one interview, a union official argued:

> It does help to some extent, but at the end of the day people will always break the law. You can take it as a piece of legislation. How many bills and legislations that we have got in this country but people still overlook those and break the law (Numsa official cited in Tshoaedi 1999: 79).

According to some women officials, the sexual harassment of women also has to do with socialisation in a patriarchal society. Thus a code of conduct was not addressing the problem, but it 'offers women some protection'. According to the Chemical Workers' Industrial Union (CWIU) education officer:

> No one thing will ever be a solution. The code of conduct is not going to change the way we have been brought up or men's attitudes towards women. It's a gradual project, until mothers teach their sons how to behave. To some extent it does assist, it gives women more to protect themselves when it does happen, but it certainly does not prevent it from happening (CWIU education officer cited in Tshoaedi 1999: 80).

The fact that cases of sexual harassment (or misconduct, as they would call it) are often presided over by the very same officials who are also involved in similar practices means that most cases of sexual harassment, particularly those involving senior officials, are 'pushed under the carpet'.

> In some cases it may be because of the environment which still favours men. It may be that all those men have also been accused of the same things [of sexual harassment], of having a multitude of relationships which is seen as a symbol of braveness, *you know the culture*. It is true that it is a deterrent to many women. It may be difficult for women to approach the same people [male officials] about sexual harassment, because they may think because they are also doing it and what can they do about that particular problem. But on the other hand, it may be that even the office bearers who are supposed to handle the case are faced with a situation where the person who is accused is very popular and powerful in the organisation and they do not know how to deal with the matter. So the only way for them is to push it under the carpet (Cosatu official cited in Tshoaedi 1999: 100).

The Cosatu official quoted above points out that unions are male dominated organisations that privilege heterosexual male behaviour. They are an environment that applauds the display of heterosexual hegemonic masculinity where being in multiple relationships is regarded as a symbol of bravery and is part of the organisational culture. What is significant about the conversation above is the acknowledgement from a senior union official that unions do not have proper mechanisms for dealing with cases of sexual harassment against powerful individuals in the unions.

SEXUAL HARASSMENT AS AN ABUSE OF POWER BY POWERFUL MEN IN THE UNIONS

About 73 per cent of the workers interviewed in the survey disagreed with the statement that 'there is no such a thing as sexual harassment' in the unions. Some Cosatu officials, in in-depth interviews, highlighted that 'sexual harassment is a sensitive issue in the trade union movement … it's an uncomfortable issue'.

> But then in the labour movement again … it's a very sensitive issue because there are female comrades and you see that in big gatherings like congresses or workshops, I mean you hear comrades saying we didn't sleep well, there

were knocks, people were knocking and that seems to be happening quiet often ... these are quite prevalent in the trade union movement ... (interview, Cosatu official, 2015).

It has long been demonstrated that sexual harassment in the unions often discourages women from taking part in trade unions and in leadership positions. Research I conducted with women administrators and women activists in the unions confirms this. In the recent survey, 59 per cent agreed that sexual harassment discourages women from taking part in trade union activities.

Most of the Cosatu members (63 per cent) interviewed in the survey agreed with the statement that 'sexual harassment is an abuse of power by powerful men in the unions'. In defining sexual harassment, one of the union officials criticised the idea of women's empowerment in the unions, where there is an expectation for women to give sexual favours in order to advance in union structures or leadership structures.

> Comrades would expect sexual favour from a female before they can help them ... that amounts to sexual harassment you know, and that means these comrades will have stifled their development ... but it shouldn't be like that, the practice should be discouraging that before they [women] get recognised or acknowledged they must give sexual favours to the leadership ... (interview, Cosatu official, 2015).

Interviews further demonstrate that decisions to support women leaders are sometimes influenced by the male leadership's personal interests, which are often sexual.

> You know my understanding about sexual harassment is ... ehh ... I will go back to this thing of a position, I'm the regional secretary, I will make an example about myself ... and remember as a regional secretary I do have certain powers that are vested upon me, maybe I can manipulate. I'm not saying I'm manipulating things, but maybe when you go to a particular congress or you go whether it's a branch or whatever, you can see this particular lady and you [are] having interest ... and you do things that will make it a point that that particular lady is coming up as a leader ... ehh ... in that branch or in the region, but some people they are having that is I want this particular person to be nearer to me ... so that is my understanding, using your position to advance your things, wrong things, in particular sexual, ja, that is the way I can call it sexual harassment (interview, Nehawu official, 2014).

Cosatu officials also pointed out that trade unions have made significant gains in addressing sexual harassment in the workplace and ensuring that employers adopt policies and procedures. However, Cosatu itself has not shown the same commitment in addressing the same problems within its own organisation and affiliates.

> Now the issue of sexual harassment ... many trade unions have fought and sorted it out in the workplace to ensure that there is reduction and no tolerance insofar as sexual harassment is concerned. But ... I think a lot must be done, it's not enough ... not only in the trade unions but across the liberation movement and the Alliance there is a sense that women remain the subject of men and so on, so forth, you can never address those issues of women [*sic*] inferiority and so on if you still have polygamy, you still have leaders who promote women [*sic*] abuse ... I think our workplaces are doing much better work than ourselves as trade unions ... (interview, Cosatu official, 2014).

The progress that has been made in the workplace by employers has been observed by Asanda Benya (2013) in her research on women mineworkers in Rustenburg. According to her study, women mineworkers who are union members had more confidence in their employer's human resource officials than in their union in terms of addressing cases of sexual harassment. Often, such cases were not taken seriously by union officials, who subjected women to more humiliation, ridicule and, worse, further harassment and accusations (Benya 2013: 59).

IS THE PERSONAL BECOMING POLITICAL IN COSATU?

The slogan 'The personal is political' was adopted by feminists to highlight the importance of women's experiences as political issues that must be recognised as part of the broader discourse on politics. The slogan challenged the conceptualisation of politics which separated the private (personal) from the public (politics), thus treating women's experiences as unimportant. Feminists criticised the idea of politics, or the public, where women, bodies, sex, emotions and intimate relationships were excluded and declared to belong in the private sphere (Holmes 2000: 305). Following this challenge by feminists, Holmes argues that 'all relationships became open to political scrutiny because of recognition that politics is about power relationships. Politics could include discussions of sexual relationships in the "private" sphere and the personal lives of political actors' (Holmes 2000: 308).

The definition of what constitutes politics has, however, always been a contested issue within Cosatu and its affiliates. As illustrated earlier, most men at the Cosatu national congress of 1989 failed to recognise sexual harassment as violence against women in the unions and therefore a significant political issue that required urgent resolution (Tshoaedi 2012). The congress was more concerned about state violence and arrests of some trade unionists, and maintained that these were more 'serious' political issues. Trade union politics are characterised by unequal power relations, where men dominate leadership and decision-making structures. Men in positions of power within Cosatu and its affiliates are publicly engaging in the definition of what is political and when certain behaviours or acts become political. In her paper 'When is the personal political? The president's penis and other stories', Mary Holmes (2000: 305) argues that interpretations of what is 'personal' and when it is politically significant rely on assumptions about the social identity and position of the people involved.

Since the accusations against Vavi in 2013, more allegations against other senior union officials have surfaced. The following incidents have been reported since then:

- In September 2013, Fikile Majola, the general secretary of Nehawu, was accused of being involved with junior office staff members and having children with two junior officials.
- In October 2013, similar allegations were levelled against the deputy general secretary of Satawu, Nicholus Maziya. He was accused of using his position to ensure that the woman he was involved with was appointed first as provincial organiser and then as acting provincial secretary in the Western Cape.
- More recently the *Sowetan* of 16 February 2015 carried a front-page story headlined 'Cosatu leader in sex row'. The official concerned was Vusi Ntshangase, the Mpumalanga secretary of Satawu. The twist in this particular story is that the same Nicholus Maziya who was accused of the same conduct was handling the disciplinary charges against Ntshangase for 'attempted rape, sexual harassment, dishonesty and bringing the organisation into disrepute' (Anon. 2015).

What is remarkable in all these stories is that most (if not all) of the officials have not acknowledged any wrongdoing. As in Vavi's case, the allegations have been dismissed as a political conspiracy with the aim of destroying the accused's trade union careers. The argument of political conspiracy serves to protect men who are accused of sexual harassment and rape, while the women involved are perceived to be causing 'disorder, a threat to political order' in the trade union movement (Holmes 2000: 310).

> ... the male part of the situation gets protected by the fact that the issue is now viewed as of a political nature, now the female part of the situation becomes a victim because she is dealt with in terms of the laws, the IR [industrial relations] laws ... actually maybe we should put this thing on record, we must clarify that she was not dismissed because of sexual encounter, the charges that led to her dismissal are away from that, that was not even part of the charge sheet for her dismissal ... (interview, Cosatu official, 2015).

According to the union official quoted above, in dealing with the allegations against Vavi we need to make a distinction between sexual harassment and a political matter. The Vavi matter is political and therefore cannot be 'simply dealt with [using] ... the code of sexual harassment because the minute you do that you are disregarding the political nature of the situation'. Defining sexual harassment as a political conspiracy has turned it into a powerful political tool, used by factions to score points. The political mud-slinging happens in the public space, as demonstrated by one 2013 *Mail & Guardian* headline: 'Vavi camp to reveal worse Cosatu affairs' (Letsoalo 2013). Men may be at the centre of exposing sexual harassment in the unions, but this is not necessarily meant to confront the real problems of patriarchal gendered relations or the power and privileges that men hold.

What happens with all these allegations going back and forth is that sexual harassment is seen as part of the culture of the unions, and the power that men possess, and how they use it, is not being addressed in all these revelations and counter-revelations – which suggests that this is 'normal' men's behaviour. 'It happens all the time, and it happens all over the world, it is not only in the unions' (interview, Sadtu official, Eastern Cape, 2014).

> Many Cosatu leaders are guilty of the same conduct [sleeping with juniors]. All the general secretaries are running the unions like their spaza shops. What did Vavi do that they did not do? What Vavi did is like a picnic compared to others (Letsoalao 2013).

This incident is no exception, as we have witnessed from similar cases, such as that of former US president Bill Clinton, also accused of sexual harassment in his office by a junior employee, Paula Jones. Holmes (2000) notes that in spite of the accusations and evidence against Clinton at the time, his ratings as he was campaigning for the US presidential elections were not tainted by the scandal. In fact, as Holmes indicates, Paula Jones became the subject of scorn for ruining Clinton's reputation. As in the Vavi case, supporters of Clinton, together with his wife, viewed the allegations as a political conspiracy motivated by white right-wing opposition aimed at discrediting Clinton. In her comparative study of the US, European Union and Germany, Kathrin Zippel (2006: xiii) observes similar tendencies delegitimising victims of sexual harassment and discrediting allegations of sexual harassment against high-profile political figures.

The tendency to normalise such behaviour or to undermine women's claims of being sexually harassed obviously justifies the reluctance of Cosatu unions to treat the matter seriously. It legitimises the perpetrators' claims of being victims of conspiracy theories, painting women as individuals with limited intellectual capacities who are being used or manipulated by political opponents for political gains.

WOMEN'S RESPONSE TO THE ALLEGATIONS

Reflecting on the scandal during the Cosatu special congress in 2015, women were critical of how the matter was handled internally by Cosatu leadership. But, more importantly, they also highlighted their failure to stand in solidarity with the woman who accused Vavi of rape and sexual harassment. Speaking on Cosatu women's silence on the matter, Kate Matlou of Satawu pointed out that 'she was ashamed they kept quiet on the matter' (cited in the *Sowetan*; see Anon. 2015) and argued that as women in Cosatu they 'failed to do justice for the employee who had sex with Vavi by not coming out in her defence'.

According to news reports, women leaders at the congress criticised the male leadership of Cosatu for not prioritising gender issues (Feketha 2015). In an interview cited by Siviwe Feketha (2015) in the *Sowetan*, Nomarashiya Caluza, the regional secretary of Sadtu in KwaZulu-Natal, expressed her disappointment:

> I am very disappointed at our structure called the central executive committee. We started this congress yesterday and we are about to close. I have never heard a single person standing firm in advancing gender struggles in relation to what has happened at Cosatu House. If we have a Cosatu that is serving as a home to all workers, it must include the women we have employed.

In the analysis of the 2008 Taking Democracy Seriously survey (Buhlungu and Tshoaedi 2012), I reflected on the representation of women's voices in Cosatu's leadership structures. In the chapter titled 'Making sense of unionised workers' political attitudes: The unrepresentation of women's voices in Cosatu', I argued that the silencing of women's voices is due to the internal operations of Cosatu, where the politics of the majority dominate. This kind of politics works to suppress the voices of women and other marginalised groups; only the views of the powerful are listened to and included in the decision-making processes. I further criticise the notion of democracy that only gives preference to the majority at the expense of the marginal groups in Cosatu:

> ... the notion of democracy that only gives significance to the powerful and influential goes against what the labour movement stands for (protecting and promoting the interests of the less powerful in society, that is the working class – and women included) (Tshoaedi 2012: 107).

CONCLUSION

The Vavi scandal highlights the gendered power relations in the trade union movement. It demonstrates the unequal power relations in trade union leadership and employment, where men are strategically located in positions of power, with unlimited access to resources. Men's control is not limited to organisational resources, but extends to controlling women's bodies through controlling their access to employment and career mobility. The gendered hierarchy in trade unions perpetuates a patriarchal system in which women are largely recognised as bodies, as sexual objects and as political tools.

The much publicised sexual harassment case against Vavi presented an opportunity for the trade unions to open the space for debating gender issues and addressing inequality. The failure to prioritise sexual harassment as an epic problem in the unions demonstrates the gendered politics of power. The 1989 congress refused to acknowledge the problem of sexual harassment in Cosatu unions, with men continuing to dominate the public space and the organisational discourse. Their powerful location in the leadership structure of Cosatu privileged them to define the agenda for the 2015 congress, which excluded the interests of women. The political contestation within Cosatu leadership and the Tripartite Alliance determined the priorities of the federation. Again, the definition excludes the gendered nature of these politics. Sexual harassment was not prioritised at the 2015 congress in spite of being a weapon used by various political opponents in Cosatu unions.

This has implications for how we view gender relations in Cosatu in post-apartheid South Africa. Trade unions in South Africa, particularly Cosatu, have played a significant role in the liberation and democratisation of the country. They are important organisations with significant power and influence in the South African political landscape. And yet these organisations have failed women, and black women in particular, when it comes to advancing gendered transformation and democratisation. This failure is noticeable within their organisational and leadership structures, resulting in a working-class agenda that consistently fails to give precedence to gendered inequalities in our labour markets. Women (black women in particular) continue to be employed in the lowest-paying occupations, with limited or no rights to basic conditions of employment, as they are often not organised by trade unions (Bezuidenhout and Fakier 2006). Cosatu unions are yet to engage in campaigns that forcefully demand equal opportunities for women and men in the labour market, challenging the gendered occupational structure and promoting the safety of women from sexual harassment and violence in the workplace. Transformation requires a conscious effort with a clear agenda for eliminating sexist patriarchal attitudes that discriminate against women as full human beings with equal citizenship rights. It requires the full commitment of male trade unionists to prioritise gender equality in collective bargaining forums. To achieve this, trade unions need to change their democratic practices and principles, which are based on the power of the majority and the exclusion of the minority.

BIBLIOGRAPHY

Acker, Joan. 1990. Hierarchies, jobs, bodies: A theory of gendered organisations. *Gender and Society* 4(2): 139–158.

Anon. 2015. Cosatu leader in sex row. *Sowetan*, 16 February.

Benya, Asanda. 2013. Gendered labour: A challenge to labour as a democratising force. *Rethinking Development and Inequality* 2(special issue): 47–62.

Bezuidenhout, Andries and Khayaat Fakier. 2006. Maria's burden: Contract cleaning and the crisis of social reproduction in post-apartheid South Africa. *Antipode* 38(3): 463–486.

Bradley, Harriet. 1999. *Gender, Power and the Workplace: Analysing the Impact of Economic Change*. Basingstoke: Macmillan.

Briskin, Linda and Patricia McDermott. 1993. *Women Challenging Unions: Feminism, Democracy and Militancy*. Toronto: University of Toronto Press.

Brunner, Laura and Maryanne Dever. 2014. Work, bodies and boundaries: Talking sexual harassment in the new economy. *Gender, Work and Organization* 21(5): 459–471.

Buhlungu, Sakhela and Malehoko Tshoaedi (eds). *Cosatu's Contested Legacy: South African Trade Unions in the Second Decade of Democracy*. Cape Town: HSRC Press.

Cobble, Dorothy S. and Monica Michal. 2002. On the edge of equality? Working women and the US labour movement. In *Gender, Diversity and Trade Unions: International Perspectives*, edited by Fiona Colgan and Sue Ledwith. London and New York: Routledge.

Connell, Raewyn. 2005a. Change among gatekeepers: Men, masculinities and gender equality in the global arena. *Signs* 30(3): 1801–1825.

Connell, Raewyn. 2005b. *Masculinities*. 2nd ed. Berkeley: University of California Press.

Connell, Raewyn and James Messerschmidt. 2005. Hegemonic masculinity: Rethinking the concept. *Gender and Society* 19(6): 829–859.

Eyre, Linda. 2000. The discursive framing of sexual harassment in a university community. *Gender and Education* 12(3): 293–307.

Feketha, Siviwe. 2015. Vavi sex scandal stalks congress. *Sowetan*, 18 July. http://www.sowetanlive.co.za/news/2015/07/18/vavi-sex-scandal-stalks-congress (accessed 25 September 2015).

Franzway, Suzanne. 1999. 'They see you coming': A comparative study of sexual politics and women union officials in (English) Canada and Australia. *Labour and Industry: A Journal of the Social and Economic Relations of Work* 10(2): 147–168.

Franzway, Suzanne. 2002. Sexual politics in (Australian) labour movements. In *Gender, Diversity and Trade Unions: International Perspectives*, edited by Fiona Colgan and Sue Ledwith. London and New York: Routledge.

Fraser, Nancy. 1992. Sex, lies and the public sphere: Some reflections on the confirmation of Clarence Thomas. *Critical Inquiry* 18(3): 596–612.

Hassim, Shireen. 2006. *Women's Organisations and Democracy in South Africa: Contesting Authority*. Madison: University of Wisconsin Press.

Healy, Geraldine and Gill Kirton. 2000. Women, power and trade union government in the UK. *British Journal of Industrial Relations* 38(3): 343–360.

Holmes, Mary. 2000. When is the personal political? The president's penis and other stories. *Sociology* 34 (2): 305–321.

Ledwith, Sue. 2006. Feminist praxis in a trade union project. *Industrial Relations Journal* 37(4): 379–400.

Ledwith, Sue. 2012. Gender politics in trade unions: The representation of women between inclusion and exclusion. *Transfer: European Review of Labour Research* 18(2): 185–199.

Letsoalo, Matuma. 2013. Vavi camp to reveal 'worse' Cosatu affairs. *Mail & Guardian,* 13 September.

McLaughlin, Heather, Christopher Uggen and Amy Blackstone. 2012. Sexual harassment, workplace authority and the paradox of power. *American Sociological Review* 77(4): 625–647.

Meyer, Warda. 2015. DA MP accused of sexual harassment. *IOL*, 24 February. http://www.iol.co.za/news/politics/da-mp-accused-of-sexual-harassment-1822639 (accessed 25 September 2015).

News24 Correspondent. 2015. EFF MPL quits party due to sexual harassment. *News24*, 26 May. http://www.news24.com/SouthAfrica/Politics/EFF-MPL-quits-party-due-to-sexual-harassment-20150526 (accessed 25 September 2015).

News24 Correspondent. 2016. Shocking details emerge in case against Fransman. *News24*, 10 January. http://www.news24.com/SouthAfrica/News/shocking-details-emerge-in-case-against-fransman-20160110 (accessed 19 January 2017).

Robinson, Kerry H. 2005. Reinforcing hegemonic masculinities through sexual harassment: Issues of identity, power and popularity in secondary schools. *Gender and Education* 17(1): 19–37.

Seale, Lebogang. 2013. Vavi 'headhunted' sex scandal woman. *IOL*, 5 August. http://www.iol.co.za/news/politics/vavi-headhunted-sex-scandal-woman-1557517 (accessed 19 January 2017).

Tshoaedi, Malehoko. 1999. Functional differentiation in trade union employment: A study of gender inequality with specific reference to women union officials. MA thesis, University of the Witwatersrand.

Tshoaedi, Malehoko. 2002. Women in the labour movement: Perceptions of gender democracy in South African trade unions. In *Gender, Diversity and Trade Unions: Interna-*

tional Perspectives, edited by Fiona Colgan and Sue Ledwith. London and New York: Routledge.

Tshoaedi, Malehoko. 2006. The marginalisation of women unionists during South Africa's democratic transition. In *Trade Unions and Democracy: Cosatu Workers' Political Attitudes in South Africa*, edited by Sakhela Buhlungu. Cape Town: HSRC Press.

Tshoaedi, Malehoko. 2008. Roots of women's union activism: South Africa 1973–2003. PhD thesis, University of Leiden.

Tshoaedi, Malehoko. 2012. Making sense of unionised workers' political attitudes: The (un) representation of women's voices in Cosatu. In *Cosatu's Contested Legacy: South African Trade Unions in the Second Decade of Democracy*, edited by Sakhela Buhlungu and Malehoko Tshoaedi. Cape Town: HSRC Press.

Williams, Christine L., Patti A. Giuffre and Kirsten Dellinger. 1999. Sexuality in the workplace: Organisational control, sexual harassment, and the pursuit of pleasure. *Annual Review of Sociology* 25: 73–93.

Zippel, Kathrin. 2006. *The Politics of Sexual Harassment: A Comparative Study of the United States, the European Union and Germany*. Cambridge University Press: Cambridge.

9

Internal Democracy in Cosatu: Achievements and challenges

Johann Maree

INTRODUCTION AND BACKGROUND

Many of the unions that came together in 1985 to form Cosatu built their power by means of democratic worker organisation (Maree 1986). The form the democracy took was by means of elected leaders who were accountable to their members. This was particularly the case at the level of the workplace, where workers elected shop stewards regularly and the shop stewards held frequent meetings with their members. The shop stewards were given mandates by their members on issues they had to take up with management, and they had to report back on the outcomes of their negotiations with management.

But this did not happen only at the level of the workplace. It was also happening at higher levels of organisation in the unions. When the Western Province General Workers' Unions (later the General Workers' Union) was established in 1978, it was structured in such a way that there was workers' control of the union. The constitution laid down that a controlling committee, consisting of two elected representatives from each of the organised workplaces, took all the major policy decisions in the union. Officials in the union, including the general secretary, then had to implement policies decided by the controlling committee (Maree 1989: 134–135).

It also happened at the federal level of unions. The Trade Union Advisory and Coordinating Council (TUACC) was the forerunner of the Federation of South African Trade Unions (Fosatu) in KwaZulu-Natal. Elected representatives from the unions on the executive council of TUACC were expected to represent the interests of their union members and to report back to their unions. The reasoning behind this was very well explained by Alec Erwin, who was the first general secretary of Fosatu. In an interview in 1979 about the challenge of building democracy in the unions, he said:

> We'd say you must have resilient structures that can hold people accountable in a real sense. We must establish more definite structures of accountability. So what we were trying to build in TUACC, and are presently trying to achieve in Fosatu, is that the democratic structure must be through a process of the factory controlling the shop steward because that man the worker sees every day in the plant, his access to him is far greater. Then the shop steward sits on the BEC [Branch Executive Committee] and the report-back system is structured and definite. So we've been trying in TUACC to build that structure up from shop steward to BEC to TUACC.
>
> Now that is a very much slower process because structures in themselves never create democracy. Only aware leadership and membership create democracy. So once having built shop stewards you then have to make them effective shop stewards. If they are effective their membership is going to be more informed, conscious and interested in knowing what they are doing. And likewise good shop stewards will make a good BEC, and a good BEC a good National Executive Committee (interview, Alec Erwin, 1979).

When the first survey of Cosatu members was undertaken shortly before the historic first democratic elections in South Africa in 1994 and fifteen years after the founding of Fosatu in 1979, one of the primary objectives was to establish whether workplace democracy was still being practised in Cosatu unions. This was found to be the case (Ginsburg et al. 1995: 30–39), and as it was such a core objective of the survey, the same questions have been retained in every survey conducted shortly before all of the subsequent four elections, in 1999, 2004, 2009 and 2014, providing a remarkable longitudinal study of the perceptions and practices of Cosatu members with regard to democracy and within the Cosatu-affiliated unions.

But the surveys did not stop there. They have also systematically examined whether there have been any indications of oligarchy in Cosatu. The approach adopted was to see whether oligarchy as conceptualised by Robert Michels in 1911 existed in the unions. Michels conceived of oligarchy as the control of organisations such as trade unions and political parties by their full-time officials and not by their members. He argued that oligarchy was inevitable owing to the increased technical and administrative complexity of the organisations as they grew larger. This is known as Michels's iron law of oligarchy (Michels 1959: 90–97).

The remainder of this chapter consists of five sections. In the first, there is a detailed presentation in tabular form of the longitudinal data from the five surveys on whether workplace democracy still exists in Cosatu affiliates. It finds that workplace democracy has remained consistently high throughout the period and that shop stewards have been kept accountable to their members.

The second section, which also presents information in tabular form, looks at what has been called the 'democratic rupture' in Cosatu between leaders and union members, an expression coined in the book based on the survey of Cosatu members in 1994 (Ginsburg et al. 1995: 64). A democratic rupture exists when leaders in Cosatu sit on national bodies where they frame policies that directly affect workers without consulting their members or providing them with feedback on their decisions. This is also what Michels called oligarchy, and section two therefore also deals with oligarchy. The finding is that the democratic rupture and oligarchy have continued to prevail up to 2014.

The third section presents the views of officials in Cosatu on democracy in the federation. A number of officials in Cosatu were interviewed after the 2014 survey of Cosatu members had been analysed by the researchers. The interview schedule for officials was drawn up in order to shed more light on certain of the findings that emanated from the survey. Almost all of the officials interviewed for this chapter identified internal democracy in Cosatu with shop-steward accountability. They emphasised time and again that shop stewards and other leaders had to be representative of union members and accountable to them. Some went as far as saying that shop stewards were mandated by their members.

The fourth section takes an excursion into contemporary theories of trade union democracy and raises a dimension that has been neglected in both the theory and practice: consensus building. Consensus building, it is argued, provides voice for ordinary and peripheral union members. It instils participatory democracy in the union, and enables members to participate in the formulation of union policies.

The fifth and final section is the conclusion that pulls the findings together and examines their implications for the trade union movement. It contends that the absence of consensus building in Cosatu helps to explain the contemporary ructions taking place within the federation. It concludes that Cosatu needs to incorporate consensus building into its understanding and practice of democracy.

This chapter does not deal with the issue of sexual harassment in Cosatu unions as it has been covered thoroughly in the preceding chapter, which demonstrates that unions often considered it as 'personal' and therefore not central to the unions – and shows that women's issues were still not considered as important as political issues. The findings on democracy in this chapter are based on the views of men and women interviewed in the 2014 survey.

WORKPLACE DEMOCRACY IN COSATU AFFILIATES 1994–2014

This section analyses the state of shop-floor democracy. Central to this in the South African tradition is the role of shop-steward committees. In their analysis of a 2012 survey of shop stewards, Themba Masondo et al. (2015: 214–215) found a number of democratic practices that act as countervailing tendencies against Michels's iron law of oligarchy. First, direct forms of democracy in the workplace – including processes of mandating – remain resilient. Second, shop stewards are still socialised into believing that they derive their power directly from workers and that leaders who bypass or ignore the will of workers should be democratically removed, or sidelined as happened in the case of the platinum belt where members left the NUM en masse. Third is the point that Michels's thesis is more applicable to national structures of representation, and that democratic practice at local levels is more vibrant than in national union structures of representation. Our findings seem to confirm all three points.

In this first section, data from all five Taking Democracy Seriously surveys are used to assess longer-term trends regarding the basic functioning of union democracy in the workplace. Indicators such as the presence of shop stewards in workplaces, how regular shop-steward elections are held and whether trade union members view mandates as important are used for the analysis.

Table 9.1 shows that the presence of shop stewards in workplaces has remained extremely high even though there has been a very slight decline from 99 per cent in 1994 to 95 per cent in 2014.

Table 9.1:   Do you have shop stewards in your workplace?

	1994	**1998**	**2004**	**2008**	**2014**
Yes	99.1%	97.5%	96.0%	97.7%	94.8%
No	0.9%	1.7%	2.5%	1.6%	3.2%
Don't know	0.0%	0.8%	1.5%	0.7%	1.9%
Total	**100%**	**100%**	**100%**	**100%**	**100%**
Number included	643	639	653	620	619

Table 9.2:   If yes, how did they become shop stewards?

	1994	**1998**	**2004**	**2008**	**2014**
Elected by workers	84.6%	92.7%	91.5%	93.0%	90.3%
Appointed by union officials	13.5%	2.7%	2.4%	2.5%	1.7%
Appointed by management	0.9%	0.8%	0.6%	1.1%	0.3%
Other	0.9%	0.3%	0.5%	0.2%	0.3%
Do not know	0.0%	3.5%	4.9%	3.3%	7.3%
Total	**100%**	**100%**	**100%**	**100%**	**100%**
Number included	638	633	627	612	587

Table 9.3:   If elected, how often are elections for shop stewards held?

	1998	**2004**	**2008**	**2014**
Once in two years or more frequently	64.8%	48.6%	44.0%	38.1%
Once in three years or less frequently	34.5%	37.9%	48.7%	48.5%
Do not know	0.7%	13.4%	7.4%	13.4%
Total	**100%**	**100%**	**100%**	**100%**
Number included	545	619	596	530

Shop stewards remain overwhelmingly elected by workers throughout the twenty-year period (Table 9.2). The proportion has remained consistently above 90 per cent except for 1994 (a bit of an outlier) with an unusually high proportion (13.5 per cent) of shop stewards reportedly appointed by management.

There has been a remarkably big drop in the frequency of shop-steward elections (Table 9.3). In 1998 almost two-thirds of shop stewards (64.8 per cent) had been elected at least once in two years. By 2014 this had fallen to only 38.1 per cent. This confirms what the Numsa official in the Western Cape said when interviewed. He

Table 9.4:   When did you last participate in electing your shop steward?

	1994	1998	2004	2008	2014
Within the last two years	79.7%	25.5%	61.7%	72.4%	59.9%
More than two years ago	12.2%	53.0%	21.1%	18.1%	22.7%
Do not know	0%	13.4%	8.4%	3.2%	10.7%
Never	8.1%	8.1%	8.9%	6.3%	6.6%
Total	**100%**	**100%**	**100%**	**100%**	**100%**
Number included	640	606	621	620	532

Table 9.5:   If you elected shop stewards, how did you elect them?

	1994	1998	2004	2008	2014
Show of hands	53.3%	45.7%	50.1%	48.7%	56.2%
Secret ballot	46.7%	54.3%	49.9%	48.7%	42.1%
Do not know	–	–	–	2.6%	1.7%
Total	**100%**	**100%**	**100%**	**100%**	**100%**
Number included	591	591	589	573	525

claimed it was becoming common practice in most unions to elect shop stewards for four-year terms of office (interview, Numsa official, 2014).

Although the findings from one survey to the other fluctuate widely and 1998 is at odds with the other years, a clear majority (60 per cent on average for the five years) of Cosatu members surveyed had participated in the election of shop stewards within two years of the survey (Table 9.4). Another 25 per cent on average had also participated in electing shop stewards, but more than two years before each survey. Thus, an overwhelming majority of workers surveyed (85 per cent) definitely participated in the election of shop stewards. Only 7.6 per cent on average said that they had never participated in the election of shop stewards.

Although there has been a gradual decline since 1998 in the proportion of shop stewards elected by secret ballot, the distribution between a show of hands and a secret ballot has remained pretty even (Table 9.5). In 1998 secret ballots exceeded a show of hands and in 2008 they were exactly equal. It is interesting to note that secret-ballot voting is therefore quite a common practice in Cosatu unions. As pointed out in the introductory chapter to this volume, this became a controversial issue in the national congresses that confirmed the expulsion of Numsa from Cosatu.

Table 9.6: When you elect a shop steward, that person …

	1994	1998	2004	2008	2014
… can represent your interests they see fit	26.5%	30.1%	18.1%	20%	28.8%
… can only do what the membership tells them to do	73.5%	49.8%	53.8%	48.6%	44%
… has discretion (choice) within a broad mandate	Not asked	20.1%	28.1%	31.4%	27.1%
Total	**100%**	**100%**	**100%**	**100%**	**100%**
Number included	630	631	626	590	520

Table 9.7: When you elect a shop steward …

	1994	1998	2004	2008	2014
… she or he must consult you every time she or he acts on behalf of workers	76.7%	59.4%	62.6 %	56.1%	58.1%
… she or he must consult you from time to time on important issues	23.3%	39.6%	36.2%	42.2%	39.3%
… she or he does not have to consult you because she or he is elected to represent your interests	0.0%	0.9%	1.3%	1.7%	1.5%
Do not know					1.1%
Total	**100%**	**100%**	**100%**	**100%**	**100%**
Number included	640	636	633	590	535

Table 9.6 confirms that Cosatu members have retained a fairly strong belief that shop stewards have to be guided by the mandate that union members give them. Roughly half of the members surveyed were of the view that members may only do what they are mandated to do, while another quarter thought that they have to act broadly within their mandate.

Table 9.7 confirms and reinforces the findings of the previous table that shop stewards have to receive mandates from their members before they act and are not just given a free hand to do as they wish once they have been elected. Fewer than 2 per cent of those surveyed thought that shop stewards do not have to consult their members. The remaining 98 per cent remained firmly of the view that shop stewards have to consult them before they act.

Table 9.8: When the shop steward acts on your behalf ... (2004, 2008 and 2014 only)

	2004	2008	2014
... they must report back to workers every time	83%	78.2%	79.2%
... they must only report back to workers on important issues	17%	20%	20%
... they do not have to report back	0%	1.1%	0.8%
Total	**100%**	**100%**	**100%**
Number included	n.a.	n.a.	581

Table 9.9: Do you agree or disagree with the following statement? If a shop steward does not do what the workers want, the workers should have a right to remove her/him.

	1994	1998	2004	2008	2014
Yes	94.9%	92.8%	94.1%	94.4%	91.8%
No	5.1%	4.7%	3.9%	4.1%	4.9%
Do not know	0%	2.5%	2%	1.5%	3.2%
Total	**100%**	**100%**	**100%**	**100%**	**100%**
Number included	633	639	648	612	587

Table 9.10: In your workplace, has a shop steward ever been removed by the workers?

	1994	1998	2004	2008	2014
Yes	30.6%	35.9%	27.3%	35.1%	34.9%
No	69.4%	58.9%	66%	56.8%	54%
Do not know	0%	5.2%	6.7%	8%	11.1%
Total	**100%**	**100%**	**100%**	**100%**	**100%**
Number included	633	633	644	609	587

Table 9.8 confirms that shop stewards are also firmly expected to be accountable. No more than 1 per cent hold the view that shop stewards do not have to report back to their members. Furthermore, four out of five members think that shop stewards must report back to members every time they act.

Table 9.9 shows that Cosatu members overwhelmingly (92–95 per cent) believe that they have the right to force shop stewards to carry out the mandate they were given by reserving the right to remove them should they fail to do so. This means that shop stewards are held accountable by their members; otherwise they get dismissed as shop stewards.

Table 9.10 shows that Cosatu union members have exercised their right to keep shop stewards accountable. On average over the five surveys, one-third of members (33 per cent) confirm that shop stewards have been removed by workers in their workplaces.

Table 9.11 shows that the major reason for dismissing shop stewards, advanced by well over half of the members surveyed, is that the shop steward was not doing the job properly. This would entail not being accountable to members. Another important reason, advanced by about a quarter of the members, is that the shop stewards were considered to be too close to management and were not representing workers' interests. Note that in 2004 more than one answer was allowed, whereas in 2008 and 2014 only one answer was allowed. Care has to be taken in comparing 2004 with the other two years, but it is nevertheless interesting to note that shop stewards have also been dismissed for having the wrong politics, and that this was at its highest in the 2014 survey. This could indicate the growing divisiveness in the trade union movement over the past few years.

In view of the rupture between full-time shop stewards of NUM and workers on platinum mines in the Rustenburg region, it was decided to research union members' views on shop stewards, especially full-time shop stewards, to see whether they were still viewed as being close to workers or whether alienation had set in between them. Questions were thus included in the survey for the first time to gauge union members' perceptions of their shop stewards and full-time shop stewards.

Table 9.11: If yes, what was the main reason for the shop steward/s being removed? (2004, 2008 and 2014)

	2004	2008	2014
Not doing their job properly	75%	63.1%	54.1%
Too close to management	27%	24.6%	26.8%
Different politics	7%	4.6%	8.3%
Too close to union officials	2%	0.0%	2.0%
Other	5%	7.5%	7.8%
Do not know	–	0.2%	1.0%
Total	**n.a.**	**100.0%**	**100.0%**
Number included			205

Table 9.12: Do you agree or disagree with the following statement? Shop stewards in this workplace represent workers' interests. (2014 only)

	Number	Percentage
Strongly agree/agree	528	89.9
Neutral/do not know	34	5.8
Strongly disagree/disagree	25	4.3
Total	**587**	**100**

It is clear from Table 9.12 that an overwhelming proportion of Cosatu members, well nigh 90 per cent, are firmly of the opinion that their shop stewards represent workers' interests.

Table 9.13 shows that shop stewards still hold meetings quite regularly, with 63.5 per cent of surveyed members stating that their stewards convened meetings at least once a month (18.5 per cent weekly and 45 per cent monthly). In addition, another 22 per cent called meetings whenever there was a crisis. This helps to explain why shop stewards are still deemed to represent workers' interests.

Table 9.13: How often do shop stewards hold meetings with members in your workplace? (2014 only)

Once a week	18.5%
Once a month	45%
Once a year	1%
Twice a year	2.4%
When there is a crisis	21.9%
Other	2.6%
Do not know/cannot remember	7%
Never	1.5%
Total	**100%**
Number included	584

Table 9.14: Do you have full-time shop stewards at your workplace? (2014 only)

	Number	Percentage
Yes	447	76.1%
No	126	21.5%
Do not know	14	2.4%
Total	**587**	**100%**

It is noteworthy that more than three-quarters of Cosatu members surveyed have full-time shop stewards at their workplaces (Table 9.14). This shows that the presence of full-time shop stewards is now more the norm than the exception wherever Cosatu unions are organised.

The question presented in Table 9.15 was only posed to workers with full-time shop stewards at their workplaces. The findings show that a sturdy majority – over 60 per cent – think full-time shop stewards have not lost touch with the shop floor. This shows that a clear majority of full-time shop stewards are fulfilling their mandate and representing workers' interests. However, a relatively high proportion (30 per cent) of Cosatu members are of the view that full-time shop stewards have lost touch with the shop floor, which implies that almost a third of Cosatu members feel estranged from their full-time shop stewards.

What can we conclude from the data on internal trade union democracy? There is still strong shop-floor democracy in Cosatu unions. Almost all the workplaces have shop stewards elected by their members. The members believe the shop stewards must be representative of and accountable to them. Meetings are still held frequently – weekly or monthly – and are well attended. Workers have retained the right of dismissal of shop stewards deemed not to be doing their work or representing workers. About a third of workers interviewed knew about or have been involved in the dismissal of shop stewards. These findings provide ample evidence that Cosatu members give their stewards mandates, thereby ensuring that they represent workers' interests. In addition, by retaining and exercising the right to remove shop stewards, they make sure that the shop stewards are accountable to them.

However, elections for shop stewards are being held less frequently, with a decline of annual or biennial elections and a rise in three- to four-yearly elections. This is in line with the statement by the Western Cape regional secretary of Numsa that shop stewards are increasingly being elected for four-year terms of office instead of

Table 9.15: Do you agree or disagree with the following statement? Full-time shop stewards in this workplace have lost touch with the shop floor.

	Number	Percentage
Strongly agree/agree	135	30.2%
Neutral/do not know	36	8.1%
Strongly disagree/disagree	276	61.7%
Total	447	100%

annually. Also, a growing number of shop stewards are being dismissed for political reasons – which takes us into the next section on the democratic rupture between union members and their leaders.

DEMOCRATIC RUPTURE BETWEEN COSATU MEMBERS AND LEADERS 1994–2014

Trade unions have grown considerably in membership and geographic coverage. This introduces additional strain on democratic practice. In the previous section we looked at the relationships between members and shop stewards at the level of the workplace. We now shift scale to introduce indicators of the state of democratic practice at the national level, starting out with Nedlac, a key forum for the participation by unions in policy formulation and collective bargaining. Again, the data allows us to track changes from 1994 to the present.

Table 9.16 shows that an overwhelming majority of Cosatu members surveyed do not know what Nedlac is. Although that there has been a gradual decline in the

Table 9.16: Do you know what Nedlac (National Economic Development and Labour Council) (National Manpower Commission, NMC, in 1994) is?

	1994 (NMC)	1998	2004	2008	2014
Yes	23.5%	8.7%	21.5%	29.3%	33.9%
No	76.5%	91.3%	78.5%	70.7%	64.6%
No answer					1.5%
Total	**100%**	**100%**	**100%**	**100%**	**100%**
Number included	630	655	637	627	619

Table 9.17: Have you ever been to a union meeting where there has been a report-back on Nedlac?

	1994 (NMC)	1998	2004	2008	2014
Yes	13.2%	30.3%	21.8%	42.8%	39.1%
No	86.8%	69.7%	78.2%	57.2%	60%
Do not know					0.9%
Total	**100%**	**100%**	**100%**	**100%**	**100%**
Number included	637	613	611	187	215

proportion who do not know, almost two-thirds still did not know what Nedlac was in the 2014 survey.

In 2008 and 2014 the data has been filtered to analyse only those who knew what Nedlac was. Because 2008 and 2014 include only those in the survey who said they knew what Nedlac was, the findings of the first three surveys are not comparable with the last two surveys. Nonetheless, it is significant that a majority of Cosatu members surveyed had never attended a meeting where there had been a report-back on Nedlac (Table 9.17).

Again, for Table 9.18, in 2008 and 2014 the data has been filtered to analyse only those who knew what Nedlac was. There are two remarkable findings in this table. First (in the years 1998 and 2004, when all Cosatu members surveyed are included in the table) is the high proportion of Cosatu union members who do not know whether Nedlac is an important body. Second is the high proportion (when only the members who knew what Nedlac was are included) who think it is an important body. Yet, on average over the four surveys when Nedlac existed (1998–2014), only one-third of members were ever at a union meeting where there was a report-back on Nedlac.

Table 9.19 shows that there is a remarkable jump of Cosatu members who knew what the RDP was, from barely 25 per cent in 1994 to around 80 to 90 per cent from 1998 to 2008. What is significant is that the figure was so low in 1994, since the

Table 9.18: Do you think that Nedlac is an important body through which Cosatu can influence policy which is of direct importance to workers?

	1998	2004	2008	2014
Yes	39.7%	41.9%	89.2%	74.3%
No	4.5%	11.2%	4.8%	13.8%
Do not know	55.8%	46.9%	5.9%	11.9%
Total	**100%**	**100%**	**100%**	**100%**
Number included	582	608	186	210

Table 9.19: Do you know what the RDP (Reconstruction and Development Programme) is?

	1994	1998	2004	2008
Yes	24.5%	82.3%	89.0%	78.5%
No	75.5%	17.7%	11%	21.5%
Total	**100%**	**100%**	**100%**	**100%**
Number included	611	633	653	627

RDP originated from within Cosatu and 'grew out of the forces struggling to transform South Africa and the demands of ordinary members of the ANC, its allies in the trade unions, civics and other social movements'. It was also 'openly debated at many conferences both inside the ANC and among its allies' (Ginsburg et al. 1995: 69). The finding suggests that the policy makers in Cosatu did not engage much with the rank-and-file members of Cosatu-affiliated unions when they drew up the RDP. If they had done so extensively, more Cosatu members would have known what the RDP was in 1994.

An overwhelming majority of Cosatu members surveyed did not know what Gear was (Table 9.20). What is more, the proportion kept on rising, from well over half in 1998 to two-thirds in 2004 and to three-quarters in 2008. Gear was initiated in 1996 and replaced by AsgiSA in 2006. It was thus still in its implementation phase during 1998 and 2004, and much discussed. It was increasingly heavily criticised by Cosatu and the SACP. That such a substantial majority of Cosatu members surveyed did not know what Gear was shows convincingly that Cosatu neither consulted nor briefed its members extensively on Gear.

Well over 60 per cent of Cosatu members did not know what the NDP was (Table 9.21) in spite of the fact that it is the ANC's officially adopted long-term plan that has been heavily criticised by Cosatu, specifically Numsa, and is one of the key reasons for the tensions between Zwelinzima Vavi and Numsa on the one hand and the current leadership of Cosatu on the other.

Table 9.20:   Do you know what Gear is? (1998, 2004 and 2008 only)

	1998	2004	2008
Yes	41.8%	32.8%	24.8%
No	58.2%	67.2%	75.2%
Total	100%	100%	100%
Number included	552	635	628

Table 9.21:   Do you know what the National Development Plan (NDP) is? (2014)

	Number	Percentage
Yes	220	35.5%
No	391	63.2%
No answer	8	1.3%
Total	619	100%

Table 9.22:   Do you support the NDP? (2014)

	Number	Percentage
Yes	158	71.8
No	60	27.3
Do not know	2	0.9
Total	**220**	**100**

Table 9.23:   Do you know what your federation's position is on the NDP? (2014)

	Number	Percentage
Yes	123	55.9
No	95	43.2
Do not know	2	0.9
Total	**220**	**100**

Note that only those who said they know what the NDP was were asked the question represented in Table 9.22. In spite of the fact that Cosatu opposes the NDP, no less than 72 per cent of the Cosatu members who actually know what it is support it. This demonstrates a serious disparity between Cosatu's policy makers and the rank-and-file membership.

Table 9.23 further elaborates. It shows that in spite of 56 per cent of Cosatu members knowing that their federation strongly opposes the NDP, 72 per cent of them support the NDP – which calls into question the extent to which Cosatu's policies represent the views of their members. This takes us to another highly contested matter – that of the so-called youth wage subsidy.

Despite frequent and vociferous opposition from Cosatu to the youth wage subsidy, only a minority of its members (37 per cent) know what it is (Table 9.24). This suggests that members' views regarding the subsidy were not widely canvassed by Cosatu leaders.

Only those who said they knew what the youth wage subsidy was were asked the question in Table 9.25. It shows that of those who do know what the youth wage subsidy is, slightly more than half (51 per cent) support it. Again, this is a troubling finding that illustrates the democratic rupture in Cosatu.

Furthermore, of those who know what the youth wage subsidy is, half support it, while well over half (55 per cent) know that Cosatu opposes it (Table 9.26). This demonstrates, first, that there is no consensus among Cosatu members on the issue and, second, that there was either no effort to achieve consensus or that efforts to build consensus failed.

Table 9.24: Do you know what the youth wage subsidy (now the Employment Tax Incentive Bill) is? (2014)

	Number	Percentage
Yes	228	36.8
No	378	61.1
Do not know	13	2.1
Total	**619**	**100**

Table 9.25: Do you support the youth wage subsidy? (2014)

	Number	Percentage
Yes	116	50.9
No	112	49.1
Total	**228**	**100**

Table 9.26: Do you know what your federation's position is on the youth wage subsidy? (2014)

	Number	Percentage
Yes	126	55.3
No	101	44.3
Do not know	1	0.4%
Total	**228**	**100**

What can we conclude from the data about the rupture between Cosatu members and leaders? With the exception of the RDP, a majority of workers do not know what national organisations their leaders serve on, nor what policy decisions their leaders have taken on their behalf. Only a small proportion of members (one-third) have ever been at a meeting where a report-back was given on Nedlac, one of the most important statutory bodies that impact on labour. In addition, a majority of members oppose the policies of their leaders on both the National Development Plan and the youth wage subsidy. Cosatu leaders are thus taking major policy decisions without consulting most of their members and that do not have the support of the majority of them. This indicates that the leaders do not represent members' views, do not hold themselves accountable to members, and fail to build a consensus among the union members or between them and rank-and-file members. Clearly, a democratic rupture exists between leaders and members, and oligarchy is rife in Cosatu.

COSATU OFFICIALS' PERCEPTIONS OF INTERNAL DEMOCRACY IN COSATU

An innovation since the first three surveys is to follow up the survey of Cosatu members with interviews of Cosatu leaders. This was done very systematically after the 2014 survey. The leaders interviewed vary widely from union leaders to national leaders, with local and provincial leaders in between. An interview schedule was drawn up by the panel of researchers while reviewing the survey findings, thereby identifying issues where leaders could shed more light and assist with interpreting the information. What follows is how various officials responded to the question 'What is the state of internal trade union democracy – of both the affiliates and of Cosatu local and regional structures?'

A Cosatu official relatively high up in the federation's hierarchy responded that Cosatu has always, from the days of Fosatu worker control, maintained a sound practice:

> ... and so all of the structures still constitutionally have a majority of workers in them where decisions are taken. The structures and the form of the constitution are well-honoured within Cosatu generally. So in practice in the affiliates, constitutional worker control principles are adhered to as far as I am exposed to them, but clearly there is an emerging tendency to centralise decisions and move them away from the workers in respect of resolving key challenges in the federation (interview, Cosatu official, 2015).

The principle of internal trade union democracy as understood in Cosatu was very clearly spelled out by a Cosatu official in the Nelson Mandela Bay local:

> What we are guided by internally is the principle of worker control and internal democracy. One of the fundamental tenants of the internal democracy is the issue of the mandate. At all times shop stewards must get mandates from members and present those mandates. The second part is that a leader must be able to be accountable, to go back to members and say this is what I have done on your behalf and how do you feel about it. Lastly, it is about transparency, about openness. Ensuring democracy in the trade union is about exposing exactly what is so that members are able to take decisions on that basis (interview, Cosatu official, 2014).

This point of view was strongly echoed by a Numsa regional official in the Eastern Cape. His view on internal democracy in Numsa is as follows:

> Numsa is a workers' control union. It's a union that is mandatory; it's a union that takes mandates from workers, a union that will go back to members in terms of what they have been requested to demand, or take up as an issue with the employers, and then those workers will always be given feedback on all those issues. Hence we say it's a workers' control organisation (interview, Numsa Eastern Cape regional official, 2015).

In response to the same question, a Numsa regional official in the Western Cape said that he observed a very different trend in other unions:

> We still believe in Numsa that democracy should be the rule of the day in the trade union. We do see that in some of the unions democracy is not being practised. Power is concentrated among the leadership and being used to control the whole union. It leads to corruption. Some are using finance to retain their position or to advance their narrow interest. You can see that many trade unions are collapsing (interview, Numsa Western Cape regional official, 2015).

This could be said to be the jaundiced view of an official of a union that has been expelled from Cosatu. However, a Cosatu official in Gauteng came up with some telling insights into current union leaders' lifestyles, even though he maintained that they listened to what workers have to say. In response to the question 'How would you characterise the trade union leadership at this current juncture?' the official answered:

> Well, for me, they are trying their best to go back to meet with members. If you look at general meetings that have been convened by leaders, they themselves directly go to see workers. That is why, for example, in provincial leadership we try to convene shop-stewards councils not less than four times per year and begin to talk to those shop stewards. That's why once a year we convene general meetings where we go to regions, what we call clusters, to engage with members. We engage on what is called 'listening campaign'. We are not going there to defend, to say anything to workers, but to sit and listen to workers, what workers say are the issues

emanating from our members. So that tells you how serious the leadership takes addressing things with members (interview, Cosatu official, 2015).

In response to a follow-up question on whether there is any difference between the current crop of leaders and pre-1994 leaders, the answer was that there is obviously a difference. The same official proceeded to explain the difference as follows:

> In pre-1994 for you to be leader of an organisation, it meant you must know that as a leader you can die, be arrested and you go into exile. Today is the opposite. I mean if you are the leader of a union, you are going to have a posh office; some of the leaders of the trade unions are moving with bodyguards, they are not even driving cars, they are sitting at the back of not just ordinary cars, Mercedes-Benz, Rolls-Royces of this world ... So the conditions are not necessarily the same. I mean nowadays for you to be general secretary of a union, you are earning above a million ... which was not the situation pre-1994. If you are a leader of the union now, it means that probably once a month you go to one of the conferences overseas, sleep in nice and posh hotels, as compared to previous situation before 1994.

When asked whether the current leadership is still in touch with the issues of the workers on the ground, the official answered in the affirmative, advancing a very interesting reason: it is a fear that the workers may remove them from office, an important power in democracy. 'A trade union official's term of office is in many instances three years, but if you don't attend to workers issues, workers will remove you. Sometimes workers even remove you no matter how good you are. They will call a vote of no confidence against you.'

This official also provided a spirited reply to the argument that trade unions are being used as a stepping stone by officials:

> If a trade unionist must not become an IR [industrial relations] manager, if trade unionists must not become councillors, if trade unionists must not become MPs, who must be? Must it mean that because you are trade unionist you must be a trade unionist for the rest of your life?

Regarding the conflict within Cosatu and between its leaders, a Gauteng official made some telling points:

I think every organisation at a certain stage will be confronted by challenges of leadership. EFF is hardly a year old and it is plunged into leadership battles and crises. So leadership contests and leadership battles are part of organisational dynamics. Anyone who expects there will be no leadership battles in the federation is not taking into account the nature of the federation. The federation is a federation of affiliates and you are not dealing with one centre but you are dealing with what used to be plus/minus twenty-one affiliates. So you deal with twenty-one different centres which are all independent and autonomous. So it is given that you will have leadership battles unless you want to tell me another way (interview, Cosatu official, 2015).

Three other Gauteng officials, however, all believed that contemporary trade union leaders have lost touch with rank-and-file members. A Cosatu coordinator in Gauteng maintains that huge disparities in salaries between workers and trade union officials have created a social distance between them. He explains how trade union leaders lose contact with workers as follows: 'When they go to aircraft, they are always in the business class ... Who sits there in the business section of the aircraft? It's the captains of the industry, so you mingle with them, then they become your friends' (interview, Cosatu official, 2015).

A Samwu official from Gauteng used the following example to illustrate how social distance is created between trade union officials and workers:

Trade union leaders go to different parties, they don't stay in the same neighbourhoods. Most leaders they stay in the northern suburbs, drive fancy cars. On the other hand the majority of workers rely on unreliable public transport to go to and from work (interview, Samwu official, 2015).

A Satawu official in Gauteng attributes the divergence between workers and trade union officials to what he calls 'stomach politics'.

Self-interest, that's what I mean by stomach politics. Self-interest comes first now rather than workers' interests. So by saying stomach politics, leadership of trade unions generally now are looking at what is going to benefit them, maximise kickbacks for them to benefit (interview, Satawu official, 2015).

What emerges as a strong theme from the interviews with Cosatu leaders is the identification of trade union democracy with representative and accountable structures and practices. It was stressed that shop stewards are given mandates by their members and that they must report back on the outcome of their meetings with management. There was also a defence, that leaders had not lost touch with workers, although this argument was less convincing considering what was perceived to be the lavish lifestyle of current leaders in Cosatu.

But that is where the understanding of trade union democracy stopped. It did not extend into proactive steps that trade union leaders could take to maintain democratic practices and build consensus within and between unions, even though it is acknowledged that Cosatu consists of numerous centres of power. It is also acknowledged that each union affiliated to Cosatu is an independent power centre with its own views. That makes the absence of consensus building all the more important, as is confirmed by contemporary international trends in trade union practice and theory. These are considered next.

INTERNATIONAL TRENDS AND THEORIES OF TRADE UNION DEMOCRACY

In an interesting chapter on trade union democracy, Matt Flynn et al. (2004: 320) put forward the argument that there are two major approaches. One is 'voice', by which is meant 'the influence which the ordinary member has over union policy, including the representation of differing constituencies with the union's membership'. The other is 'control', which is 'how ordinary members exert influence over those responsible for implementing policy'.

Flynn and others contend that academic literature and trade union legislation in Britain in the 1980s and early 1990s had largely focused on control, 'viewing democracy as regulating the interests of ordinary members against those of leaders' (Flynn et al. 2004: 320). The reason for such a focus on trade union democracy was to try to prevent what Michels foresaw as inevitable: the rise of oligarchic leaders effectively formulating policy and controlling the members, instead of members controlling the leaders (Flynn et al. 2004: 322). Flynn and his co-authors argue that since as early as the 1980s, 'the notion of democracy as control over leaderships has lost force and the notion of democracy as voice for partial constituencies has gained importance' (Flynn et al. 2004: 321). Voice is exercised democratically in a union by means of an iterative process of consensus building 'in which all members can influence union policy, which everyone then unites behind' (Flynn et al. 2004: 328). Ordinary members and members from peripheral constituencies thus share an active role in shaping union policy.

In Britain, efforts 'to staunch the drain in union numbers since the late 1970s' led to unions recruiting 'workers who had been historically under-represented in the trade union movement'. As unions sought to recruit new kinds of members, they had to adapt their democratic structures and practices by engaging in consensus building (Flynn et al. 2004: 329–330). The new kinds of members that the unions started recruiting are indicative of changes in the social composition of workers and in the social norms of society. Flynn et al. list the following social groups being recruited: women, black workers, youth, lesbians and gays, the wider community, and trade and occupationally differentiated groups (Flynn et al. 2004: 330–335). In order to give these social groups voice, it became necessary to engage in consensus building so that their voices could be heard. This amounts to a participative form of democracy rather than representative democracy, one in which there is 'active involvement of groups of workers in order to articulate their views' and contributing to policy formulation (Flynn et al. 2004: 348).

CONCLUSION: INTERNAL DEMOCRACY IN COSATU

In this chapter, democracy within Cosatu over the past twenty years has been carefully analysed. It was found that there is still a strong tradition of democracy at the workplace in that union members are keeping the shop stewards they elected representative of them and accountable to them. Although the frequency with which shop stewards are elected has declined as their terms of office have become longer, there is still a strong perception among union members that if shop stewards are not accountable the members can dismiss them.

However, at higher levels of union and federal organisation this accountability has broken down. It is a breakdown that goes back to 1994, when the first survey was conducted. With the exception of the RDP, a majority of members surveyed have consistently not known what the organisations are on which their leaders are meant to represent them. Furthermore, only a small proportion have ever been at union meetings where their leaders have reported back to them about Nedlac, a statutory body in which Cosatu plays an extremely important role. In addition, a majority of members also do not know what the government plans and laws are, about which their leaders have formulated policy decisions that have an impact on them as workers. In the latest 2014 survey it was established that a majority of members who do know what the government plans and laws are hold views opposite to the policies their leaders have adopted.

It is thus clear that there is a democratic rupture between the rank-and-file members and the union and federation leaders. This rupture can be explained in two ways. It can be understood as the existence of oligarchy within Cosatu (for another discussion and findings of previous surveys, see Maree 2012). Oligarchy exists when a union or federation is controlled and dominated by its leaders, not by its members. Robert Michels, who pioneered the work on oligarchy, argued that leaders still control and dominate organisations even when they go through the motions of consulting members (Michels 1959: 21–34; Maree 1982: 42). In Cosatu, only a small minority of members are consulted or provided with feedback by leaders on what they do at national level. It is therefore very easy for leaders to brush aside the feedback they receive from members and, instead, formulate policies based on their own preferences and ideologies.

A second explanation of the rupture within Cosatu between members and leaders is that it is due to a lack of consensus building by the unions and the federation. Consensus building is a participative process in which the members are proactively given the opportunity to formulate their needs, interests and demands, followed by a dialogue between the different constituencies within the union and, finally, the framing of policies that take the diverse voices within the union into consideration. It is a form of participative democracy and provides members with voice inside the organisation. Cosatu leaders have failed to build consensus within and between unions in the federation. None of the Cosatu leaders who were interviewed in 2015 mentioned consensus building as part of their understanding of democracy within Cosatu.

Another aspect of consensus building is that it entails reaching out to peripheral workers who have been overlooked or neglected by unions. It can also be a way of growing the unions. In Cosatu's case, it would apply to recruiting atypical workers such as temporary labour-broker workers, as no less than 90 per cent of Cosatu members surveyed are in permanent full-time posts.

Finally, the rupture between the unions in Cosatu and the expulsion of Numsa is in part due to the failure of Cosatu leadership to engage in consensus building between the unions and within the federation. This has happened at both the leadership and the rank-and-file levels. A rift started to develop ever since Cosatu played a key role in getting Jacob Zuma elected as president of the ANC in Polokwane in 2007. That rift gradually widened into a chasm that could not be bridged owing to the failure of building a consensus among the leaders of Cosatu. The rift has cascaded down to the unions as well, resulting in the expulsion of Numsa from Cosatu. It is too late to prevent a rupture within Cosatu. But the federation and its affiliated unions need to incorporate consensus building as a vital part of their understanding of trade union democracy. They need to ensure that workers have voice inside the unions and participate in formulating policies that represent their needs and aspirations.

BIBLIOGRAPHY

Buhlungu, Sakhela and Malehoko Tshoaedi (eds). 2012. *Cosatu's Contested Legacy: South African Trade Unions in the Second Decade of Democracy*. Cape Town: HSRC Press.

Flynn, Matt, Chris Brewster, Roger Smith and Mike Rigby. 2004. Trade union democracy: The dynamics of different forms. In *Trade Unions and Democracy: Strategies and Perspectives*, edited by Mark Harcourt and Geoffrey Wood. London: Transaction Publishers.

Ginsburg, David, Edward Webster, Roger Southall, Geoffrey Wood, Sakhela Buhlungu, Johann Maree, Janet Cherry, Richard Haines and Gilton Klerck. 1995. *Taking Democracy Seriously: Worker Expectations and Parliamentary Democracy in South Africa*. Durban: Indicator Press.

Maree, Johann. 1982. Democracy and oligarchy in trade unions: The independent trade unions in Transvaal and the Western Province General Workers' Union in the 1970s. *Social Dynamics* 8(1): 31–42.

Maree, Johann. 1986. An analysis of the independent trade unions in South Africa in the 1970s. PhD thesis, University of Cape Town.

Maree, Johann. 1989. The General Workers' Union, 1973–1986. In *The Angry Divide: Social and Economic History of the Western Cape*, edited by Wilmot James and Mary Simons. Cape Town: David Philip.

Maree, Johann. 2012. Cosatu, oligarchy and the consolidation of democracy in an African context. In *Cosatu's Contested Legacy: South African Trade Unions in the Second Decade of Democracy*, edited by Sakhela Buhlungu and Malehoko Tshoadi. Cape Town: HSRC Press.

Masondo, Themba, Mark Orkin and Edward Webster. 2015. Militants or managers? Cosatu and democracy in the workplace. In *Cosatu in Crisis: The Fragmentation of an African Trade Union Federation*, edited by Vishwas Satgar and Roger Southall. Johannesburg: KMMR Publishing.

Michels, Robert. 1959. *Political Parties*. New York: Dover Publications. (First published in 1911 in German.)

10

Public Sector Unions in Cosatu

Christine Bischoff and Johann Maree

INTRODUCTION

Public sector unions have grown in size, power and significance in Cosatu over the past twenty-four years and have instigated two of the largest strike actions, in 2007 and 2010, ever witnessed in South Africa. Cosatu's public sector unions have increased their membership from a mere 7 per cent of total union membership in 1991 to 39 per cent in 2012 (Cosatu 2012: 7). This constitutes a tenfold increase in membership, from 85 000 in 1991 to 854 000 in 2012. According to Cosatu (2015: 4), '... union density in the private sector was constant from 1995 to 2005 at 32.4 per cent whilst in the public sector, it increased from 50 per cent to 68.4 per cent.' In 2013 the contribution of public sector unions to Cosatu's income was 38 per cent. According to Cosatu's financial statements, this proportion rose to 60 per cent in 2014 (Marrian 2015). This is in part due to the expulsion of Numsa from Cosatu and the decline of the NUM as members defected to Amcu, but also to an increase in the membership of public sector unions affiliated to Cosatu.

The perceived dominance of public sector unions in Cosatu has already led to anxieties and tensions, illustrated by the response by Nehawu to the ANC secretary general Gwede Mantashe's statements made at the national congress of the NUM in

June 2015. Mantashe had reportedly said that 'the federation's dominance by public sector unions would turn Cosatu into a yellow federation' and, quoted directly, that '[o]nce you have a federation that is dominated by the public sector, then you are in trouble' (Nehawu 2015). (The term 'yellow union' typically refers to unions set up by authoritarian states to do their bidding and to pre-empt real independent unions from emerging. The term was specifically used during the Cold War, when many such unions were funded by the Central Intelligence Agency (CIA) of the US government, often in anti-communist East Asian countries.) Gwede Mantashe urged Cosatu 'to focus on recruiting more industrial workers'. Nehawu spokesperson Sizwe Pamla, who later became Cosatu's spokesperson, wrote in a press release: 'The problem with this statement is that it reduces public sector unions to unreliable and ahistorical organisations and sets the workers against each other ... In fact, it's the role of Cosatu to dominate all sectors of the economy including the public sector. Cosatu public sector unions have more than 50 per cent membership already in the sector and this should be encouraged' (Mahlakoana 2015).

In view of their growing importance it was decided by our research team to conduct an analysis of survey findings specifically related to Cosatu's public sector unions for the first time since the Cosatu membership surveys began in 1994. This chapter consists of a detailed statistical survey of Cosatu's public sector union members in comparison with private sector union members. It is based on the Taking Democracy Seriously survey of Cosatu members carried out shortly before the 2014 elections, and shows where the public sector unions and their members differ significantly from the private sector unions and their members – as well as where they are similar.

Before commencing with the analysis we clarify what constitutes a public sector trade union. Glenn Adler (2000) offers a breakdown of what is considered as the public sector in South Africa: it is characterised by employees working for the public service (that is, in the national and provincial departments); employees who work for the state-owned enterprises (except for ones that have been privatised); those who work for the local authorities (the city councils, the municipalities and town councils); and employees of universities and universities of technology and associated institutions. Furthermore, the public sector is characterised by employees who are covered by the same legislation (that is, the Public Service Act 1994) and represented by the trade unions bargaining in the Public Service Coordinating Bargaining Council (PSCBC) (Adler 2000: 4) or, in the case of the municipal workers, in the South African Local Government Bargaining Council (SALGBC). Public sector unions do not, therefore, have private sector employees as members.

PROFILE OF PUBLIC SECTOR UNION MEMBERS

The profile of public sector union members in our sample here is contrasted against those from the private sector. We interviewed 233 (37.6 per cent of the sample) members from public sector unions and 386 (62.4 per cent of the sample) members from private sector unions. We should remind the reader that Numsa was still an affiliate of Cosatu when the survey was conducted. Our sample of public sector union members came from the unions represented in Table 10.1 below.

Table 10.1 shows that the proportion of union members surveyed was roughly in proportion to the union's total membership. The larger the union, the higher the number of members interviewed, with an over-representation of members from Popcru. Interviewees came from Gauteng (47, or 20.2 per cent), North West (2, or 0.9 per cent), KwaZulu-Natal (54, or 23.2 per cent), Eastern Cape (83, or 35.6 per cent) and the Western Cape (47, or 20.2 per cent). Of those interviewed, 123 were male (53 per cent) and 109 female (47 per cent). A considerably higher proportion of female public sector union members (almost half of the total surveyed) than female private sector union members (fewer than a quarter) were interviewed.

Table 10.1: Cosatu public sector union members surveyed

	Members surveyed April 2014	Membership of union 2012
Popcru	58	149 339
	24.9%	16.5%
Samwu	35	153 487
	15%	16.9%
Denosa	14	74 883
	6%	8.3%
Sadtu	51	251 276
	21.9%	27.7%
Nehawu	67	260 738
	28.8%	28.8%
Pawusa	8	17 146
	3.4%	1.9%
Total	**233**	**906 869**
	100%	**100%**

Union membership for 2012 from Cosatu (2012: 7)

There is a noticeable difference in the age distribution of private sector and public sector union members in that the private sector members are younger (Table 10.2). Of the union members under twenty-five years of age, 6.3 per cent are private sector union members and 0.9 per cent are public union members. In a larger age group, 41 per cent of private sector union members are below the age of thirty-five, whereas only 29 per cent of public sectors member are below that age. Conversely, 35 per cent of public sector union members are older than forty-six as opposed to 26 per cent of private sector union members.

Migrant labour has become a major feature of employment relations since the mining of diamonds and gold in the nineteenth century. It persists to this day and it is therefore important to examine the extent and impact of migrant labour on public sector union members.

Table 10.2:   Age distribution of private and public sector union members

	Private sector unions	Public sector unions	Total
18–25	24	2	**26**
	6.3%	0.9%	**4.3%**
26–35	133	64	**197**
	34.8%	27.9%	**32.2%**
36–45	124	82	**206**
	32.5%	35.8%	**33.7%**
46–55	78	65	**143**
	20.4%	28.4%	**23.4%**
56–65	23	16	**39**
	6%	7%	**6.4%**
Total	**382**	**229**	611
	100%	**100%**	**100%**

Table 10.3:   Answers to question 'Are you a migrant worker?'

	Private sector unions	Public sector unions	Total
Yes	133	58	**191**
	34.5%	24.9%	**30.9%**
No	253	175	**428**
	65.5%	75.1%	**69.1%**
Total	**386**	**233**	619
	100%	**100%**	**100%**

Although the overwhelming majority of Cosatu union members in both the private and public sector unions do not consider themselves to be migrant workers, the private sector unions have a significantly higher proportion (more than a third) of members who do consider themselves to be migrant workers; the proportion for public sector union members is only a quarter.

Because migrant workers are cut off from their spouses and children for long periods at a time, they often strike up relations with new partners near their place of work and start a second or even a third or fourth family. It is therefore useful to see the extent to which this has happened among public sector migrant workers. As indicated in Table 10.4, more than half the civil servants in our sample who are migrant workers support more than one household on their wages.

Even so, Cosatu public sector members who are migrant workers tend to support a smaller number of households than their private sector counterparts. Ninety-one percent of public sector migrant workers support one or two households at most, as opposed to 82 per cent of private sector migrants. Conversely, 17 per cent of private sectors migrant workers support three or more households, but only 9 per cent of public sector migrant workers do so. An average of 4.05 people depend on the wages of public sector union members. Private sector union members have a slightly higher average of dependents: 4.39 people (a dependent is defined in the survey questionnaire as a person who depends on the respondent for financial support).

Table 10.4: Number of households supported by migrant workers

	Private sector unions	Public sector unions	Total
Do not know	1	0	1
	0.8%	0%	0.6%
One household	44	22	66
	35.5%	40%	36.9%
Two households	58	28	86
	46.8%	50.9%	48.0%
Three households	14	3	17
	11.3%	5.5%	9.5%
Four and more households	7	2	9
	5.6%	3.6%	5%
Total	124	55	179
	100%	100%	100%

Although the distribution of the type of residence private and public sector union members live in is broadly similar, there are two significant differences. A far greater proportion of public sector union members live in their own family house or flat (60 per cent as opposed to 44 per cent), but the reverse is the case for living in RDP houses (Table 10.5). Only 3 per cent of public employees live in RDP houses, whereas 14 per cent of private employees do, almost five times as many.

As could be expected, public sector union members have considerably higher levels of formal education than private sector union members (Table 10.6). No less

Table 10.5: Type of residence

	Private sector unions	Public sector unions	Total
Single-sex hostel	9	4	**13**
	2.3%	1.7%	**2.1%**
Own family house/flat (fully owned or with mortgage)	168	139	**307**
	43.5%	59.7%	**49.6%**
RDP house	54	7	**61**
	14%	3%	**9.9%**
Rented family house	33	22	**55**
	8.5%	9.4%	**8.9%**
Rented flat	31	24	**55**
	8%	10.3%	**8.9%**
Rented room in a house/flat	27	11	**38**
	7%	4.7%	**6.1%**
Shack	20	7	**27**
	5.2%	3%	**4.4%**
Rented room in a shack	3	2	**5**
	0.8%	0.9%	**0.8%**
Backroom (in a yard)	19	5	**24**
	4.9%	2.1%	**3.9%**
Other	20	11	**31**
	5.2%	4.7%	**5%**
Do not know	2	1	**3**
	0.5%	0.4%	**0.5%**
Total	**386**	**233**	**619**
	100%	**100%**	**100%**

Table 10.6:   Level of education of respondents

	Private sector unions	Public sector unions	Total
No formal education	3	0	**3**
	0.8%	0%	**0.5%**
Std 2 or lower/ Grade 4 or lower	4	2	**6**
	1%	0.9%	**1%**
Std 3–5/Grades 5–7	13	2	**15**
	3.4%	0.9%	**2.4%**
Std 6–8/Grades 8–10	63	7	**70**
	16.3%	3%	**11.3%**
Std 9–10/Grades 11–12	202	78	**280**
	52.3%	33.5%	**45.2%**
Technical diploma	67	54	**121**
	17.4%	23.2%	**19.5%**
University degree	25	78	**103**
	6.5%	33.5%	**16.6%**
Other	9	12	**21**
	2.3%	5.2%	**3.4%**
Total	**386**	**233**	**619**
	100%	**100%**	**100%**

than a third of public sector union member surveyed have university degrees, while only one in fifteen private sector union members have a degree. On the other hand, more than one-fifth of private sector union members range from having received no formal education up to a maximum of Grade 10, whereas only one in twenty public sector union members have such low educational qualifications.

The education gap between private and public sector union members is also found in the skill and occupational distribution of the two groups (Table 10.7). Almost 40 per cent of private union members surveyed are either unskilled or semi-skilled, whereas only slightly more than 11 per cent of public service employees fall into those two categories. On the other hand, 40 per cent of public sector union employees are in professional posts, six times higher than the proportion of private sector union members. The overwhelming majority of both private and public sector union members are permanent full-time employees. In both sectors roughly 90 per cent of union members are full-time permanent employees.

Table 10.7:   Skills and educational profile

	Private sector unions	Public sector unions	Total
Unskilled	39	9	48
	10.1%	3.9%	7.8%
Semi-skilled	113	17	130
	29.3%	7.3%	21%
Skilled	166	64	230
	43%	27.5%	37.2%
Supervisor	19	16	35
	4.9%	6.9%	5.7%
Clerical	17	27	44
	4.4%	11.6%	7.1%
Professional	26	93	119
	6.7%	39.9%	19.2%
Other	4	2	6
	1%	0.9%	1%
Do not know / refused to answer	2	5	7
	0.5%	2.1%	1.1%
Total	386	233	619
	100%	100%	100%

Table 10.8:   Average earnings of Cosatu members surveyed

	Private sector unions	Public sector unions
Mean	10 760.92	14 108.58
Median	8 000	13 550
Minimum	1 086	3 000
Maximum	45 000	42 000
Range	43 914	39 000
Number of Cosatu members	214	196

Public sector union members are paid considerably more than private sector union members (Table 10.8). The minimum wage in the public sector is two-and-three-quarters times higher than in the private sector; the mean (or average) wage is 31 per cent higher; and the median wage 69 per cent higher. It is only for the maximum wage that the private sector comes out on top. These results fit in with the educational and occupational distribution of private and public sector union members. In summary, the data confirms what one would expect – that members of public sector trade unions are, on average, better educated and in more secure jobs than their private sector counterparts.

We now turn to a comparative analysis of what the data tells us about trade union structures and democratic practice in public and private sector workplaces.

SHOP STEWARDS AND ORGANISATIONAL PRACTICE IN THE WORKPLACE

A slightly higher proportion of public sector trade union members reported that they had shop stewards in their workplaces (227, or 97.4 per cent). In the private sector 360 (or 93.3 per cent) reported the same. In both cases these shop stewards tended to be elected by workers (89 per cent for the public sector and 91.1 per cent for the private sector). In a very few cases stewards were appointed by management (the balance of 7.7 per cent for the public sector and 6.5 per cent for the private sector was made up by those who did not know whether their stewards were elected). Interestingly, elections are held considerably more often in the public sector than in the private sector (Table 10.9). In the public sector, 52 per cent of shop-steward elections take place at least once every two years, whereas in the private sector only 30 per cent of shop-steward elections take place as often as that. Looking at it another way, 60 per cent of shop-steward elections in the private sector take place only once every three years or more, whereas this is the case for only 30 per cent of public sector shop-steward elections.

A majority of both public and private sector union members elect their shop stewards by a show of hands, secret ballots being more common in the private sector. Here, 45 per cent of union members indicated that they had elected their stewards by secret ballot, whereas only 37 per cent of civil servants indicated the same.

Members from both the private sector and the civil service (55 per cent of members of public sector unions and 61 per cent of members of private sector unions) expect their shop stewards to consult members every time they act on behalf of workers. Although there is only a 6 per cent difference between the two, this may suggest that the tradition of worker control and participatory democracy may be more established in the private sector. An overwhelming majority of union members from both categories agree or strongly agree that shop stewards represent their interests as workers. The practice of full-time shop stewards seems to be more

Table 10.9:   If shop stewards are elected, how often are elections held?

	Private sector unions	Public sector unions	Total
Cannot remember / do not know	35	36	71
	10.7%	17.8%	13.4%
More than once a year	12	6	18
	3.7%	3%	3.4%
Once a year	58	44	102
	17.7%	21.8%	19.2%
Once in two years	27	55	82
	8.2%	27.2%	15.5%
Once in three years	130	55	185
	39.6%	27.2%	34.9%
More than three years ago	66	6	72
	20.1%	3%	13.6%
Total	328	202	530
	100%	100%	100%

common in the private sector than the public sector, with 70.5 per cent of public sector union members reporting their presence in the workplace and a slightly higher proportion of private sector union members (79.7 per cent) reporting the same.

The question as to whether shop stewards had lost touch with members did not draw significantly different responses from the two sectors. This question was only asked of union members with full-time shop stewards. A majority of members (over 60 per cent) from both public and private sectors thought that full-time shop stewards have not lost touch with the shop floor, but there is a significant minority (30 per cent) who think that they have. There is a strong belief of union members in both private and public sectors that they have the right to remove shop stewards who do not represent their interests. Over 90 per cent hold that belief (90.3 per cent in the public sector and 92.8 per cent in the private sector). Nevertheless, actual practice seems to differ. In the public sector only 22.5 per cent of those interviewed indicated that a shop steward had been removed in their places of work, with a much more significant proportion of private sector union members (42.8 per cent) reporting the same. The reasons for such actions against shop stewards did not differ significantly between the two sectors – as can be seen from Table 10.10 below.

Table 10.10:   What was main reason for removing a shop steward?

	Private sector unions	Public sector unions	Total
Not doing their job properly	85	26	**111**
	55.2%	51%	**54.1%**
Too close to management	42	13	**55**
	27.3%	25.5%	**26.8%**
Different politics	13	4	**17**
	8.4%	7.8%	**8.3%**
Too close to union officials	3	1	**4**
	1.9%	2%	**2%**
Other	10	6	**16**
	6.5%	11.8%	**7.8%**
Do not know/ refused to answer	1	1	**2**
	0.6%	2%	**1%**
Total	**154**	**51**	**205**
	100%	**100%**	**100%**

Table 10.11:   How often do shop stewards hold meetings with members in your workplace?

	Private sector unions	Public sector unions	Total
Do not know/refused to answer	14	27	**41**
	3.9%	11.9%	**7%**
Never	4	5	**9**
	1.1%	2.2%	**1.5%**
Once a week	95	13	**108**
	26.4%	5.7%	**18.4%**
Once a month	162	101	**263**
	45%	44.5%	**44.8%**
Once a year	2	4	**6**
	0.6%	1.8%	**1%**
Twice a year	5	9	**14**
	1.4%	4%	**2.4%**
When there is a crisis	62	66	**128**
	17.2%	29.1%	**21.8%**
Other	13	2	**15**
	3.6%	0.9%	**2.6%**
Total	**357**	**227**	**584**
	100%	**100%**	**100%**

An interesting difference between the two sectors emerges from an analysis of how often shop-steward meetings take place. Monthly meetings are the norm in both public and private sectors. However, weekly meetings seem to be more common in the private sector. In the public sector, crisis meetings seem more common (see Table 10.11). This finding is confirmed by an analysis of responses to how often members attend such meetings.

STRIKES AND COMMUNITY PROTEST

We have already mentioned the public sector strikes of 2007 and 2010 in the introduction to this chapter. Interestingly enough, a smaller proportion of trade union members from the public sector (52.4 per cent) answered in the affirmative to the question 'Have workers in this workplace been involved in any industrial action since the last elections (in 2009)?' than from the private sector (61.4 per cent). This result is somewhat puzzling. It may mean that those civil servants interviewed did not participate in the strike of 2010, or they do not recall doing so. Those interviewed who did recall strikes mostly reported that they were supported and organised by unions. A slightly higher proportion of strikes in the private sector were not supported by unions, with only 2.5 per cent of civil servants reporting the same. Violence during such strikes seemed uncommon in both private and public sector strikes. There was no violence in slightly more than 80 per cent of the workplace strikes, with very similar results for both public and private sector strikes. What is very interesting is that violence was instigated by union members more frequently than by the police or the youth (violence was instigated in almost a third of cases by union members, about a quarter by police and around a fifth by the youth). Private sector union members instigated violence about 50 per cent more frequently than public sector union members.

The overwhelming majority of both private and public sector union members surveyed did not support the use of violence against non-striking workers. Nonetheless there are some interesting differences between private and public union members on how to deal with non-striking workers. A larger proportion of private sector union members thought that non-striking workers should be taught a non-violent lesson or engaged with politically, whereas a larger proportion of public sector members thought that non-striking workers should be left alone (see Table 10.12 below).

Table 10.12: In relation to strikes, which of the statements do you agree with?

	Private sector unions	Public sector unions	Total
There are times when it becomes necessary to use violence against non-striking workers	16	12	**28**
	4.1%	5.2%	**4.5%**
Violence is not acceptable but non-striking workers should be taught a lesson in non-violent ways	109	55	**164**
	28.2%	23.6%	**26.5%**
Non-striking workers should be engaged with politically to convince them to join the strike	150	73	**223**
	38.9%	31.3%	**36%**
Non-striking workers should be left alone to go to work if they so decide	83	61	**144**
	21.5%	26.2%	**23.3%**
Do not know/refused to answer	28	32	**60**
	7.3%	13.7%	**9.7%**
Total	**386**	**233**	**619**
	100%	**100%**	**100%**

Trade union members of private sector unions (29.5 per cent) tend to be more involved in community protests than their civil servant counterparts (22.7 per cent). The difference becomes more pronounced when one analyses the results for shop stewards only. Of shop stewards from private sector unions, 51.8 per cent report involvement in community protests, against only 36.5 per cent of shop stewards from the civil service (still a relatively high proportion). The overwhelming majority (more than three-quarters on average) were non-violent community protests – however, private sector employees participated in more than double the proportion of violent community protests than did public sector employees. A large majority of private and public sector union members are not involved in local government or community-based development initiatives. When members do engage in community initiatives, they do so mainly as community members or as members of a political party.

DEMOCRACY AND POLITICAL ORIENTATION

In this section we draw on a number of indicators to compare the political attitudes of members of public and private sector trade unions. We start out with a number of questions around institutions of democracy, then move on to contentious policy issues, and finally we look at options on the Alliance and voting preferences.

We start with Nedlac, an important forum for worker participation in policy formulation. When asked whether they knew what Nedlac was, 31.8 per cent of public sector employees answered in the affirmative. A slightly higher proportion of private sector union members answered the same (35.2 per cent).

A much lower proportion of public sector employees (23 per cent) than private sector employees (49.3 per cent) confirmed that they had attended a report-back session on Nedlac (Table 10.13). These findings already suggest that in terms of participation in policy formulation there seems to be a schism between the public and the private sectors. But we have to make a more general point about Nedlac here: if union members who did not know what Nedlac is have never been at a meeting where Nedlac was discussed, it implies that only 7.3 per cent (23.0 per cent of the 31.8 per cent who said they knew what Nedlac was) of all public sector union members surveyed have ever been to a meeting where there was a report-back on Nedlac. Even though the proportion is considerably higher for private sector union members (17.4 per cent), it still means that only about one in six private union members had ever received a report-back on Nedlac. Just about three-quarters of private and public sector union members who know what Nedlac is think that it is an important body through which Cosatu can influence policy. This highlights just how inadequate is Cosatu leaders' accountability to the unions' members in this regard.

As pointed out earlier in this volume, the National Development Plan (NDP) remains a controversial topic and is seen as one of the main reasons for the expulsion of Numsa from Cosatu. Only slightly more than a third of both private and

Table 10.13: For those who know what Nedlac is: Have you ever been at a meeting where there has been a report-back on Nedlac?

	Private sector unions	Public sector unions	Total
Yes	67	17	84
	49.3%	23%	40%
No	67	57	124
	49.3%	77%	59%
No answer	2	0	2
	1.5%	0%	1%
Total	136	74	210
	100%	100%	100%

Table 10.14: Of those who know what the NDP is, do you support it?

	Private sector unions	Public sector unions	Total
Yes	90	68	**158**
	67.2%	79.1%	**71.8%**
No	42	18	**60**
	31.3%	20.9%	**27.3%**
No answer	2	0	**2**
	1.5%	0%	**0.9%**
Total	**134**	**86**	**220**
	100%	**100%**	**100%**

public sector union members know what the NDP is. Criticisms of the ideological content of the NDP aside, it is rather shocking that so few unionised civil servants are even aware of the plan they are supposed to implement – this despite the fact that the NDP has frequently been criticised publicly in the media by Cosatu.

Furthermore, both private sector and public sector union members who know what the NDP is support it strongly (see Table 10.14 above). A majority of union members who actually know what the NDP is also know what Cosatu's position is on the NDP (52.3 per cent of public sector union members and 58.2 per cent of private sector union members). In spite of that, the overwhelming majority hold a view contrary to Cosatu's: that is, they support the NDP, while Cosatu leaders officially oppose it. This shows that Cosatu leaders' policy on the NDP is unrepresentative of its unions' members, especially public sector union members. This further underlines how disconnected some Cosatu campaigns are from members' views.

A similar trend emerges when one considers the youth wage subsidy (or the Employment Tax Incentive Bill). A majority of union members from both public and private sectors do not know what the youth wage subsidy is.

An interesting divide opens up when one further disaggregates (by sector) those who know what the youth wage subsidy is, and whether they support the policy (see Table 10.15). Here, 60.7 per cent of civil servants support the measure, compared to only 45.1 per cent of members of private sector unions. This is a marked difference between the level of support for the youth wage subsidy between private and public sector union members who know what it is, and one of the most striking indications that there may be significant differences in interests and ideological orientation emerging between members of civil service unions and their private

Table 10.15:　Of those who know what the youth wage subsidy is, do you support it?

	Private sector unions	Public sector unions	Total
Yes	65	51	**116**
	45.1%	60.7%	**50.9%**
No	79	33	**112**
	54.9%	39.3%	**49.1%**
Total	**144**	**84**	**228**
	100%	**100%**	**100%**

sector counterparts. In addition, there is a difference between private and public sector union members who know what the youth wage subsidy is and what Cosatu's position is on it – 59.7 per cent of private sector union members know what this is, compared with fewer than half of public sector union members. This implies that there are still many public sector union members who support the youth wage subsidy even though they know that Cosatu opposes it.

When it comes to views on parliamentary democracy, both public and private sector union members hold very strong views that the political party they vote for must consult its supporters on all issues, or at least on important issues affecting them. Over 95 per cent of private sector and public sector trade union members hold this view. This is very similar to their views on the accountability of shop stewards in the workplace. When asked the question 'When a party makes decisions in Parliament that affect its supporters it must report back to the people that voted for it', a slight but potentially important nuance emerges, with 78 per cent of private sector employees choosing 'every time' and 71.7 per cent of public sector employees choosing the same. Of private sector employees, 20.7 per cent expect report-backs on 'only on major issues', whereas 27 per cent of public sector employees expect the same. In deciding to vote for a party, responses were very similar, with 'past performance' scoring 33.5 per cent with civil servants and 28.8 per cent with private sector union members; 'loyalty to a political tradition' scoring 20.2 per cent with civil servants and 19.7 per cent with private sector union members; 'leadership' scoring 13.5 per cent with civil servants and 15 per cent with private sector union members; and 'policies' scoring 27.9 per cent with civil servants and 31.1 per cent with private sector union members. This may suggest that 'past performance' is slightly more important to members of public sector unions and 'policies' somewhat more important to members of private sector unions, but these variations are too small to suggest the presence of different voting cultures between the two groups.

Possibly more suggestive differences emerge when asked about the Tripartite Alliance. Levels of support are higher among civil servants, with 46.4 per cent responding that the Alliance 'is the best way of safeguarding workers' interests in Parliament' and 43.3 per cent of private sector union members responding similarly. Note that support for the Alliance has dropped to less than half for both categories of Cosatu members. The second most popular view is that Cosatu should not be aligned with any political party. No less than 31 per cent of private and 28 per cent of public sector union members are of this opinion. The third most popular view is that workers should form their own political party. This view is held by a rather small proportion of members: only 9 per cent of private and 6 per cent of public sector union members. Nonetheless, it is interesting to note that this is a considerably higher proportion than members who contend that workers' interests in Parliament should be represented by the South African Communist Party (SACP) alone. It is also worth noting that a fairly large proportion (12 per cent of private and 16 per cent of public sector union members) either refused to answer the question or did not know how to answer it.

When asked whether the Alliance should continue and contest elections, once again private and public sector union members broadly share opinions (Table 10.16). However, in this case there is a fairly significant difference between the two groups in that a considerably larger proportion of public sector union members think that the Tripartite Alliance should continue and contest the next election (50 per cent of public as opposed to only 42 per cent of private sector union members). On the other hand, a considerably larger proportion of private than public sector union members are of the view that Cosatu should not be aligned with any political party. Almost a third of private sector union members surveyed would prefer Cosatu not to be aligned to any political party. Although small, a not insignificant number of members were of the view that Cosatu would be better off forming its own political party. Once again, the support for the SACP is very low. Only 1.6 per cent of private and 0.9 per cent of public sector union members think that Cosatu should maintain its alliance with the SACP.

The first thing to note about Table 10.17 is that when asked who they were going to vote for in the upcoming elections (2014), 38 per cent of the Cosatu union members interviewed did not give an indication – because they did not want to tell, or did not know, or did not intend to vote. Hence only 62 per cent of union members interviewed indicated how they intended to vote. The most significant finding is that, of all union members surveyed, less than a majority (49 per cent) said they were going to vote for the ANC – this in spite of the fact that Cosatu is in an alliance with the ANC. Nevertheless, no other party came even near the ANC. The EFF

Table 10.16: Do you think that this Alliance should continue and contest the election after 2014 (in 2019)?

	Private sector unions	Public sector unions	Total
Yes	162	116	**278**
	42%	49.8%	**44.9%**
No. Cosatu should not be aligned with any political party	122	49	**171**
	31.6%	21%	**27.6%**
No. Cosatu would be better off forming its own party	37	21	**58**
	9.6%	9%	**9.4%**
I think that Cosatu should maintain its alliance with the SACP only	6	2	**8**
	1.6%	0.9%	**1.3%**
I think that Cosatu should maintain its alliance with the ANC only	6	6	**12**
	1.6%	2.6%	**1.9%**
Do not know/refused to answer	53	39	**92**
	13.7%	16.7%	**14.9%**
Total	**386**	**233**	**619**
	100%	**100%**	**100%**

came next with 6.5 per cent and the DA third with 3.2 per cent of union member support. All the other parties could only muster 1 or 3 union members out of 619 surveyed who would vote for them. Party political support was very similar between the Cosatu public and private sector union members, although a close majority of public sector members indicated that they would vote for the ANC. Support for the EFF and DA was considerably lower among public sector union members

What does the data tell us about differences between public and private sector union members regarding views on parliamentary democracy and the Tripartite Alliance? The expectations of parliamentary democracy are remarkably close to what union members demand from their shop stewards. Over 95 per cent of both public and private sector union members insist that parliamentarians must consult them on issues, and no less than 99 per cent that they must report back. The only noteworthy difference between public and private sector union members is that a lower proportion of public sector members expect parliamentarians to report back on *every* issue.

Although the union members' expectations of the level of accountability of their members of Parliament are unrealistic, the grounds on which they decide to vote

Table 10.17: Which party are you going to vote for in the forthcoming (2014) national elections?

	Private sector unions	Public sector unions	Total
ANC	187	119	**306**
	48.4%	51.1%	**49.4%**
EFF	34	6	**40**
	8.8%	2.6%	**6.5%**
DA	15	5	**20**
	3.9%	2.1%	**3.2%**
Agang	2	1	**3**
	0.5%	0.4%	**0.5%**
Azapo	1	0	**1**
	0.3%	0%	**0.2%**
IFP	1	0	**1**
	0.3%	0%	**0.2%**
PAC	1	0	**1**
	0.3%	0%	**0.2%**
UDM	0	3	**3**
	0%	1.3%	**0.5%**
Other	2	1	**3**
	0.5%	0.4%	**0.5%**
My vote is my secret	107	69	**176**
	27.7%	29.6%	**28.4%**
Do not intend to vote	18	9	**27**
	4.7%	3.9%	**4.4%**
Do not know/refused to answer	16	18	**34**
	4.1%	7.7%	**5.5%**
Question not asked	2	2	**4**
	0.5%	0.9%	**0.6%**
Total	**386**	**233**	**619**
	100%	**100%**	**100%**

for a party are soundly based. Slightly fewer than a third base their decision on a party's past performance and about the same proportion on the policies of the party, while another 14 per cent base it on leadership. The proportion basing their vote on loyalty to the party is, however, quite high (at 20 per cent for both public and private sector union members). A majority of both public and private sector union members no longer think that the Tripartite Alliance is the best way of safe-guarding workers' interests, but a large proportion of members still do so – around 44 per cent of public and private union members still hold this view, with very little difference between them. This is a massive decline from 1994, when 82 per cent thought it was the best way and, as late as 2008, 62 per cent still held this view. On the other hand, a growing number contend that Cosatu should not be aligned with any political party (31 per cent of private and 28 per cent of public sector union members). In 1994 only 15 per cent of all Cosatu union members surveyed held this view.

A similar proportion of union members held the view that the Alliance should contest the next election – slightly fewer than 50 per cent of public sector and 42 per cent of private sector members. In 1994, 76 per cent of members thought that the Alliance should contest the next election. On the other hand, 21 per cent of public and 32 per cent of private sector members held the view that Cosatu should not be aligned to any party (an average of 28 per cent for all members surveyed). This is a dramatic increase over the mere 3 per cent who thought so in 1998.

Finally, around 50 per cent of both public and private sector union members said they would vote for the ANC in the election – a dramatic fall from the 75 per cent who said they would do so in 1994.

Overall, there is dwindling support among both private and public sector union members for the Tripartite Alliance and the ANC, with the public sector union members still slightly more supportive of both than are their private sector comrades.

CONCLUSION

The main distinction between public and private sector union members surveyed is that the public sector members are older, more educated, in higher occupational positions, and better remunerated than private sector members. The minimum earnings in the public sector is 2.75 times higher than that in the private sector, the average 31 per cent higher, and the median 69 per cent higher.

Not only in their employment are public sector union members better off, but also in their social lives. A smaller proportion of them are migrant workers, and of those who are, a smaller proportion support more than two households. A larger proportion of public sector union members live in their own houses and flats.

Public sector union members are more conservative in the sense that they have not changed their views and loyalties to the same extent as have private sector members. A greater proportion of them still want Cosatu to remain in the Tripartite

Alliance, and vote for the ANC, than do private sector members. The evidence in this chapter shows that they have considerable material interests in maintaining the status quo.

BIBLIOGRAPHY

Adler, Glenn (ed.). 2000. *Public Service Labour Relations in a Democratic South Africa*. Johannesburg: Wits University Press.

Congress of South African Trade Unions (Cosatu). 2012. *11th Cosatu Congress Secretariat Report: 2nd Draft for Internal Circulation 24th August 2012*. Johannesburg: Cosatu.

Cosatu. 2015. *Organisational Report to 12th National Congress 23 to 26 November 2015*. Johannesburg: Cosatu.

Mahlakoana, Theto. 2015. Union berates 'divisive' Mantashe. *IOL*, 4 June. http://www.iol. co.za/news/politics/union-berates-divisive-mantashe-1.1867811#.VmazyW8aLZ4 (accessed 8 December 2015).

Marrian, Natasha. 2015. Who is fighting for worker rights? Because it's not Cosatu. *Rand Daily Mail*, 27 November. http://www.rdm.co.za/politics/2015/11/27/who-is-fighting-for-worker-rights-because-it-s-not-cosatu (accessed 8 December 2015).

National Education, Health and Allied Workers' Union (Nehawu). 2015. Nehawu rejects the notion that the public sector union's domination of Cosatu risks turning it into a 'yellow' federation. Media statement, 4 June. https://www.nehawu.org.za/files/THURSDAY,-04-JUNE,-2015-NEHAWU-rejects-the-notion-that-the-public-sector-union-s-domination-of-Cosatu-risks-turning-it-into-a-yellow-federation.pdf (accessed 19 March 2017).

11

Are Cosatu's Public Sector Unions Too Powerful?

Johann Maree

INTRODUCTION

Cosatu's public sector unions have grown stronger and stronger since the federation was founded. At its launch in November 1985, the membership of public sector unions totalled only 24 486, constituting only 5 per cent of all the founding unions' membership (Baskin 1991: 55). By 1991, public sector union membership still comprised only 7 per cent of total Cosatu membership, but by 2012 it had risen to a hefty 39 per cent. By then, some of the federation's largest unions were public sector unions, such as Nehawu with 260 738 members, Sadtu with 251 276, and Popcru with 149 339 (Cosatu 2012: 7).

Over the years, the Cosatu public sector unions had flexed their muscles for all citizens in South Africa to see and feel. For instance, in 2007 and 2010 they played leading roles in public sector strikes that were the largest strikes ever experienced in South Africa up to that time (in terms of working hours lost). This has given rise to the question of whether the Cosatu public sector unions have become too powerful insofar as they, along with other public sector unions, have used their bargaining power to acquire excessive earnings and too large a share of the state's expenditure for their members – these acquisitions then prevent the state from providing adequate services to the public. In addition, it can be asked whether the public sector unions have also been too powerful to concede that their members have to improve service delivery to the public as their earnings rise.

This chapter commences with an overview of public sector employment relations, focusing mainly on developments since the advent of democracy in 1994. The question whether public sector unions in general, and Cosatu's public sector unions in particular, have become too powerful, is finally addressed. The focus is on whether the substantial resources allocated by the state to remunerate public servants are commensurate with the improvement in service delivery. As a case study, it examines school education and the role of Sadtu, a Cosatu-affiliated union. It also looks at some of the internal political disputes within Sadtu and briefly explores Sadtu shop stewards' support for the ANC and the SACP in comparison to that of shop stewards in other Cosatu unions.

PUBLIC SECTOR UNIONS AND COLLECTIVE BARGAINING IN SOUTH AFRICA

This section starts off by providing a brief historical background of the emergence of public service collective bargaining in South Africa. It then looks at the evolution of public service trade unions as well as labour legislation and institutions of public sector collective bargaining. Finally, it explores the outcome of collective bargaining and industrial action in the public sector up to 2014.

Emergence of collective bargaining in public services

The original body that regulated the remuneration and working conditions of public servants in South Africa was the Public Service Commission (PSC). It was established in 1912 and had the power unilaterally to determine remuneration and working conditions (Adler 2000: 7). The Public Servants Association (PSA), established in 1920, was the first employees' association. It represented only white permanent civil servants, almost all males, and was purely an advisory body without any real influence (Du Toit 2005: 24; Macun and Psoulis 2000: 95).

This type of regulation remained more or less the same until sporadic outbursts of protest action in health services, education, police and correctional services took place during the late 1980s and early 1990s. This was linked to the emergence of militant black trade unions in these three occupational fields: Nehawu, established in Cosatu in 1987; Sadtu, launched in Cosatu in 1990; and Popcru, which affiliated to Cosatu in 1994. Between 1989 and 1993 these three unions played a major role in initiating the biggest strike wave in the history of the public service up to that time (Adler 2000: 10–11; Macun and Psoulis 2000: 99).

As a result of these unions' actions, a new labour relations dispensation was introduced by the apartheid regime. Negotiations started soon after the strikes ended. The outcome was new legislation, the Public Service Labour Relations Act (PSLRA) of 1993 that extended core labour rights to public servants for the first time. The Act brought labour relations in public services in line with the system operating in the private sector (Adler 2000: 11).

The PSLRA granted statutory recognition to trade unions organising public services. This established a permanent foothold for the unions that expanded rapidly. By 1995 there were nineteen unions and staff associations that participated in collective bargaining with the state. The unions and associations were divided into two camps: the cautious and conservative predominantly white unions that emerged from the established staff associations, and the recently emerged militant black unions (Du Toit 2005: 29–30).

The PSLRA also set up new structures for collective bargaining at central, provincial and departmental levels (Macun and Psoulis 2000: 100). At central level, the Public Service Bargaining Council (PSBC) was established for workers employed under the Public Service Act. It excluded educators and police personnel, hence the Education Labour Relations Council (ELRC) was set up for educators and the National Negotiating Forum (NNF) for uniformed police personnel (Patel 2000: 129–130).

Establishment of public service bargaining councils and rapid growth of unions

The transformation of labour relations in public service that commenced under the apartheid regime was continued by the new regime. The Labour Relations Act 66 of 1995 (LRA) granted the same labour relations and collective bargaining rights to employees in public service as to employees in the private sector. Section 35 of the Act established the Public Service Coordinating Bargaining Council (PSCBC) statutorily, while section 37 granted it the right to designate a sector of the public service for the establishment of a bargaining council (see LRA section 36(2)(a) and (b), and section 37(5)).

The PSCBC took over the PSBC, while the ELRC and NNF were elevated to the status of bargaining councils by the LRA (Adair and Albertyn 2000: 824, n.57; Adler 2000: 5). The NNF was combined with the Department of Safety and Security Departmental Bargaining Council and called the Safety and Security Sectoral

Bargaining Council (SSSBC). In addition, the PSCBC created two more bargaining councils: the Public Health and Social Development Sectoral Bargaining Council (PHSDSBC) that covers the whole of the health and welfare sector, and the General Public Service Sectoral Bargaining Council (GPSSBC) that covers all employees who do not fall within the scope of any of the other sectoral bargaining councils (Adair and Albertyn 2000: 826–827).

Once the state had officially recognised public sector trade unions for public workers and public sector bargaining councils had been established, trade union membership in the public sector grew rapidly. In the early 1980s, the PSA was the largest organisation, with about 80 000 members. By 1999, there were nineteen unions in the public sector, representing more than 980 000 employees with a union density of 96 per cent. The PSA, with 186 000 members, was no longer the largest union as it had been overtaken by Sadtu with 204 500 members (Macun and Psoulis 2000: 101, 109).

Table 11.1 provides a breakdown of Cosatu public sector union membership at three-yearly intervals from 1991 to 2012. It shows that Cosatu's public sector union membership shot up more than ninefold between 1991 and 2000. This was mainly due to the phenomenal growth of Nehawu and Sadtu as well as the subsequent establishment of Denosa and Popcru in 1997. Thereafter, membership levelled off for six years, but started increasing again for the following six years.

In 2012, the seven Cosatu unions bargaining on the PSCBC had a total membership of 698 728. This constituted 59 per cent of the total membership of 1 184 728 of all the unions on the PSCBC, a clear majority (PSCBC 2012). Note that Samwu does not negotiate on the PSCBC.

Table 11.1: Cosatu public sector union membership, 1991–2012

	1991	1994	1997	2000	2003	2006	2009	2012
Denosa	n.a	n.a.	73 000	70 000	71 000	64 000	68 450	74 883
Nehawu	18 000	64 000	163 000	235 000	235 000	204 000	230 445	260 738
Pawusa	n.a	n.a.	n.a.	n.a.	n.a.	17 000	16 169	17 146
Popcru	n.a	n.a	45 000	71 000	67 000	96 000	125 732	149 339
Sadtu	n.a	59 000	146 000	219 000	215 000	224 000	236 843	251 276
Sama	n.a	n.a.	n.a.	n.a.	n.a.	5 000	7 246	7 759
Samwu	60 000	100 000	117 000	120 000	120 000	118 000	135 906	153 487
Sasawu	n.a	n.a.	n.a.	18 000	18 000	9 000	7 804	7 074
Total	**78 000**	**223 000**	**544 000**	**733 000**	**726 000**	**737 000**	**828 595**	**921 702**

Source: Cosatu (2012: 6)

The statistical analysis of public sector union members surveyed in 2014 revealed that public sector union members earned 31 per cent more on average than the private sector members surveyed, while their median income was 69 per cent higher. This could, in part, be due to the fact that the education level of public sector members is higher than that of private sector members – more than half (57 per cent) of public sector members have a university degree or technical diploma, while fewer than a quarter (24 per cent) of private sector members have attained that level of education. Although the overwhelming majority of both private and public sector union members surveyed enjoy full-time permanent jobs, a slightly higher proportion of public sector members have such posts (92 per cent as compared to 89 per cent of private sector union members). A smaller proportion of public sector members are migrant workers (25 per cent compared to 35 per cent of private sector members). Finally, a larger proportion of public sector members live in their own homes or flats (60 per cent as compared to 44 per cent of private sector members).

Collective bargaining outcomes in public services 1994–2014

Collective bargaining in the public service in South Africa after the political transformation in 1994 has been extremely eventful and filled with unprecedented action and record-breaking events. It commenced in 1996, when a three-year agreement was reached. The increase of wages in the first year was phenomenal: the lowest-paid Grade 1 workers received a 29.5 per cent increase, while Grade 2 to Grade 6 workers all received wage increases higher than 35 per cent. The 'rank and leg' system of promotion made the increases even larger than they appeared. This was because all employees on Grade 1 in 1996 were automatically advanced to Grade 2 whether or not they qualified under a performance review. In the following two years (1997 and 1998), the wage increases were at least as high as the rate of inflation (Adler 2000: 18).

Thereupon employment in the public service declined, with the lowest grades hardest hit. Overall employment during the same period (1996–1998) declined by more than 13 per cent (a loss of nearly 170 000 jobs), with the reduction of the Grades 1 to 5 workforce over 19 per cent. There was a simultaneous increase in jobs of over 7 per cent for the middle category (Grades 6 to 9). State employment fell to its lowest level of 1.125 million in 2001, after which it started increasing steadily (Van Rensburg 2014). In spite of the fall in employment, total personnel costs as a percentage of budget expenses over the three-year period increased from 46.6 per cent to 50.1 per cent, while the state's salary bill increased on average by 12.2 per cent per year. This increase was said to be 'crowding out' other state spending (Adler 2000: 22–23; Baskin 2000: 146).

The 1999 round of negotiations produced the first-ever legal strike of public service workers. With only slightly more than one percentage point separating the unions' demand from the government's offer (7.5 per cent demand and 6.3 per cent offer), a number of unions went on a legal strike. It was the first time that the radical unions and previously cautious staff associations had jointly engaged in industrial action. Leading ANC figures attacked public servants and their unions for being selfish, and on 7 September 1999 the ANC government unilaterally imposed and implemented its final offer (Adler 2000: 26–27). This demonstrated that there were still many unresolved issues in the collective bargaining relationship between the state and the unions representing its employees. In spite of that, collective bargaining in public services was relatively uneventful for the following seven years. A single-year agreement in 2000 was followed by two three-year agreements from 2001–2003 and 2004–2006. However, it was the three-year agreement negotiated in 2007 that highlighted the inadequacies and unresolved issues in public service collective bargaining as it unleashed the largest and most damaging strike up to that time in the country's history.

The strike lasted for twenty-eight days and caused the loss of an estimated 8.1 million working days (Department of Labour 2007: 38). The largest strike prior to this was the 1987 mineworkers' strike, with 7 million lost working days (Baskin 1991: 229–235). At the core of the strike was the dispute over wage increases. The public service unions opened negotiations with a demand for a 12 per cent increase, while the state's first offer was an overall average increase of 5.3 per cent. The state was reluctant to improve substantially on its offer, and so 700 000 public service employees went on strike. As the strike carried on, the state incrementally increased its offer to 6.5 per cent, then 7.25 per cent and finally to 7.5 per cent. The unions had hoped for higher increases, but had underestimated the state's resolve not to increase the public service wage bill excessively. Each one percentage point increased the cost to the state by an additional R1.8 billion (Bloch 2007; Hassen 2007a: 7–8). The education unions refused to sign the agreement, as they deemed the wage increase offered by the state to be too low. Other aspects of the agreement included a 1 per cent increase above inflation for the following year and the extension of medical and housing assistance to the bulk of public service employees (Hassen 2007b).

The 2007 strike was followed three years later by another major strike by public servants in 2010 that set a new record for working days lost in one year (see Figure 11.1).

According to Katherine Joynt and Mariane Tsoeu (2011: 9), the 2010 strike demands were an outflow of the 2007 strike settlement because the government had failed to act upon it. In the 2010 strike public servants had demanded a wage increase of 8.6 per cent. The government initially offered 7 per cent, which it increased by only 0.5 per cent during negotiations. A reason put forward for the low increase was that government coffers had been depleted by the Fifa World Cup (Ceruti 2011: 6). This fuelled the anger of poorly paid civil servants, as they considered the R110 million spent by ministers and department officials on World Cup tickets to be a misuse of the public purse (Joynt and Tsoeu 2011: 9). Shortly after the conclusion of the football World Cup, the public service strikes erupted and lasted for twenty days. The final settlement included an average wage increase of 7.5 per cent and an increase of 60 per cent in the housing allowance from R500 to R800 per month (Joynt and Tsoeu 2011: 10).

During both the 2007 and 2010 strikes, reports of intimidation, damage to property and the use of force and violence appeared in newspapers around the country, costing civil servants, especially nurses and teachers, considerable public and media support (Anon. 2007).

In spite of the limited gains made by civil servants during the 2007 and 2010 strikes, their increase in pay over the past sixteen years has been considerable, especially when taking into consideration the rise of more than 30 per cent they received in 1996. Since the PSCBC was established in 1998, entry-level wages in government have increased from R19 002 in 1998 to R67 806 in 2014. In real terms (adjusting for inflation) this constitutes a 110 per cent increase, more than a doubling of the lowest salaries. High (level 12) salaries increased even more, by 159 per cent over the same period, while government employment increased by 26 per cent from 1.22

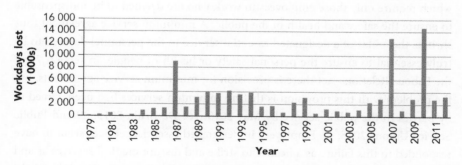

Sources: SAIRR (2012: 46) for 1979 to 2010; Department of Labour (2012: 6, Fig. 2) for 2011 and 2012

Figure 11.1:   Workdays lost due to strikes, 1979–2012

million to 1.54 million (Van Rensburg 2014). According to *Rapport*, this has raised the state's expenditure on civil servants' remuneration to around 40 per cent of total non-interest expenditure (Van Rooyen 2015).

POWER AND PERFORMANCE OF PUBLIC SECTOR UNIONS IN SOUTH AFRICA

Economic power of public sector unions

As has been shown above, public sector unions have managed to achieve massive increases in the wages and salaries of public service employees. The public sector unions also staged two strikes in 2007 and 2010 in which a record number of working hours were lost. Public sector unions are therefore very strong. Their striking power is so high because collective bargaining of all civil servants takes place centrally on the PSCBC. When the unions all go on strike, more than a million workers thus stop working, severely disrupting the economy and services to the public.

Public service strikes in South Africa harm the citizens more than their employers, the state. This is because when public service employees who provide direct services to the public, such as nurses and teachers, go out on strike, they remove care of the sick and hinder the education of the nation's children. Even though nursing has been declared an essential service under the Labour Relations Act, nurses still go on strike. When an occupation or sector has been declared an essential service, it is illegal for any employees in that occupation or sector to go out on strike – however, in many countries there is provision for minimum service agreements which require only those employees to work who are deemed to be indispensable to ensure the safety and health of the public. A minimum service agreement thus shrinks the ambit of a designated essential service to the personnel deemed to be truly essential to ensure the personal safety or health of people. In section 72 of the Labour Relations Act there is provision for minimum service agreements, but the problem with this provision is that no minimum services had been agreed to by parties in the public service by May 2015 (see De Bruin 2013: 29 and Public Service Unions 2015: 1). Employees in designated essential services seem to have responded to this failure as a licence to strike and disrupt medical services as and when they please. For instance, during the 2007 public services strike health workers, including people in essential jobs, trashed sterile operating theatres, damaged instruments and equipment, and stopped all operations and surgical procedures at Tygerberg Hospital (Esbach 2007).

Economic effect of bargaining power of public sector unions

The question arises of what the economic effects are of the bargaining power of public sector unions. Two economic consequences are briefly explored below: first, whether it has raised the remuneration of public servants above that of private sector employees, and second, whether it has increased the proportion of the Treasury budget spent exclusively on remunerating public servants.

Effect on earnings differentials between public and private sector employees

Regarding the first question, a finding from the data collected in the 2014 survey of Cosatu members was that, on average, public sector employees earned 31 per cent more than private sector employees, while the median income of public sector members was 69 per cent higher. The minimum earnings of the public sector employees was no less than two-and-three-quarter times higher than the minimum of private sector employees (see Table 10.8 in Chapter 10).

A South African Reserve Bank study in 2005 came up with a similar finding. It established that the median monthly wage of public sector employees was two-and-a-half times higher, at R5 000, compared to the R2 000 of private sector employees (Bosch 2006: 21, Table 3.2). But for both these studies there was no control for factors that could influence compensation (education, occupation, age, and so on). Correcting for this to some extent, the Reserve Bank study established that public sector remuneration was higher than that of private sector employees for all levels of schooling, from no schooling up to matric. However, for employees with degrees the median salary was higher in the private than the public sector, as well as for professionals and employees with vocational qualifications (Bosch 2006: 21, Table 3.2).

Ingrid Woolard, an economist at the University of Cape Town, carried out a more sophisticated study which came up with similar findings. Using the February 2000 Labour Force Survey of Statistics South Africa, she established that public sector median wages were higher at all levels of schooling up to matric, but private sector median wages were higher for degreed and vocationally qualified employees as well as professionals (Woolard 2002: 7, Table 1). By means of a regression analysis she also established that the wage premium was purely for working in the public sector. She concluded:

> The regressions show that, after controlling for education, age, location and occupation, public sector employees earn more than their private-sector

counterparts … Being employed in the public sector multiplies your earnings by a premium of about 18 per cent (Woolard 2002: 13).

Woolard does not attribute the wage premium to strong trade unions in the public
sector. She maintained that 'trade union membership slightly enhances earnings in
both the public and private sectors and by about the same amount' (Woolard 2002:
13). It is, however, not clear how reliable this is for public sector employees, as the
wage rates determined at the PSCBC are extended to all public sector employees
whether or not they are union members. The public sector wage premium could be
due to the public sector having rapidly and more thoroughly corrected the racial
wage differentials inherited from the apartheid era. This is borne out by the fact that
the wage premium for African public sector employees was found to be substantial,
while for their white counterparts it was almost insignificant. Woolard (2002: 13)
found that 'the average African public servant is earning 32 per cent more than his
equally experienced, equally qualified counterpart in the private sector.'

In other countries, earnings premiums for public servants are not uncommon,
nor are they universal. In Britain, the premium is much lower than in South Africa.
The UK Office for National Statistics (2014: 1) estimated that in April 2013, 'on average, the pay of the public sector was between 2.2 per cent and 3.1 per cent higher
after adjusting for the different jobs and personal characteristics of the workers'. In
addition, the average pay difference in favour of the public sector had narrowed
since 2010, which, in part, reflected the restraints on public sector pay.

In Canada, the premium of public servants is larger, but not as high as the South
African premium. Researchers at the Fraser Institute, using the Labour Force Survey for April 2011, established that

> [a]fter controlling for such factors as gender, age, marital status, education,
> tenure, size of firm, province, city, type of job, and industry, public sector
> workers (including federal, provincial, and local) enjoyed a 12.0 per cent
> wage premium, on average, over their private sector counterparts in Canada.
> When unionization status is factored in the analysis, the wage premium for
> the public sector declines to 9.5 per cent (Palacios and Clemens 2013: 5).

Therefore, trade unions in Canada lower the earnings premium of public servants
over private sector employees.

In the USA the situation appears to be reversed. There, according to one study,
public servants generally earn less than their private sector counterparts in the same
occupations. Keith Bender and John Heywood have estimated the average earnings

differentials for public servants at state and local government levels over the period 2000 to 2008. Their findings are:

> Wages and salaries of state and local employees are lower than those for private sector workers with comparable earnings determinants (e.g. education). State employees typically earn 11 per cent less; local workers earn 12 per cent less. Over the last twenty years, the earnings for state and local employees have generally declined relative to comparable private sector employees (Bender and Heywood 2010: 3).

This differential observed in the USA is not due to the power of trade unions in the private sector, because union density is considerably higher in the public sector than in the private sector. The proportion of contracts covered by unions over the 2000–2008 period was 38 per cent in the state sector, almost three times higher than the private sector, where it was only 13 per cent (Bender and Heywood 2010: 7, Table 1).

From the above it is clear that the public sector wage premium that exists in other countries cannot be attributed to the power of public sector trade unions. Yet this is not the same as the situation in South Africa, nor is it as clear. The massive increase in compensation that has been achieved through bargaining by the public sector unions from 1996 to 2014 is certainly due in part to their bargaining power on the PSCBC. However, it could also be due in part to a government that was committed to employment equity and keen to remove racist wage structures inherited from the apartheid era. This would explain why Woolard found that African public sector employees' wage premium was so high and that of white public sector employees almost insignificant.

Effect on proportion of the Treasury budget spent on remunerating public servants

On the other hand, the strong bargaining power of the public sector unions has resulted in the steady increase in the proportion of the Treasury budget spent exclusively on remunerating public servants. When social contributions and all other costs are added, it is known as the wage bill. The wage bill in 2012 amounted to R336 billion, which was 2.3 times more than the 1994 wage bill in real terms (that is, allowing for inflation). By the end of 2014, only two years later, it increased by another R104 billion to R440 billion. In real terms this constituted an 18 per cent increase from 2012 to 2014 (Harper 2014; StatsSA 2015). The wage bill makes up 35

Table 11.2:   Wage bill as percentage of expenditure by region (average 2000–2008)

	Central government	General government
Middle East and North Africa (n=12)	36	37
Latin America and Caribbean (n=27)	32	38
Sub-Saharan Africa (n=45)	27	32
OECD (n=24)	16	26
Eastern Europe and Central Asia (n=28)	18	26
East Asia and Pacific (n=10)	23	32
South Asia (n=8)	22	28

n = number of countries

Source: Based on Mills et al. (2011: 8, 10)

per cent to 40 per cent of total Treasury expenditure, according to different estimates. The *City Press* finding is that the wage bill constitutes 35 per cent of total expenditure for the whole budget, while the *Sunday Times* finding is that it is higher, at 40 per cent (see Harper 2014; Isa 2015). This is among the world's highest, if not the highest. Unfortunately, comparative figures for 2014 could not be found, but Table 11.2 provides supporting evidence for the period 2000–2008.

Table 11.2 shows that, for each of the major regions of the world, the average wage bill for both central and general government expenditure over the period 2000–2008 was below 40 per cent of total government expenditure. Moreover, in only two of the seven regions did it exceed 35 per cent, whereas in two of the regions it did not exceed 26 per cent.

Service delivery and performance of the public sector

The question arises whether the escalation in public servants' remuneration has been matched by an improvement in their service delivery to the public. The head of a constitutional advisory body, the Financial and Fiscal Commission (FFC), told the *Sunday Independent* that the government was not getting matching value for the growing wage bill. The warning was sounded that the public sector wage bill, which has consistently constituted the largest component of the government's expenditure, has the potential of undermining the state's fulfilment of its service delivery mandate (Sidimba 2014).

Although public service employees' earnings have more than doubled over the past decade, it is by no means clear that their performance has improved to the same extent, or even that it has improved at all. There is an abundance of anecdotal evidence that public services have not improved over the past decade or more. A Treasury survey in 2014 found that there was 'little evidence of a corresponding improvement in service delivery' (Rose 2015). Research by the Public Sector Accountability Monitor at Rhodes University found that public services were too poor to justify wage increases (Brand-Jonker 2014).

It was reported by the *Sunday Independent* in July 2014 that the Public Service Commission (PSC) and the FFC were jointly conducting research on the link between performance in the public sector and the government's wage bill (Sidimba 2014). At the time of writing (May 2015) there has been no indication what stage that research has reached. Nothing has as yet been released to the public. What is clear, however, is that there is at least one Cosatu public sector union, Sadtu, that has consistently opposed linking remuneration of teachers with their performance. It also does not hesitate to act to the detriment of learners in pursuit of its own members' interests.

Sadtu's performance

Sadtu's general approach is always to support increases of teachers' remuneration regardless of their performance. It also fights hard for the improvement of teachers' working conditions and any additional training to enhance their skills. The union holds that poor working conditions and low pay demotivates teachers and hence, by implication, they perform badly. In this regard Sadtu looks well after its members' interests. On the other hand, Sadtu firmly opposes linking teachers' remuneration to their performance at school as measured by how their students are performing (Sadtu Secretariat 2009). It is against the annual evaluation of pupils in Grades 3, 6 and 9 on the grounds that it takes time away from teaching (Maregele 2013). The union has also resisted the testing of teachers to mark final-year (matric) exam papers to ensure that only competent teachers mark papers. It also opposes biometric registration of the arrival and departure times at school as a way of countering absenteeism on the part of teachers (Masondo 2015b; Motshekga 2014). In short, Sadtu opposes a range of measures that would improve teachers' effectiveness in raising their pupils' performance.

Sadtu came out against the 2009 findings of the National Education Evaluation and Development Unit (Needu) report that recommended minimum performance standards for schools. These standards were to be set while bearing schools' different histories and capacities in mind. The schools' performance was to be tracked by means of a sophisticated monitoring and evaluation system (Needu 2009: 68–69). Sadtu's response was to state that 'the report is concerned with measuring outputs, rather than improving inputs into the teaching and learning system'. It went on to state: '... the main concern of the report is with monitoring and evaluation to hold the teachers to account. Development must take place elsewhere' (Sadtu Secretariat 2009).

In 2009 the Western Cape government announced a new ten-year plan for education that would require teachers and principals to sign performance contracts. This was to combat the increased number of failing schools with diminished literacy and numeracy levels. By introducing the contracts, the provincial government would be able to hold teachers, principals and schools accountable for achieving targets. It has been established by research conducted at the University of Stellenbosch that incentives to teachers who produce good results do help pupils' academic performance. Researchers at the Socio-economic Policy Unit of the university analysed studies conducted in India, Brazil, Chile, Israel, Kenya and North Carolina, USA, and found that the mere existence of a bonus system tended to improve the performance of teachers and their students. They established that schools in which teachers spent a larger proportion of time on instruction had a much greater likelihood of achieving bonuses based on performance. The researchers also found that an incentive system could push lazy and unmotivated teachers to do well and could help identify poorly trained and weak teachers (Anon. 2015). Sadtu, nonetheless, opposed the plan, maintaining that any change to the conditions of employment for teachers would have to be negotiated nationally (Mtyala 2009).

Over the past two years far more serious allegations have been made against Sadtu members and officials. Sadtu officials and members have proactively taken steps that undermine and weaken the quality of school education in South Africa. A Needu report in 2013 that was suppressed for two years stated that Sadtu wielded its power over human resource departments to have unqualified teachers appointed to positions of authority, thereby undermining efforts to provide quality education to schoolchildren. Furthermore, it found that, because of Sadtu meddling, senior teachers such as heads of department and principals were promoted to positions in district and provincial offices without demonstrating the requisite level of knowledge or management skills. These findings were widespread. Needu evaluators who visited right across the country were informed that this was happening in more than 50 per cent of the provincial and district offices. The report pointed out that, once made, inappropriate appointments retarded development for many years and even decades (Jansen 2015).

But worse was still to come. In April 2014 the *City Press* claimed that it '... can reveal that plum posts, including those of principal and deputy principal, are routinely sold for upwards of R30 000 each in KwaZulu-Natal' by Sadtu members.

Investigations of similar rackets in Limpopo and North West provinces were also under way (Harper and Masondo 2014a). A week later *City Press* revealed that this corruption was far more widespread than it had reported initially, and there was a flood of tip-offs from teachers in Gauteng, Mpumalanga and Free State (Harper and Masondo 2014b) and that 'in at least two cases sitting principals were violently forced out of their posts and threatened with death' by Sadtu members (Harper 2014).

Sadtu vehemently denied that it was engaged in the selling of posts and in death threats. The general secretary of Sadtu, Mugwena Maluleke, took strong exception to *City Press*. He did not deny that it was happening, but claimed that individuals had done so in their personal capacities (Maluleke 2014).

Six months later, in November 2014, *City Press* again reported two more well-documented cases of Sadtu pressure to have weaker-qualified Sadtu members appointed to teaching posts. In one case, the headmaster of the school said that their lives and those of their families would be in danger if they did not do so (Masondo 2014).

A year later, an investigation commissioned by the minister of basic education released its initial findings. The investigation team of ten was headed by Professor John Volmink. Its findings confirmed not only what *City Press* had revealed a year before, but also that the malpractices were more widespread than the newspaper had reported. The investigation found that 'not only is education in KwaZulu-Natal being run by rogue union members, but Sadtu members have been found to have violated the system in the provincial education departments of Gauteng, North West, the Eastern Cape, Mpumalanga and Limpopo' (Masondo 2015a).

Numerous other allegations were uncovered by the investigation. Evidence showed that a number of senior Sadtu members in the Eastern Cape received cows, sheep and goats as payment for several principals' positions throughout the province. The very serious finding was made that Sadtu officials were demanding that union members be appointed to thirty-seven chief education specialist posts. When the positions were initially advertised, the prerequisite for candidates was a degree. 'But because most of Sadtu's favoured candidates did not have degrees, the advertisement was withdrawn and the requirements were amended to a diploma' (Masondo 2015a).

The National Executive Committee (NEC) of Sadtu released a statement condemning the sale of jobs for teachers 'in strongest terms and made it clear that the union never sanctioned such' (Sadtu 2015). At the same time it implicitly acknowledged that Sadtu members and officials were complicit: 'Sadtu will also not allow those who are benefiting from this barbaric and counter-revolutionary practice to damage the image and reputation of the union. The union will root out all those union members who will be fingered by the Volmink Enquiry' (Sadtu 2015). But instead of proceeding to act against leaders of the union who had been identified and named in a letter to him, the Sadtu general secretary denied that he had been provided with their names (Masondo and Harper 2015).

The final Volmink Report to the minister of basic education was submitted in May 2016. Although it was the final report, part of it was embargoed as a forensic investigation was still under way. In addition, the names of persons dealing with allegations of irregular appointments of educators at schools were expunged because the forensic investigations were still ongoing (Volmink et al. 2016: 46, 197).

The report confirmed its initial finding that Sadtu had effectively taken control of basic education in six of the nine provinces in the country. It presented its findings exhaustively and unambiguously as follows:

> The Department of Basic Education has retained semblances of managerial and administrative control in three of South Africa's nine provinces. These are the Free State, the Western Cape and the Northern Cape. In all other provinces, Sadtu is in de facto control. According to the data given to and gathered by the Task Team, this domination by a union has been achieved by using combinations of the following ways and means:
> - By being an industrial and adversarial trade union;
> - By means of its incorporation of office-based educators as members;
> - Its use of a repertoire of strategies to coerce teachers, principals, officials and others to accede to its demands;
> - By using teacher militancy to pressurise its members to be unionists first and professionals second;
> - By practising cadre deployment to ensure that high percentages of managers, decision-makers and others with power and influence in education are placed in well-paid positions where they can prioritise the union's interests;
> - By using undue influence at different stages of the appointments process to ensure that its candidates are appointed (Volmink et al. 2016: 119).

Evidence in support of these statements is provided for the North West Province, where the task team found that 'more than 85 per cent of the senior staff in the Department [of Education] have been deployed there by Sadtu after having served as union office-bearers ... These individuals have been rewarded for service to the union with well-paid jobs in the Department whether there is a vacancy or not and/ or whether the individual has appropriate skills and qualifications or not' (Volmink et al. 2016: 82, 106).

Sadtu was given the opportunity to respond to the report in writing and did so in a twenty-three page annexure. In its response, Sadtu acknowledges that the selling of posts is extensive:

> The practice of selling posts whether through the exchange of money or other favours such as sexual favours is widespread though under-reported. The under-reporting can be attributed to the fact that the sellers and buyers of posts operate in high secrecy and, in certain instances, accompanied by intimidation or threats of intimidation (Volmink et al. 2016: 241).

Sadtu continued to state emphatically that it does not condone or encourage the selling of posts. Furthermore, 'whenever information came to Sadtu's attention regarding such practices, it took steps to deal with matters raised, for example, the allegation relating to Kalfontein Primary School in 2006, in which Sadtu reported the matter to the Gauteng Department of Education for investigation and appropriate action' (Volmink et al. 2016: 241). The problem is compounded by the fact that there is usually no prosecution after such an investigation. For instance, in 2014 the Gauteng Department of Education (GDE) appointed a firm of attorneys to investigate claims made by the *City Press* that posts were being sold for cash. The investigation found that this was indeed the case, but that there was a climate of fear that prevailed. 'The GDE then moved to take disciplinary action, but the majority of witnesses did not wish to give signed statements' (Volmink et al. 2016: 20–21).

In the words of the Volmink Report, 'Sadtu is highly conscious of the negative public image it has been given over the matter of buying and selling posts' (Volmink et al. 2016: 105). It therefore defends itself aggressively against the Volmink Report's findings. Its two most frequently used criticisms of the report are that it has not produced any hard evidence or a single witness against Sadtu and that the Ministerial Task Team (MTT) was conducting investigations outside its term of reference (Volmink et al. 2016: 243–244, 245, 247, 250, 251, 252). It also asserts that the MTT was biased against Sadtu (Volmink et al. 2016: 242). It goes as far as to say that the MTT 'was hell-bent to condemning Sadtu in its investigation and findings', that 'it has a closed mind when it comes to Sadtu', and that it was out 'to tarnish Sadtu' (Volmink et al. 2016: 244, 248, 249).

Regarding the lack of evidence, it is disingenuous of Sadtu to claim the MTT has not produced evidence or witnesses when there are acts of intimidation and threats – even death threats – made to people who do speak up against Sadtu. As for bias against Sadtu, in one after the other newspaper report individuals have pointed the finger at Sadtu, as did many of the people interviewed by the MTT. Finally, the criticism that the MTT examined issues beyond its term of reference points to defensiveness, denialism, and unwillingness on the part of Sadtu to take responsibility for either causing or fixing the malpractices. The MTT was essentially exploring ways of putting an end to the malpractice of appointing inappropriate and incompetent people into teaching and other education posts in a desperate effort to improve the standard of education at most schools in South Africa. But Sadtu would have none of it (see also Paton 2016).

On top of all of this is Sadtu's propensity to strike. It participated in the August 2010 national strike by public service unions. The Sadtu NEC released a statement beforehand that the union had taken a unanimous decision that it would embark on a full-scale indefinite strike over wages with a total shutdown. Sadtu demanded an 8.6 per cent wage increase, while the state offer was standing at 7.0 per cent. Sadtu was therefore engaging in a national strike over a 1.6 per cent salary adjustment (Sadtu 2010a). The final settlement was a 7.5 per cent increase, only an 0.5 per cent increase on what the state was already offering.

Sadtu has repeatedly shown itself willing and ready to strike, even at a critical time such as when students are preparing to write their matric (final-year) exams. For instance, in September 2013, 60 000 Sadtu members in KwaZulu-Natal went on a strike that disrupted the crucial matric trial examinations. The reasons advanced for the strike were unpaid strike pay, unfilled posts, and the province's failure to implement grade adjustments since 2009. At the commencement of the strike Sadtu announced that it intended to go on an indefinite 'work to rule' and to disrupt examinations (Anon. 2013).

But Sadtu had gone even further and persuaded pupils at schools to join them in their protest action. Earlier in the year, during April 2013, Sadtu had gone on a national strike over the withdrawal of collective bargaining agreements by the Department of Basic Education. In Cape Town, hundreds of pupils joined several thousand teachers in a march to Parliament to present their demands. Most of the pupils wore Sadtu T-shirts (Mtyala 2013).

Columnists and reporters who commented about the national strike in April 2013 pointed out that it was essentially children from schools in townships and rural areas who bore the brunt of the Sadtu strike. The Department of Education's spokesman, Panyaza Lesufi, said that 'learners who were affected are exclusively children from poor communities' (HSRC Press 2013). These learners are already enormously disadvantaged compared to those at former Model C schools. According to the minister of basic education, Angie Motshekga, 'Teachers in former African schools teach an average of 3.5 hours a day compared with 6.5 hours a day for former Model C schools. This amounts to a difference of three years of schooling' (Mahlangu and

Prince 2016). The minister also pointed out that a study in North West Province found that teachers taught only 40 per cent of scheduled lessons, while a national study by the Human Sciences Research Council in 2010 found that almost 20 per cent of teachers were absent on Mondays and Fridays (Mahlangu and Prince 2016).

Gwede Mantashe, the ANC general secretary, made a blistering attack on Sadtu while it was still threatening to strike. He accused Sadtu of 'sabotaging education' and intimated that Sadtu did not care about the education of black children. In response, Mugwena Maluleke said that 'our members are very angry with Mantashe's attitude. We can expect a very huge, huge strike because of the attitude towards our members' (Moshoeshoe and Macupe 2013).

In spite of the negative perceptions Sadtu generates in the public's mind and the damning findings of the Volmink Report, Sadtu has persisted in resisting measures taken by educational authorities to improve the quality of basic education. In September 2016 it vowed that it would boycott the systemic tests to be conducted at Western Cape schools the following month, advancing numerous reasons, some of which are far-fetched, for their opposition to the tests. Their most trenchant reasons are that the tests make the teachers look like failures, give them extra work, and do not assist them in any way (Malgas 2016; GroundUp 2016). The systemic tests are language and mathematics tests conducted every year by the Western Cape Education Department (WCED). Each learner in Grades 3, 6 and 9 has to take the test. The objective of the tests, according to the department, is to identify schools that need support and to assist them. The annual tests help the department to track progress, set annual targets, inform teacher training and support, and evaluate the impact of its interventions (Shelver 2016). The department claims the programme has been a success, as Grade 3 pass rates had risen from 47.5 per cent in 2011 to 57.6 per cent in 2015, Grade 6 pass rates from 23.4 per cent to 37.6 per cent, and Grade 9 pass rates from 10.4 per cent to 22.2 per cent (Damba-Hendrik 2016).

But Sadtu went beyond just boycotting the tests. It disrupted primary schools where the tests were being written and used students from high schools to do the disruption for them. In order to do so, Sadtu in Khayelitsha invited the Congress of South African Students (Cosas) to a meetings where it was decided that no school should write the systemic tests. The two organisations then took action to stop the tests from being written. An example of the disruption is one that happened on Thursday morning, 13 October 2016, when a group of learners from Bulumko and Joe Slovo senior secondary schools in Khayelitsha, accompanied by members of Sadtu, entered Injongo Primary School to stop the systemic tests which learners were writing. According to one of the learners, a Cosas Provincial Executive Committee member, the headmaster called police and 'in no time, there were parents armed with whips. They chased us, beating us.' She tried to explain to the principal, from whom she tried to grab the test papers, that 'we are doing what our teachers have asked us to do' (Damba-Hendrik 2016).

The WCED was forced to get a court interdict against Sadtu and Cosas, as 10 per cent (146 out of 1 473) of the schools could not write or complete the tests because of the disruptions. The Western Cape Division of the High Court of South Africa issued an order instructing Sadtu and Cosas to inform their members not to disrupt systemic tests commissioned by the WCED (Shelver 2016). Sadtu in the Western Cape claimed to welcome the order issued by the high court (Rustin 2016). Its provincial secretary went as far to say, 'We condemn the use of violence in the strongest terms' (Nkalane 2016). However, a mere two days after the court order was issued, Sadtu members disrupted tests being written at St Helena Bay Primary, Masiphathisane Primary and Diazville Primary (Herman 2016).

In its constitution Sadtu lists the following objectives: 'to promote and further the interests of its members' (clause 6.3); 'to promote and maintain high standards of ethical conduct, professional integrity and efficiency in the promotion and maintenance of standards of teaching and learning' (clause 6.10); and 'to encourage the development of the aesthetic aspects of the learner's life and to help promote his or her educational, spiritual and physical development' (Sadtu 2010b). Except for promoting and furthering the interests of its members as it sees fit, it is not living up to the goals it has set itself. It is not maintaining high ethical standards nor doing its best to promote learners' educational development. Instead, it seems to be doing its best not to promote teachers and learners' educational development.

The political rupture Cosatu has experienced over its support for the Tripartite Alliance and the expulsion of Vavi reverberated in Sadtu as well. The fallout is discussed next.

Expulsion of Sadtu president and the formation of a new public service trade union

In August 2013, Sadtu's NEC suspended its president, Thobile Ntola, for allowing the general secretary of Cosatu, Zwelinzima Vavi, a platform to address Sadtu members at a regional meeting to apologise for his sexual indiscretions (for having an affair with a junior female colleague). Furthermore, Sadtu was furious with Ntola for publicly commenting that Vavi's apology had been accepted by the teacher union's Eastern Cape region (eNCA 2013). Ntola was described as a 'staunch' Vavi supporter.

Ntola attracted such condemnation from his own trade union because at the time Vavi was under suspension within Cosatu. Sadtu's NEC subsequently dismissed Ntola in May 2014. He accused Cosatu of a political conspiracy to silence him (eNCA 2014). Sadtu's deputy general secretary responded by claiming that the dismissal of Ntola was not linked to the Vavi saga and that Ntola had been charged with misconduct relating allegedly to his 'inappropriate relationship' with a service provider. Ntola publicly denied the allegations, claiming his innocence and contending that he was being targeted by the members of the NEC and that the real reason was the tension in the federation over the suspension of Vavi (Makhafola 2014). Vavi was briefly reinstated as general secretary only to be finally expelled as general secretary of Cosatu at a special CEC meeting convened from 30 to 31 March 2015. Sadtu's Eastern Cape region challenged Sadtu NEC's actions and demanded that Ntola be reinstated.

The expulsion of Ntola is revealing of the pressures in Cosatu and among and even within its affiliates for a number of reasons. The expulsion of Ntola, and Vavi's court case, exposed the deep divisions within Cosatu. The expulsion of Vavi revealed the rivalry between the factions within some of the affiliates – between those who called for Vavi to be ousted and those who are allies of Vavi and the affiliate or affiliate leader who supports him. This could possibly be linked to the political tensions within Cosatu whether to support, or not to support, the ANC and the SACP. In this regard it does not seem as if Sadtu is an outlier in Cosatu, at least not as far as its shop stewards are concerned. In an extensive survey of Cosatu shop stewards conducted in 2012, it was found that Sadtu shop stewards' support for the ANC and the SACP was within the same range as for all the other Cosatu unions – in fact, it was almost in the median position of the unions' support for the ANC and the SACP. In response to the question 'Which political party or parties do you support?', 82 per cent of Sadtu shop stewards said they supported the ANC and 13 per cent that they supported the SACP (Case 2013: 81, Figure 55). Support for the ANC among Cosatu unions, excluding one outlier, ranged from 73 per cent to 93 per cent, and for the SACP from 2 per cent to 17 per cent. The outlier was Pawusa, where only 64 per cent of shop stewards support the ANC, while 16 per cent support the DA.

In December 2014, Ntola, along with what is described as other 'disgruntled' unionists, have now collaborated to form a rival public service trade union to take on the other public sector affiliates in Cosatu. Ntola has made it clear that the new union will not be aligned to any political party and that it does not care who workers vote for in the elections. The new public service trade union is called the South African Public Service Union, and it aspires to target over 1.3 million public servants, covering those in education, health, the judiciary, safety, security, defence and local government, and administrators, social workers and general workers. The new union will negotiate for a basic minimum wage for workers in the public sector (Dlamini 2014). The focus on the minimum wage is necessary, according to Ntola, as he feels that 'workers in the public sector need a united voice and those leaders who had been assigned to them had failed workers by joining the government. History tells us that most of the leaders, especially in the federation in the public sector, ultimately land in bureaucracy or parliament ... They think if I am unable to improve the minimum wage for the workers, let me improve the minimum wage for myself' (Dlamini 2014).

CONCLUSION

This chapter has focused on Cosatu's public sector unions in view of their growing importance within Cosatu. By 2012 four of the seven largest unions were located in the public sector (Nehawu, Sadtu, Samwu and Popcru) and 39 per cent of all Cosatu members worked in the public sector.

In order to place the analysis of the unions in a broader context, the South African public sector collective bargaining institutions and the outcome of bargaining within the sector since 1994 were presented first. The main features are that there are four sectoral bargaining councils and a single coordinating bargaining council, the PSCBC. Collective bargaining is highly centralised and takes place in the PSCBC between the state and all public service employees. This has given the unions considerable bargaining power, with the result that public servants' earnings have increased remarkably since the PSCBC was established in 1998. The question is, then, whether the increase in earnings of public servants achieved by the public sector unions where Cosatu unions played a leading role has been matched by improved performance of public servants. No such evidence has been found. A case study of one public sector union, Sadtu, was thus presented. The finding is that instead of improving the performance of teachers, thereby lifting the low standard of education in South Africa's poorest schools, Sadtu and its members have consistently adopted policies and taken action that has led to the further deterioration of education in these schools. This not only affects education negatively, but also seriously undermines school-leavers' ability to find employment and potentially condemns them to lifelong poverty.

While it is commendable that public sector employees are well remunerated and that Cosatu public sector unions have played a role in this achievement as well as in facilitating the successful achievement of racial redress in the public sector, it is equally disturbing that there is no evidence that this has resulted in improvement of performance of public servants. The performance of Sadtu, which has systematically opposed measures that could improve teachers' performance in the country's poorest schools and whose rogue members are illegitimately undermining the quality of school education, can only be condemned in the strongest terms and requires urgent intervention.

BIBLIOGRAPHY

Adair, Barbara and Sue Albertyn. 2000. Collective bargaining in the South African public sector: The emergence of sector based bargaining. *Industrial Law Journal* 21: 813–829.
Adler, Glenn. 2000. The neglected role of labour relations in the South African public service. In *Public Service Labour Relations in a Democratic South Africa*, edited by Glenn Adler. Johannesburg: Wits University Press.
Anon. 2007. Editorial: Unions, stop the thuggery. *Sunday Times*, 10 June.
Anon. 2013. MEC, Sadtu in talks as strike disrupts matric trial exams. *City Press*, 2 September. http://www.news24.com/Archives/City-Press/MEC-Sadtu-in-talks-as-strike-disrupts-matric-trial-exams-20150430 (accessed 11 May 2015).
Anon. 2015. Carrots not apples for teachers. *City Press*, 22 February. http://www.news24.com/Archives/City-Press/Carrots-not-apples-for-teachers-20150429 (accessed 29 November 2016).
Baskin, Jeremy. 1991. *Striking Back: A History of Cosatu*. Braamfontein: Ravan.
Baskin, Jeremy. 2000. Public service bargaining: An assessment of the three-year wage agreement. In *Public Service Labour Relations in a Democratic South Africa*, edited by Glenn Adler. Johannesburg: Wits University Press.
Bender, Keith and John Heywood. 2010. *Out of Balance? Comparing Public and Private Sector Compensation over 20 Years*. Washington, DC: National Institute on Retirement Security. http://www.mnpera.org/vertical/Sites/%7BCB6D4845-437C-4F52-969E-51305385F40B%7D/uploads/%7BDBA0E14A-9DD0-49C3-8B6B-B1C3F-756F1A2%7D.PDF (accessed 17 May 2015).
Bloch, Graeme. 2007. Let strike teach us, for children's sake. *Business Day*, 12 July.
Bosch, Adél. 2006. Determinants of public and private sector wages in South Africa. South African Reserve Bank, *Labour Market Frontiers* 8 (October): 17–24. https://www.resbank.co.za/Lists/News%20and%20Publications/Attachments/345/Determinants%20of%20public%20and%20private-sector%20wages%20in%20SA.pdf (accessed 17 May 2015).
Brand-Jonker, Nellie. 2014. 15 per cent dalk die laaste strooi [15 per cent possibly the last straw]. *Rapport*, 5 October.
Ceruti, Claire. 2011. 2007 and 2010 public sector strikes: Maturing contradictions. *South African Labour Bulletin* 35(1): 6–8.
Community Agency for Social Enquiry (Case). 2013. *Cosatu Shop Steward Survey Findings Report*. Commissioned by the Forum for Public Dialogue (FPD). Braamfontein: Case.
Congress of South African Trade Unions (Cosatu). 2012. *11th Cosatu Congress Secretariat Report: 2nd Draft for Internal Circulation 24th August 2012*. Johannesburg: Cosatu.
Damba-Hendrik, Nombulelo. 2016. Violence as Sadtu disputes tests in Khayelitsha. *GroundUp*, 17 October. www.groundup.org.za/article/violence-sadtu-disrupts-tests-khayelitsha (accessed 3 November 2016).

De Bruin, Frikkie. 2013. Essential services: The implication of a minimum service agreement for the public service. Presentation to Third Biennial Labour Relations Conference, Centurion, 22–24 October.

Department of Labour. 2007. *Annual Industrial Action Report*. Pretoria: Department of Labour.

Department of Labour. 2012. *Annual Industrial Action Report*. Pretoria: Department of Labour.

Dlamini, Penwell. 2014. Ex-Sadtu chief to lead new union. *TimesLive*, 5 December. http://www.timeslive.co.za/thetimes/2014/12/05/ex-sadtu-chief-to-lead-new-union (accessed 29 November 2016).

Donnelly, Lynley. 2015. Nene hits public sector pay. *Mail & Guardian*, 27 February. http://mg.co.za/article/2015-02-27-nene-hits-public-sector-pay (accessed 31 May 2015).

Du Toit, Jacqueline. 2005. Employee relations in the public service of three southern African countries: South Africa, Namibia and Botswana. Master's dissertation, University of Cape Town.

eNCA. 2013. Tensions brew in Tripartite Alliance. *eNCA.com*, 26 October. http://www.enca.com/south-africa/tensions-brew-tripartite-alliance (accessed 29 November 2016).

eNCA. 2014. Sadtu president expelled. *eNCA.com*, 19 May. https://www.enca.com/sadtu-president-expelled (accessed 29 November 2016).

Esbach, Bronwynne. 2007. Strikers trash operating theatres at Tygerberg. *Saturday Weekend Argus*, 9 June.

Harper, Paddy. 2014. The case of two kidnapped principals. *City Press*, 11 May.

Harper, Paddy and Sipho Masondo. 2014a. How Sadtu sells its posts. *City Press*, 27 April.

Harper, Paddy and Sipho Masondo. 2014b. More jobs for sale in Sadtu racket. *City Press*, 4 May.

Hassen, Ebrahim-Khalil. 2007a. Interpreting the public service strike. *South African Labour Bulletin* 31(3): 7–8.

Hassen, Ebrahim-Khalil. 2007b. Public service strike: What was finally agreed? *South African Labour Bulletin* 31(4): 10.

Herman, Paul. 2016. Protestors disrupt tests at three West Coast schools. *News24*, 29 October. http://www.news24.com/SouthAfrica/News/protestors-disrupt-tests-at-three-west-coast-schools-20161029 (accessed 3 November 2016).

HSRC Press. 2013. Pupils join teachers for Sadtu strike over withdrawal of collective bargaining agreements. *BooksLive*, 26 April. http://hsrcpress.bookslive.co.za/blog/2013/04/26/pupils-join-teachers-for-sadtu-strike-over-withdrawal-of-collective-bargaining-agreements/ (accessed 11 May 2015).

Isa, Mariam. 2015. Pay-hike battle a threat to SA finances. *Sunday Times*, 1 March.

Jansen, Leanne. 2015. Unions wield power over schools. *Sunday Independent*, 19 April.

Joynt, Katherine, and Mariane Tsoeu. 2011. Public sector strike: Was it successful? *South African Labour Bulletin* 35(1): 9–11.

Macun, Ian and Christine Psoulis. 2000. Unions inside the state. In *Public Service Labour Relations in a Democratic South Africa*, edited by Glenn Adler. Johannesburg: Wits University Press.

Mahlangu, Dominic and Chandré Prince. 2016. Angie reads riot act. *City Press*, 24 January.

Makhafola, Gertrude. 2014. Ntola caused divisions – Sadtu. *IOL*, 21 May. http://www.iol.co.za/news/politics/ntola-caused-divisions---sadtu-1691777 (accessed 29 November 2016).

Malgas, Natalie. 2016. WC Sadtu to challenge systematic testing. *EWN*, 12 September. http://ewn.co.za/2016/09/12/WC-Sadtu-to-challenge-systematic-testing (accessed 3 November 2016).

Maluleke, Mugwena. 2014. Sadtu: We're not to blame. Interview with Sadtu General Secretary Mugwena Maluleke. *City Press*, 11 May.

Maregele, Barbara. 2013. Teachers' union wants evaluations scrapped. *Cape Times*, 15 January.

Masondo, Sipho. 2014. Sadtu still giving jobs to pals. *City Press*, 2 November.

Masondo, Sipho. 2015a. Sadtu still selling posts. *City Press*, 17 May.

Masondo, Sipho. 2015b. Education is held hostage by the Sadtu mafia. *City Press*, 24 May.

Masondo, Sipho and Paddy Harper. 2015. How Sadtu boss lied. *City Press*, 24 May.

Mills, Zac, with Sudyumna Dahal, Colum Garrity and Nick Manning. 2011. *Wage Bill and Pay Compression Summary Note*. Washington, DC: PREM Public Sector & Governance Unit, World Bank. http://siteresources.worldbank.org/PUBLICSECTORANDGOV-ERNANCE/Resources/285741-1343934891414/WageBillandPayCompressionSumma-ryNote.pdf (accessed 17 May 2015).

Moshoeshoe, Monare and Bongekile Macupe. 2013. Sadtu sabotaging education – Mantashe. *Sunday Independent*, 10 March.

Motshekga, Angie. 2014. Sadtu does not rule. *City Press*, 13 October. http://www.news24.com/Archives/City-Press/Sadtu-does-not-rule-20150430 (accessed 29 November 2016).

Mtyala, Quinton. 2009. Sadtu slams plan for education in Cape. *IOL*, 25 November. http://www.iol.co.za/news/south-africa/sadtu-slams-plan-for-education-in-cape-1.465683?ot=inmsa.ArticlePrintPageLayout.ot (accessed 28 April 2015).

Mtyala, Quinton. 2013. Pupils join teachers in march to Parliament. *SowetanLive*, 25 April. http://www.sowetanlive.co.za/news/2013/04/25/pupils-join-teachers-in-march-to-parliament (accessed 11 May 2015).

National Education Evaluation and Development Unit (Needu). 2009. *Ministerial Committee on a National Education Evaluation and Development Unit Final Report*. Government Gazette Vol. 526, No. 32133, Pretoria, 17 April.

Nkalane, Michael. 2016. Teacher union slams test disruption. *Cape Times*, 20 October. http://www.iol.co.za/capetimes/teacher-union-slams-test-disruption-2082124 (accessed 3 November 2016).

Office for National Statistics (UK). 2014. *Public and Private Sector Earnings – March 2014*. http://www.ons.gov.uk/ons/dcp171776_355119.pdf (accessed 17 May 2015).

Palacios, Milagros and Jason Clemens. 2013. *Comparing Public and Private Sector Compensation in Canada*. Vancouver: Fraser Institute Studies in Labour Markets.

Patel, Imraan. 2000. Growing pains: Collective bargaining in the public service. In *Public Service Labour Relations in a Democratic South Africa*, edited by Glenn Adler. Johannesburg: Wits University Press.

Paton, Carol. 2016. SA schools under Sadtu dominion. *Business Day*, 20 January.

Public Service Coordinating Bargaining Council (PSCBC). 2012. PSCBC membership statistics as at 31 December 2012. http://www.pscbc.org.za/wp-content/uploads/Union-Audited-Membership-National-31-December-2012.pdf (accessed 29 May 2015).

Public Service Unions. 2015. *Report on Public Service Negotiations on Outstanding Issues and 2015/2016 Wage Demands*. http://www.sadtu.org.za/docs/pr/2015/update.pdf (accessed 3 April 2015).

Rose, Rob. 2015. It's the austerity, stupid! But just don't squeeze the fat cats. *Sunday Times*, 1 March.

Rustin, Jonavon. 2016. Protest against systemic tests is lawful – Sadtu. *Politicsweb*, 27 October. http://www.politicsweb.co.za/news-and-analysis/protest-against-systemic-tests-is-lawful--sadtu (accessed 3 November 2016).

South African Democratic Teachers' Union (Sadtu). 2010a. Sadtu embarks on an indefinite strike over wages. Press release, 17 August. http://www.sadtu.org.za/show.php?id=2461 (accessed 11 May 2015).

Sadtu. 2010b. South African Democratic Teachers' Union Constitution. https://groups.google.com/forum/#!topic/sadtu-political-education-forum/Y9Qf79v5wnc (accessed 31 May 2015).

Sadtu. 2015. We do not condone sale of teaching jobs – Sadtu NEC. *Politicsweb*, 25 May. http://www.politicsweb.co.za/politics/we-do-not-condone-sale-of-teaching-jobs--sadtu-nec (accessed 31 May 2015).

Sadtu Secretariat. 2009. Sadtu response to the Needu Report: Top heavy on evaluation, light on development. http://www.sadtu.org.za/show.php?id=2493 (accessed 27 April 2015).

Shelver, Jessica. 2016. High court orders Sadtu, Cosas, not to disrupt systemic tests. *Politicsweb*, 27 October. http://www.politicsweb.co.za/politics/high-court-orders-sadtu-cosas-not-to-disrupt-system (accessed 3 November 2016).

Sidimba, Loyiso. 2014. State's wage bill growing 'too fast' to be good value. *Sunday Independent*, 27 July.

South African Institute of Race Relations (SAIRR). 2012. *South Africa Survey 2012*. Johannesburg: SAIRR.

Statistics South Africa (StatsSA). 2015. *Consumer Price Index History from 1960*. Report No. P141. Pretoria: StatsSA. http://www.statssa.gov.za/publications/P0141/CPIHistory.pdf (accessed 4 May 2015).

Van Rensburg, Dewald. 2014. State gears up for wage war. *City Press*, 5 October.

Van Rooyen, Gerrit. 2015. Cosatu hou SA weer as gyselaar aan [Cosatu holding SA hostage again]. *Rapport*, 8 March.

Volmink, John et al. 2016. *Report of the Ministerial Task Team Appointed by Minister Angie Motshekga to Investigate Allegations into the Selling of Posts or Educators by Members of Teachers Unions and Departmental Officials in Provincial Education Departments*. Final report, 18 May. Pretoria: Department of Basic Education.

Woolard, Ingrid. 2002. *A Comparison of Wage Levels and Wage Inequality in the Public and Private Sectors, 1995 and 2000*. Working Paper 02/62, Development Policy Research Unit, University of Cape Town.

12

Labour Beyond Cosatu, Other Federations and Independent Unions

Andries Bezuidenhout

INTRODUCTION

For roughly four decades, starting with the formation of Cosatu in 1985, the South African labour landscape was dominated by this labour federation with, at its high point, the 2.2 million members of its affiliated trade unions. South African labour scholarship is also dominated by studies of the history of Cosatu, its leadership figures and its affiliated unions. This is, perhaps, not surprising, as the federation played an important role in the struggle against apartheid, and that phase of its history has been described as an example of social movement unionism (Von Holdt 2002; Webster 1988). The federation also wielded immense political influence owing to its mass base and because it was (and remains) in an alliance with the ANC as the ruling party. Cosatu, along with Fedusa with its 550 000 members and Nactu with approximately 300 000 members, represented organised labour in Nedlac.

Despite attempts by Fedusa and Nactu to merge, this landscape remained stable for twenty years. Two events fundamentally altered this stability. The first is the rise of Amcu, which gave Nactu a new lease on life, most probably also ending the possibility for unity with Fedusa. The second is the expulsion of Numsa from Cosatu, which opens up the future to a number of possibilities. Whether Cosatu will remain the dominant player is largely dependent on how the boundaries and spheres of influence are redrawn on this new labour landscape.

In addition to the three major players, and now Numsa as a potential fourth national player (at the time of writing Numsa was still in the process of setting up the South African Federation of Trade Unions (Saftu)), we should mention the increasingly active role played by the neo-nationalist Afrikaner trade union Solidariteit (or Solidarity, in English), along with its civil society arm AfriForum and a range of affiliated training institutions. Solidariteit is affiliated to the Confederation of South African Workers' Unions (Consawu), but is the only major union in this federation. It has been agitating to become a member of Nedlac, but up to now has not been successful in this.

Then there are a number of independent unions not affiliated to any labour federation. In terms of membership figures the most significant of these is probably the PSA. A number of new players have also emerged in the organising vacuums left by existing unions in sectors such as agriculture. One of the most intriguing examples of these is the Bawsi Agricultural Union of South Africa (Bawusa), led by the enigmatic Nosey Pieterse, which shot to notoriety at the time of agricultural strikes in the Western Cape at the end of 2012.

This chapter provides a brief historical map of the emergence of each of these groupings and how we got to this lay of the labour landscape. The terms economic, political, social movement and entrepreneurial unionism are used to frame the analysis. The chapter goes on to discuss in more depth the impact of recent events – the tectonic shifts caused by the emergence of Amcu and the expulsion of Numsa – on the potential for labour unity and the danger posed by further fragmentation of organised labour. Finally, the chapter speculates on possible future scenarios. The main focus in this chapter is on trade unions and political alliances, rather than organising strategies and ways in which members are organised, serviced and represented in their places of work, although the conclusion to the chapter briefly returns to these matters.

VARIATIONS OF UNIONISM

Trade unions are typically described as craft, general, industrial or company unions (see Bendix 1996: 167–170). When one considers the role trade unions play in terms of social and political engagement and the structuring of this in relation to political parties and movements (the focus of this chapter), a more useful classification would be the concepts economic, political and social movement unionism. To this list we would like to add entrepreneurial unionism. Each of these concepts has an etymology that can be traced to original formulations, revisions and reformulations. We do not have the space to trace each of these here, and therefore use a recent South African formulation by Devan Pillay (2013) as our point of departure. He argued that Cosatu had morphed from social movement unionism to political unionism after the transition to democracy. This argument is supported here in broad terms. However, the recent rupture does open up possibilities for a different configuration to emerge. More about this later. First, an outline of definitions:

(i) *Economic unionism* is sometimes referred to as collective bargaining unionism or business unionism (see Webster 1988). Pillay defines economic unions as

… independent unions which confine their activities to the workplace (and are market focussed). Their sole interest is the improvement of the working conditions of their members, and they may be highly institutionalised, usually conservative but at times militant (such as airline pilots' unions) – but only to use their monopoly power to defend their own narrow interests, whether or not they transgress the interests of other members of the working class (Pillay 2013: 13).

(ii) *Political unionism* adds to the representation of members a focus on what Pillay calls 'state-political struggle'. Such unions, however, are often 'closely allied or tied (and often subordinate) to a political party'. He elaborates:

Like business unionism, it is often hierarchically organised, with an oligarchic form of representative democracy (i.e. while regular elections are held for office-bearers, elected leaders operate with a high degree of autonomy from the membership). Leaders are usually senior party officials. Once political democracy is achieved, these unions offer strong support for their parties during elections, usually provide party funding, and sometimes having block votes in party congresses (Pillay 2013: 14; see also Buhlungu 2010: 11).

(iii) *Social movement unionism* is a highly contested concept and has led to a number of debates on how useful the concept is in the first place (see Moodie 2012; Seidman 2011). Karl von Holdt has argued that this form of trade unionism only emerges under very specific conditions. His definition:

Social movement unionism is embedded in a network of community and political alliances, and demonstrates a commitment to both internal and democratic
practices as well as to the broader democratic and socialist transformation of
authoritarian societies (Von Holdt 2002: 285).

This form of unionism therefore differs from political unionism insofar as the
union is not dominated by a political party and is internally democratic. According
to Von Holdt, the model is peculiar to authoritarian regimes in the global South.
However, a number of Northern scholars have convincingly drawn our attention to
this form of unionism emerging elsewhere as well (see Chun 2009; Clawson 2003;
Fantasia and Voss 2004). Pillay includes both the Southern and Northern models in
his definition and defines social movement unionism as

... by definition progressive, given their orientation towards progressive social
change in the interests of the broader working class. As such they draw on traditions of open Marxism as well as other participatory-democratic schools of
thought, such as syndicalism. Social movement unions can be divided into two
sub-types, the more reformist 'social justice' unions, typically found in the USA,
and the more explicitly anti-capitalist, or anti-systemic, type. The latter type is
often most robust during the phases of struggles for democracy, but, if allied to
a political party, tends to drift towards social justice or political unionism once
political power has been achieved (Pillay 2013: 15).

(iv) In our mapping of the changing South African labour landscape we have run
up against the limits of these three categories. Cosatu's organisational report
to its twelfth national congress makes a similar observation:

The South African labour market remains highly fragmented with 180 registered trade unions. There are also twenty-three registered trade union federations in the country ... The question that must be posed is, 'why are there so
many trade unions in the country yet only 27 per cent of the workforce is unionised?' A possible answer to this question is that the majority of these unions
are mere fly-by-night enterprises. They are not there to genuinely represent the
interests of their members, but the financial interests of their leaders. It is a
crude form of business unionism (Cosatu 2015: 5).

However, this 'crude form of business unionism' should be distinguished
from business unionism as a category. The term suggested in this chapter is

entrepreneurial unionism, which moves the focus from members to the interests of officials. At times the union may look like a social movement union
and may be characterised by leaders who make appeals to notions of social
justice or even socialism, but the internal practices of these unions do not
conform to basic standards of democratic representation and their finances
are not open to outside scrutiny or review by members. Such unions may be
run by Weberian charismatic leaders who mobilise around issues and, in setting up unions, accumulate personal wealth and benefit in terms of status and
national attention. Like the cults that form around such Weberian charismatic
leaders, these unions tend to be unstable and may decline rapidly once their
leaders are discredited or move on to other entrepreneurial activities. Such
unions may also be controlled by low-profile operators who move under the
radar of public scrutiny – the 'fly-by-night' unions Cosatu refers to.

THE LAY OF THE LAND

Fedusa

Fedusa was established in 1997, from a merger between the Federation of Organisations Representing Civil Employees (Force) and the much larger Federation of
South African Labour (Fedsal), which was formed in 1985, initially mainly representing skilled white employees, many of them in the civil service. Over time, its
affiliated unions attracted more black members, now a majority in Fedusa's affiliated
unions. Fedusa's members are mainly drawn from among 'technicians, administrative employees, pilots, flight engineers, general assistants, nurses, doctors, teachers
and other skilled and semi-skilled employees from both the public and private sector of the economy' (see http://www.fedusa.org.za/about).

At the end of 2014, Fedusa had twenty-one affiliates, of which the most prominent were most probably the Health and Other Services Personnel Trade Union of
South Africa (Hospersa), the United Associations of South Africa (Uasa) (which
organises mainly in the mining industry), the National Union of Leather and Allied
Workers (Nulaw), the South African Typographical Union (Satu) (which is one
of South Africa's oldest craft unions) and SAOU (a union for Afrikaans-language
teachers). These unions affiliated to Fedusa always maintained that they were politically independent and that involvement in politics would dilute unions' attention
to focusing on servicing their members and collective bargaining. Put differently,
and in the federation's own words:

> [A] growing number of employees from all walks of life felt the need for a much stronger, party-politically independent, non-racial and stable trade union federation with unions who can advance the interests of employees and of the economy of South Africa in an independent and responsible manner.

As such, Fedusa unions' collective bargaining strategies never took on the kind of mass protests that characterised the social movement tradition of Cosatu. Again, in the federation's own words:

> Although often not as vocal or militant as other unions, Fedusa unions tend to accomplish more through sophisticated strategic interventions in board-rooms ... Also, because Fedusa is not crippled by ideological and party-political ties, it can focus on its real mandate, namely workplace matters and issues that affect its members. For this reason Fedusa focuses its capacity and energy on national and international representation to effect real influence in policy and implementation.

Fedusa also does not follow Cosatu and Nactu's principle of 'one industry, one union', maintaining that competition between unions is a good thing. More individualistic in its approach to the economy, Fedusa's unions focus on individual representation and well-informed collective bargaining, rather than social and political campaigns. As such Fedusa is a good example of economic unionism.

Nactu

Nactu was formed out of a merger between the Council of Unions of South Africa (Cusa), the federation that initially had tasked Cyril Ramaphosa to form the National Union of Mineworkers (NUM) in 1982, and the Azanian Congress of Trade Unions (Azactu). Cusa agreed with Cosatu unions on principles of non-racialism, but had a strong commitment to black leadership, along the lines of the Pan Africanist Congress (PAC). Azactu came out of the Black Consciousness Movement. When NUM left Cusa in 1985 to form Cosatu with Fosatu and a number of community unions, Cusa and Azactu decided to form a new federation in 1986, later called Nactu.

Nactu's affiliated unions, the most prominent of which are probably the Building, Construction and Allied Workers' Union (Bcawu), the Media Workers Association of South Africa (Mwasa), the South African Chemical Workers' Union (Sacwu) and, more recently, Amcu, mostly compete directly with Cosatu's unions. The spectacular rise of Amcu on the platinum belt after 2012 has probably significantly boosted Nactu's membership figures. Although its website is silent on the issue, Nactu claims a membership of 350 000. The lack of audited figures is cited as one of the reasons unity talks with Fedusa faltered.

While loosely tied to the PAC and Azapo, and formally stating its commitment to the liberation struggle, Nactu never entered into a formal alliance with these fractions of the liberation movement, maintaining this position when they became political parties after 1994. In 1990, the federation affirmed its commitment to political non-alignment with a formal congress resolution.

Nactu explains its policy on political alliances on its website (http://www.nactu. org.za) as follows:

> Nactu believes that workers join unions because of the material condition at their workplaces not because of party political preferences. No workers should be denied trade union membership because of party political affiliation. In addition, Nactu at its 1990 Congress took a decision that Nactu office-bearers may not be office-bearers of political parties. This, however, does not bar Nactu office-bearers from belonging to political parties of their choice and participation in activities.

Because of this approach, Cosatu's commitment to its alliance with the ANC and the SACP consistently stood in the way of unity with Nactu. We would classify Nactu as an example of economic unionism, but with elements of political unionism. The federation, however, has been careful not to be subverted by the interests of political parties, and maintains an arm's-length relationship with the PAC, Azapo and its post-apartheid splinter offshoots.

Solidariteit

The trade union Solidarity, or Solidariteit in Afrikaans, emerged in post-apartheid South Africa from a depleted and all but bankrupt white Mynwerkersunie (Mine Workers Union). Originally founded in 1902 by English and Australian mineworkers, the union became one of the key organisations that represented the Afrikaner working class under apartheid. Along with the state and the mining industry, it was key in maintaining the occupational and wage colour bars that protected white workers against competition from their black counterparts. The Mynwerkersunie had a close relationship with the National Party under apartheid, which unravelled in 1985 at the time of the formation of both Cosatu and the Konserwatiewe Party (Conservative Party) (KP), an ultra-right splinter group from the National Party

(Boersema 2012; Visser 2006, 2008). The KP became the official opposition in Parliament in the dying days of apartheid. The Mynwerkersunie's Arrie Paulus became a KP member of Parliament and was ridiculed by the protest singer James Phillips for vile and racist statements made there.

Around the time of the transition to democracy, the Mynwerkersunie attempted to reinvent itself as a general union, incorporating Yster en Staal (Iron and Steel), another Afrikaner union, but its membership dwindled to less than a paltry 30 000 by the mid-1990s. It was held back by its tarnished image as an ultra right-wing union. In 1997, the university-educated Flip Buys took over as the union's chief executive officer and started a process of union renewal. In 2001, it was launched with its new name and started to take on the cases of Afrikaner members who felt that they had been unfairly treated through the implementation of the Employment Equity Act. Membership figures increased dramatically to 120 000 members, attracting a larger component of women and, surprisingly, a number of black members, up to the point that the NUM became concerned about rivalry from both Fedusa's Uasa as well as Solidariteit.

Along with claiming a language of minority rights through its own court challenges to elements of the employment equity programmes as well as its 'civil rights' organisation called AfriForum, Solidariteit started mobilising around notions of belonging and self-help, creating a fund, Helpende Hand (Helping Hand), that assisted poor Afrikaners, as well as its own technical training college and even a university called Academia. The language of instruction in these institutions is Afrikaans and the union took care to include black speakers of Afrikaans as beneficiaries in order to pre-empt allegations of racism (Boersema 2012). Nevertheless, while not exclusively white, these institutions predominantly benefit white Afrikaans-speaking members.

In classifying Solidariteit, one could argue that it started out as an example of economic unionism in the early 1900s, but soon morphed into political unionism under the leadership of Afrikaner nationalists. In post-apartheid South Africa it maintained elements of this, but its model of member representation also looked like Fedusa's approach to individual servicing of membership needs – Solidariteit opened call centres and even insurance schemes for members – which contains elements of both economic and entrepreneurial unionism, but most probably with a stronger emphasis on economic unionism. More recently, however, with its civil rights arm, AfriForum, one could argue that it shows an element of social movement unionism, even though some elements of this may not be all that progressive in the context of its history and the fact that its members were beneficiaries of apartheid.

PSA and others

The PSA claims to be the 'largest, politically non-affiliated, fully-representative union' in South Africa's public service. With a membership of 235 000, it is also one of South Africa's oldest employees' organisations. It represents public servants in the civil service and in state-owned enterprises, as well as public service pensioners. It pitches its approach to potential members as follows: 'The PSA is one of very few trade unions in South Africa which attends to the individual disputes of members free of charge. It has an impressive success rate in resolving workplace-related cases.' In addition to being a registered trade union, the PSA states on its website (https://www.psa.co.za/overview) that it operates as a registered Section 21 company, meaning that it is formally registered as a non-profit organisation.

The PSA is not affiliated to any national federation and maintains a politically neutral stance. It describes one of its objectives as 'tak[ing] such steps as are deemed necessary to secure and maintain cordial relations and the fullest measure of cooperation with the government and the general public in matters affecting the public service with a view to efficiency and economy combined with the well-being of those employed: Provided that the PSA shall not endeavour to secure advantages to members by the exercise of political or other undue influence'. The PSA is a clear example of economic unionism, with a strong focus on individual representation.

Bawusa

Bawusa, along with its charismatic leader Nosey Pieterse, rose to national prominence during the 2012 strike wave in the Western Cape agricultural sector, especially around the town De Doorns. Bawusa, oddly, was formed by Pieterse's employers' organisation, the Black Association for the Agricultural Sector (Bawsi). The union's name – Bawsi Agricultural Union of South Africa – therefore refers to the name of an employers' organisation. Pieterse was earlier unsuccessfully involved in establishing a wine label, Phetogo. With the closure of this entity, Bawsi reportedly maintained a shareholder presence in the KWV (a privatised wine co-op). During the strike, Bawusa's membership increased significantly, but subsequent research found that the union was not able to sustain the momentum. Jesse Wilderman argues:

> Unlike some of the other unions, Bawusa under Pieterse's leadership spoke directly to the energy of the protests and, after establishing himself as a key leader and spokesperson, he directly led some of the more confrontational actions, including being shot repeatedly by rubber bullets during the confrontations with the police. Yet the difficultly of translating this

charismatic leadership and energy-oriented action into expanded and sustained organisation lies in the challenge of creating effective structures and empowering worker leadership beyond those at the top; Bawusa did not seem to be able find that balance over the longer term (2014: 72).

Wilderman's description points to Bawusa as an example of entrepreneurial unionism, since collective action in this case, which has the embryonic form of some kind of social movement unionism, did not translate into a movement but, rather, an entity that operates as a trade union but without the kind of member-driven union democracy that may lead to a transformative influence on society. Rather, as Wilderman argues:

> Pieterse made sure to put himself at the centre of most activities – whether it was constantly being the spokesperson for the protest in the media or having the union's conference room decorated with dozens of pictures and newspaper articles featuring himself in different struggles, Pieterse was effective at promoting himself, potentially at the expense of developing the broader leadership required to turn participation in the strike into organisation. In addition, Bawusa might have held a sort of scepticism in the often slower process of establishing more formal structures because they could be deadening to the real builder of change-action … In these ways, Bawusa's approach to organising seizes the moment but undercuts the structure and leadership development necessary for longer-term organisation building (2014: 72–73).

TECTONIC SHIFTS

The year 2012 can most probably be described as a turning point insofar as the labour landscape is concerned. This is the year when the state massacred thirty-four striking mineworkers at Lonmin's Marikana mine. A second major event is the decision by Numsa to break with the Alliance at its national congress in December 2013. Numsa showed Rehad Desai's documentary video *Miners Shot Down*, which subsequently won a Grammy Award in 2015, at this congress and invited relatives of deceased miners to address the gathering, putting it in direct opposition to NUM. A year later, Cosatu made a decision to expel Numsa. The two events – the massacre of mineworkers at Marikana and the decision by Numsa to break with the Alliance – are therefore not unrelated.

The emergence of Amcu

The massacre of 16 August 2012 at Lonmin's Marikana mine focused world attention on social and labour conditions in Rustenburg specifically and South Africa's platinum mining industry more generally. What has been described as a paradox of victory – the fact that the labour movement's spectacular successes could also lead to a process of demise – became all too apparent in light of this attention (Buhlungu 2010; see also Buhlungu and Bezuidenhout 2008). In part, this is because a number of high-profile public figures involved in the events and their aftermath had cut their teeth as senior leaders in the labour movement, specifically the NUM. First, there is Cyril Ramaphosa, involved as owner and member of Lonmin's board of directors, but also as the deputy president of the ANC. Ramaphosa, of course, is a former general secretary of the NUM. Second, there is Gwede Mantashe, involved in his role as general secretary of the ANC and as politician. Mantashe, too, is a former general secretary of the NUM. Third, there is Kgalema Motlanthe, involved as the country's deputy president and later as chairperson of a task team to address the crisis in mining. Motlanthe was also a former general secretary of the NUM. As a trade union, the NUM was one of the key supporters of Jacob Zuma's campaign against Motlanthe to be re-elected as the ANC's president at its congress in Mangaung, shortly before the tragic events at Marikana. A leading figure in this campaign was Frans Baleni, then the serving general secretary of the NUM. The events underscored the overlapping interests and personal ties, at times cooperative and at times competitive, between the NUM, mining capital and the state.

As spectacular as the NUM's rise was from its formation in 1982 onwards, so was its demise in Rustenburg. The rise of Amcu in Rustenburg and in some of the gold mines, particularly in Carletonville, meant that the NUM lost about 100 000 members in a year. But what about Amcu? Has this new union been able to revitalise some of the social movement elements of the NUM of the 1980s? It may be too soon to make a balanced assessment, but existing academic work seems sceptical that this may be the case. Joseph Mathunjwa's qualities as a charismatic leader are seen as both the union's strength and a hindrance to the development of a more sustainable union in the long run. According to Julia Foudraine, '[t]here is some evidence that suggests that Amcu is mainly being ruled by Mathunjwa. For this reason, it remains the question whether people mean the entire organization of Amcu or specifically Joseph Mathunjwa when talking about the union' (2015: 83). Furthermore:

What will be interesting to see is how Amcu is going to evolve in the coming years. After the 'Marikana Massacre' and the six months long strike, which were connected to each other and attracted many new members, it might be that the popularity of this 'new kid on the block' is eventually going to fade away, for example when Mathunjwa does not develop the institutional structures of the union more or when the union stays too wary of leftist sentiments. Many mineworkers took the brave decision to leave the powerful NUM and join the relatively new union. If Mathunjwa and his union in the end [turn] out to be a disappointment for these workers as well, the workers can abandon their president relentlessly as they did with the NUM (Foudraine 2014: 83–84).

Like Bawusa, Amcu's rise to national prominence was sparked by spectacular collective action. Unlike Bawusa, Amcu was able to translate this into a more stable membership base, as well as leading the longest strike in the history of the mining industry. It remains to be seen whether Amcu can translate this into a more sustained challenge to the status quo. A pessimistic reading of the union would point to the entrepreneurial elements involved and questions around the openness of and democratic control over the union's finances. A more optimistic reading would see the three-year wage agreement the union reached with platinum mining companies at the end of 2016 (see Rahlaga 2016) as an opportunity to turn Amcu into a more stable force. Much will depend on whether Amcu is able to incorporate independent workers' committees into democratic, worker-controlled trade union structures (Mathekga 2015; Sinwell and Mbatha 2016).

The expulsion of Numsa

The expulsion of Numsa from Cosatu is indeed a tectonic shift on the labour landscape. The aim here is not to provide an analysis of the details of the process that brought about this split in the federation but, rather, to reflect on the implications. Events developed really fast in the course of conducting the survey and the process of analysing the findings and reflecting on them. Our interactions with Numsa brought to light a fundamental tension in the union itself and within the United Front (UF) set up by Numsa to explore political alternatives.

On one hand, Numsa had to defend itself from a new rival, the Liberated Metalworkers Union of South Africa (Limusa), which was set up by Cosatu and Numsa's former general secretary in opposition to its former affiliate. It also had to deal with industry restructuring and continued pressure on industries where it organises because of the downturn in China's economy and therefore an oversupply of steel on the global market. On the other hand, Numsa had to redefine its political role outside the Alliance with the ANC and the SACP. For this end, as mentioned, it set up the UF, but the relationship between Numsa and the UF was not uncomplicated. At the very basic level, complications related to finances. Shortly after setting up the UF, Numsa lost a major source of income from agency shop fees paid by non-union members whose wages and working conditions were regulated by bargainings councils even though they were not trade union members themselves. In effect, the union lost an income stream of more than R4 million a month. At a more ideological level, there were also different visions of what opposition politics outside the Alliance would look like. Some, and particularly those involved directly in the UF, wanted a social movement approach to opposition politics, very much like the United Democratic Front (UDF) of the 1980s. This implied a gradual process of building up community structures alongside other social movements in which Numsa would be a participant (see Ashman and Pons-Vignon 2014; Ruiters 2014). Others, especially some of Numsa's national leaders and some of their advisers, had in mind a different version of the SACP, just not the SACP under its current leadership. This more Leninist approach would involve a different kind of politics that was, at some points of ideology and strategy, at odds with the social movement model. This suggests that there is a tension in Numsa between going the social movement unionism route or the political unionism route.

This realignment leaves the field open for Numsa and Nactu to enter into some kind of arrangement. During the student protests of 2016, Zwelinzima Vavi and Joseph Mathunjwa jointly addressed students and interacted with them, which signals some kind of loose cooperation between these two charismatic figures. However, the position that Numsa will take on political alliances will also shape how this process plays out. If Numsa decides to set up a political party, it will bring it into conflict with the EFF and, potentially, Nactu. If, however, Numsa decides to take a non-aligned position, there is the potential of bridging divides between Nactu and Fedusa and extended potential for trade unions outside the Cosatu fold under the political leadership of Numsa. That the UF did not do well in the 2016 local government elections, even in Nelson Mandela Metro, means that both Numsa and the UF will have to revisit their approach to politics. Table 12.1 summarises the main points made about what future alignments and realignments might look like.

Table 12.1: Variations of trade unionism after the Cosatu rupture

Social movement unionism	Political unionism	Economic unionism	Entrepreneurial unionism
	Cosatu (with elements of entre-preneurial unionism – investment companies)	Fedusa	Bawusa (as example; many others)
	Nactu (with elements of entrepreneurial unionism in the form of Amcu)	Solidariteit (with elements of both social movement and entrepreneurial unionism)	
	Numsa (with the potential to shift to social movement unionism, UF)	PSA	

FUTURE LANDSCAPES

South Africa's labour landscape remains in flux. It is hard to make predictions, since developments at the level of national politics may lead to shifts on the labour front as well – the two domains remain intertwined. The printing presses for books take much longer than those for newspapers, and more so than news instantly released on social media. If the personality of the current president, Jacob Zuma, is removed from the picture, there may even be overtures to reunite opposing federations. Nevertheless, towards the end of 2016 Cosatu again threw its hat into the political ring by formally endorsing former trade unionist Cyril Ramaphosa as their candidate for the presidency of the ANC and the country (Gallens 2016). This immediately led to condemnations from Numsa. Irvin Jim, Numsa's general secretary, described Ramaphosa as 'a director of Lonmin, [who] was directly implicated in the massacre of thirty-four Marikana workers ...' (TMG Digital 2016).

At the time of writing, Numsa, alongside Zwelinzima Vavi, was in the process of setting up a new federation, called the South African Federation of Trade Unions (Saftu). Fawu was the first union to formally disaffiliate from Cosatu in order to join a new federation in-the-making (Mahlakoana 2016). Forming such a federation takes years of preparation and work, as was the case with Cosatu in the mid-1980s, when it took approximately four years to reach agreement. Nevertheless, the launch committee moved relatively fast and had registered the new federation formally with the Department of Labour at the end of March 2017 and was due to hold a launch congress at the end of April. At the time of its formal registration, Saftu comprised twenty-one trade unions, accounting for approximately 700 000 members. The organising committee gave an indication that a further eighteen trade unions, including Cosatu affiliates, intended to affiliate, but that these decisions had to be made by national congresses. Saftu's leadership seems to have taken an approach to their journey whereby the taxi leaves the rank without a full load of passengers, with the intention of picking up some along the way. A notable absence at the time of registration was Amcu.

For now, the two dominant strands of trade unionism in South Africa are political unionism, as represented by Cosatu, and economic unionism, as represented by Fedusa, the PSA and other non-aligned unions. A worrying trend is creeping entrepreneurial unionism, with labour leaders cannibalising the need for representation by ordinary workers for personal gain. This parasitic behaviour is not limited to any one of the groupings. Yet, there remains the promise of a revitalised social movement unionism and some have argued that this is most likely to emerge from the newly formed federation.

Edward Webster (1996) first used the term 'rupture' in 1996, when Cosatu's disillusionment with the ANC's adoption of Gear started to settle in. At the time, Webster (1996: 3) quoted a Cosatu official: 'This is a transitional period, that's why we have a [Government of National Unity], that's why you have to hug the hyenas of the past in order to make advances in the future.' On tensions in the Alliance between Cosatu, the ANC and the SACP, Webster (1996: 3) rightly commented at the time: '[T]o see … strains inside the Alliance as signs of possible rupture would be premature.'

It took roughly twenty years for that rupture to happen, but even before then it started out as fragmentation. Over time 'hyenas' have changed shape, becoming figures seen as corrupting the movement from the inside, rather than enemies from the old apartheid order. Also, the rupture Webster refers to has now happened, not only in the labour movement, but fragmentation has set in in all three Alliance partners: the SACP has seen split-offs in the form of the Democratic Left Front and the Democratic Left Movement, the ANC has seen split-offs in the form of Cope and the EFF, and Cosatu with numerous of its affiliates has split and splintered into opposing labour federations and trade unions.

Until today, political rivals to the ANC have not achieved significant electoral success. The EFF, in spite of its skilful media spectacles inside and outside Parliament, remains locked into roughly 10 per cent of voter support. It is early days for the UF, but its performance in local government elections was unimpressive. The result for the ANC, however, has been the loss of three of the country's major metropolitan

231

governments, Johannesburg, Tshwane and Nelson Mandela Bay. Indeed, our survey had already anticipated this shift, especially through the dramatic decline in electoral support for the ANC among workers in Gauteng Province. Immediately after the local government elections the ANC experienced further internal divisions, with battles for control over the Treasury leading to new political fault lines and fissures. As some had argued, democracy itself was at stake (Calland 2016).

Ironically, as others have pointed out, in 2008 Cosatu campaigned to bring Jacob Zuma to power in the hope that he would shift the ANC's economic policies to the left. The Treasury was seen as the locus of state neoliberalism. By 2016, Zwelinzima Vavi publically defended the minister of finance against the same man he had supported earlier. As *Eyewitness News* reported: 'Vavi says while they are not a fan of Gordhan because of being anti-working class, they won't fold their arms while he's being harassed.' The report quotes Vavi directly: 'We will not allow yet another state capture by the president; hands off Pravin' (Manyathela 2016).

These shifts, twists and turns show just how complicated the business of taking democracy seriously has become over the twenty years that the survey has been conducted. We quoted the first publication from 1994 in the Preface to this volume: 'It will be difficult but not impossible for the labour movement to remain in the Alliance but not be co-opted, and to neither alienate itself from its base nor lose its militancy' (Ginsburg et al. 1995: 109). As Sakhela Buhlungu (2010) argued, Cosatu's gaining influence has also led to unions losing power. Given the rupture, the federation's remaining influence also runs the risk of becoming a nostalgic memory.

Our survey suggests that taking democracy seriously in 2017 and beyond would imply a process of rebuilding trade union power by revitalising internal processes of democracy and reconnecting with working-class communities in all their diversity. It would also imply taking changes in the economy and the labour market seriously – there is a dire need to organise precarious sections of the labour market. There is also a need to reconsider the nature and possibilities of working-class solidarity in the context of a nation that remains divided on the grounds of 'race' as well as gender, language, geography, generation and citizenship. This happens in the context of the resurgence globally of working-class nationalism (Brexit, the election of Donald Trump in the USA).

To be sure, this points to a need for the left globally to reconsider democratic politics. Our survey has shown that some of the traditions of participatory democracy and social movement unionism remain. It will be difficult but not impossible for the labour movement, Cosatu and labour beyond Cosatu, to creatively reconnect with those traditions and for the critically engaged tradition of South African labour studies to be part of this.

BIBLIOGRAPHY

Ashman, Sam and Nicolas Pons-Vignon. 2014. Numsa, the working class and socialist politics in South Africa. *Socialist Register* 51.

Bendix, Sonia. 1996. *Industrial Relations in the New South Africa.* Cape Town: Juta.

Boersema, Jacob R. 2012. Between recognition and resentment: An Afrikaner trade union's brand of post-nationalism. *African Studies* 71(3): 408–425.

Botiveau, Raphaël. 2015. Negotiating union: South Africa's National Union of Mineworkers and the end of the post-apartheid consensus. PhD dissertation, La Sapienza Università di Roma – Université Paris I Panthéon-Sorbonne.

Buhlungu, Sakhela. 2010. *A Paradox of Victory: Cosatu and the Democratic Transformation in South Africa.* Pietermaritzburg: University of KwaZulu-Natal Press.

Buhlungu, Sakhela and Andries Bezuidenhout. 2008. Union solidarity under stress: The case of the National Union of Mineworkers in South Africa. *Labor Studies Journal* 33(3): 262–287.

Calland, Richard. 2016. Opinion: High-stakes drama as Zuma and Gordhan square off. *EWN*, 17 March. http://ewn.co.za/2016/03/17/OPINION-High-stakes-drama-as-Zuma-and-Gordhan-square-off (accessed 30 November 2016).

Chun, Jennifer J. 2009. *Organizing at the Margins: The Symbolic Politics of Labor in South Korea and the United States.* Ithaca, NY: Cornell University Press.

Clawson, Dan. 2003. *The Next Upsurge: Labor and the New Social Movements.* Ithaca, NY: Cornell University Press.

Congress of South African Trade Unions (Cosatu). 2015. *Organisational Report to 12th National Congress 23 to 26 November 2015.* Johannesburg: Cosatu.

Davis, Rebecca. 2013. In the eye of the winelands storm: Nosey Pieterse. *Daily Maverick*, 14 January. http://www.dailymaverick.co.za/article/2013-01-14-in-the-eye-of-the-winelands-storm-nosey-pieterse/#.V16x6U0VjZ4 (accessed 13 June 2016).

Fantasia, Rick and Kim Voss. 2004. *Hard Work: Remaking the American Labor Movement.* Berkeley: University of California Press.

Foudraine, Julia 2014. Mortal men: The rise of the Association of Mineworkers and Construction Union under the leadership of Joseph Mathunjwa and the union's move to the political left, 1998–2014. MA thesis, Leiden University.

Gallens, Mahlatse. 2016. Cosatu endorses Cyril Ramaphosa as next ANC leader. *News24*, 24 November. http://www.news24.com/SouthAfrica/News/cosatu-endorses-cyril-ramaphosa-as-next-anc-leader-20161124 (accessed 30 November 2016).

Ginsburg, David, Edward Webster, Roger Southall, Geoffrey Wood, Sakhela Buhlungu, Johann Maree, Janet Cherry, Richard Haines and Gilton Klerck. 1995. *Taking Democracy Seriously: Worker Expectations and Parliamentary Democracy in South Africa.* Durban: Indicator Press.

Mahlakoana, Theto. 2016. Fawu quits Cosatu. *IOL*, 24 August. http://www.iol.co.za/news/politics/fawu-quits-cosatu-2060583 (accessed 30 November 2016).

Manyathela, Clement. 2016. Vavi warns Zuma: Hands off Gordhan. *EWN*, 1 September. http://ewn.co.za/2016/09/01/Zuma-must-get-his-hands-off-Gordhan-or-face-protests (accessed 30 November 2016).

Mathekga, Mmanoko J. 2015. Fighting the battles of the mine workers: The emergence of the Association of Mineworkers and Construction Union (Amcu). *South African Journal of Labour Relations* 32(2): 190–204.

Moodie, T. Dunbar. 2012. Social movement unionism: From enthusiasm to delivery – a response to Gay Seidman. *South African Review of Sociology* 43(1): 81–86.

Pillay, Devan. 2013. Between social movement and political unionism: Cosatu and democratic politics in South Africa. *Rethinking Development and Inequality* 2: 10–27.

Rahlaga, Masego. 2016. Amcu signs three-year wage agreement with big platinum players. *EWN*, 31 October. http://ewn.co.za/2016/10/31/amcu-signs-three-year-wage-agreement-with-big-platinum-players (accessed 30 November 2016).

Ruiters, Greg. 2014. Spaces of hope: Rethinking trade union-community alliances and citizenship in a post-alliance era in South Africa. *Politikon* 41(3): 421–441.

Seidman, Gay. 2011. Social movement unionism: From description to exhortation. *South African Review of Sociology* 42(3): 94–102.

Sinwell, Luke and Siphiwe Mbatha. 2016. *The Spirit of Marikana: The Rise of Insurgent Trade Unionism in South Africa*. Johannesburg: Wits University Press.

Steemkamp, Lizel. 2010. Political hyenas in feeding frenzy – Vavi. *News24*, 26 August. http://www.news24.com/SouthAfrica/Politics/Political-hyenas-in-feeding-frenzy-20100826 (accessed 30 November 2016).

TMG Digital. 2016. Numsa slams Cosatu's endorsement of Ramaphosa to lead ANC. *TimesLive*, 25 November. http://www.timeslive.co.za/politics/2016/11/25/Numsa-slams-Cosatu%E2%80%99s-endorsement-of-Ramaphosa-to-lead-ANC (accessed 25 November 2016).

Visser, Wessel. 2006. From MWU to solidarity – a trade union reinventing itself. *South African Journal of Labour Relations* 30(2): 19–41.

Visser, Wessel. 2008. *Van MWU tot Solidariteit: Geskiedenis van die Mynwerkersunie, 1902–2002*. Pretoria: Solidariteit.

Von Holdt, Karl. 2002. Social movement unionism: The case of South Africa. *Work, Employment and Society* 16(2): 283–304.

Webster, Edward. 1988. The rise of social-movement unionism: The two faces of the black trade union movement in South Africa. In *State, Resistance and Change in South Africa*, edited by Philip Frankel, Noam Pines and Mark Swilling. London: Croom Helm.

Webster, Edward. 1996. Cosatu: Old alliances, new strategies. *Southern Africa Report* 11(3): 3.

Wilderman, Jesse. 2014. Farm worker uprising in the Western Cape: A case study of protest, organising, and collective action. Research report, Global Labour University, Department of Sociology, University of Witwatersrand.

Zvoutete, Jackie Tatenda. 2012. Impact of institutional diversity on unions and NGOs' efforts to represent and articulate farm workers' grievances: Case study of the 2012 Western Cape farm workers' strike and protest action. Master's dissertation, University of Cape Town.

CONTRIBUTORS

Andries Bezuidenhout is an Associate Professor in the Department of Sociology at the University of Pretoria. He holds a PhD from the University of the Witwatersrand. Previously, he worked as a researcher at the Sociology of Work Unit (now the Society, Work and Development Institute) at the University of the Witwatersrand, to which he is still attached as an associate.

Christine Bischoff (née Psoulis) works for the Wits City Institute at the University of the Witwatersrand, Johannesburg. She has worked on most of the earlier surveys of Cosatu members and has co-authored book chapters and journal articles on the findings of the longitudinal study. She is currently working on her PhD at the University of Pretoria.

Janet Cherry is a South African activist and academic. She is currently Professor of Development Studies at Nelson Mandela Metropolitan University in Port Elizabeth. Her main areas of research are human rights, democratic participation, social and political history, gender and sustainable development.

Nkosinathi Paul Jikeka is currently a Numsa educator and a student of Development Studies at Nelson Mandela Metropolitan University. He was formerly SACP organiser in Mbuyiselo Ngwenda district (Nelson Mandela Bay).

Boitumelo James Malope is a PhD candidate at the University of Stellenbosch in the Department of Sociology and Social Anthropology, part of the DST/NRF SARChI Sociology of Land, Environment and Sustainable Development team. His areas of interests are labour markets and youth unemployment. He was previously at the University of Pretoria, where he did his BA, honours and master's degrees.

Johann Maree is Emeritus Professor of Sociology at the University of Cape Town. He has published extensively in the field of trade unions and employment relations.

Among his publications are *The Independent Trade Unions, 1974–1984* (editor and co-author) and *Taking Democracy Seriously* (co-author with eight others), the first book based on a survey of Cosatu members conducted shortly before the historic 1994 election.

Sandla Nomvete is an Industrial Sociology and Labour Studies doctoral fellow at the University of Pretoria. His work focuses specifically on the dynamics of continued mining migrant labour post-apartheid. Previously, he has worked with medical doctors in his quest to understand the rationale behind South African doctors migrating upon completion of their studies. His research interests also include social and political movements.

Ntsehiseng Nthejane has a BA in Social Work from the National University of Lesotho. In 2013, she moved to South Africa to further her studies in the Department of Sociology at the University of Pretoria, obtaining an honours degree in Industrial Sociology and Labour Studies. She is currently pursuing a master's degree in the same field. Her research interests are the phenomenon of illegal mining and the involvement of Basotho migrant workers.

Ari Sitas is a sociologist and writer. He heads the Department of Sociology at the University of Cape Town and chairs the National Institute for Humanities and the Social Sciences. His latest publication (in 2016) is a reissue of his labour movement writings from the 1980s, *The Flight of the Gwala-gwala Bird*.

Bianca Tame is a Lecturer in the Department of Sociology at the University of Cape Town. She previously worked as a researcher at the Industrial Organisational and Labour Studies Unit at the University of KwaZulu-Natal. Her current research focuses on private employment agencies operating in the domestic sector, the commodification of an intimate work culture, the future of work, and gender and migration.

Malehoko Tshoaedi is a Senior Lecturer in the Department of Sociology at the University of Pretoria. She holds a PhD from the University of Leiden in the Netherlands. She has lectured in Sociology at the University of Johannesburg and at the University of South Africa, and has also worked as a researcher in the Sociology of Work Unit (now the Society, Work and Development Institute) at the University of the Witwatersrand.

Page numbers in *italics* refer to figures and tables.

Printed and bound by CPI Group (UK) Ltd, Croydon, CR0 4YY

16/04/2025

14658441-0003